TWINKA THIEBAUD
AND THE
ART OF THE POSE

TWINKA THIEBAUD
AND THE
ART OF THE POSE

Edited by Jayme Yahr, Ph.D.

HIRMER

CROCKER
art museum

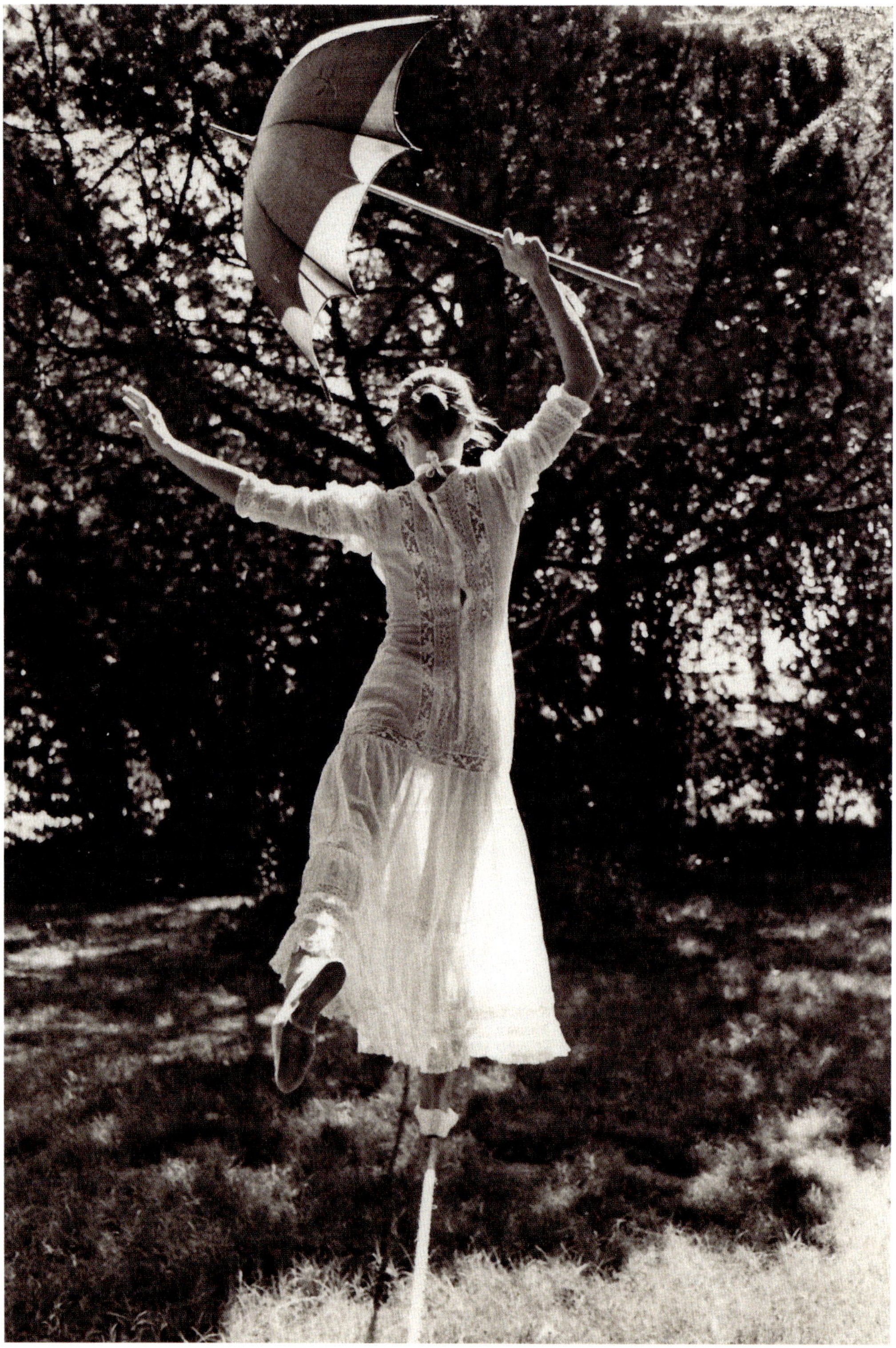

FIG. 1 Kathryn Beltrami, Twinka Thiebaud on a tightrope, 1978. Courtesy of Twinka Thiebaud.

TABLE OF CONTENTS

FOREWORD AND ACKNOWLEDGMENTS

Twinka Thiebaud and the Art of the Pose features more than 100 artworks that speak to the role of Twinka Thiebaud as an artist's model and to the working relationships and friendships she developed with artists during her career. Comprised of paintings, drawings, pastels, and photographs that date from the 1940s to the present, this exhibition begins with Thiebaud's childhood modeling work for her father, renowned Sacramento-based artist Wayne Thiebaud. The father-daughter dynamic is also visible in later works, including Wayne Thiebaud's paintings from the 1960s. As Twinka Thiebaud moved into a career as an artist's model, she worked with photographers Judy Dater, Jack Welpott, Eikoh Hosoe, John Reiff Williams, Arnold Newman, and Robert Heinecken, among many others, revealing her ability to transform her body and gaze based upon the surrounding environment and the artist's vision for the work. In the 2000s, she extended her professional relationships to additional photographers and painters, including Aline Smithson, Susan Seubert, Kim Campbell, Lorijo Daniels, Bradford J. Salamon, and Fred Dalkey. This exhibition, which brings together work by more than thirty artists, will be the first to highlight Thiebaud's long career and her influence as an artist's model, while also exploring American West-Coast experimentation and the intersection of the human body and nature.

We are grateful to all the artists featured in the exhibition and extend our gratitude to those who supplied images and loaned artworks, including Tami Bahat, Alexandra Becker-Black, Kim Campbell, Elizabeth Opalenik, Bradford J. Salamon, Pete Saloutos, Susan Seubert, Aline Smithson, Mallary Ann Thiebaud, John Reiff Williams, Crystal Bridges Museum of American Art, and the Wayne Thiebaud Foundation. In addition to having work in the exhibition, photographers John Reiff Williams and Judy Dater also served as gracious and intriguing interview subjects, with Claire Sykes expertly bringing together the nuanced details of their artist-model relationships with Thiebaud. Sykes also conducted an interview with Thiebaud herself. We posthumously acknowledge writer Henry Miller's meaningful essay on Thiebaud. Crystal Bridges Museum of American Art, the Museum of Fine Arts, Houston, and the Wayne Thiebaud Foundation each provided image and research support.

At the Crocker, we acknowledge the Co-Trustees and the Crocker staff, especially Scott A. Shields, Ph.D., for initially working with Twinka Thiebaud to conceptualize the exhibition, and Mariah Briel, who served as catalogue project manager, coordinating checklists and photography sessions, and editing essays. Others directly involved in the project were Caitlin Schwarz, who provided organizational

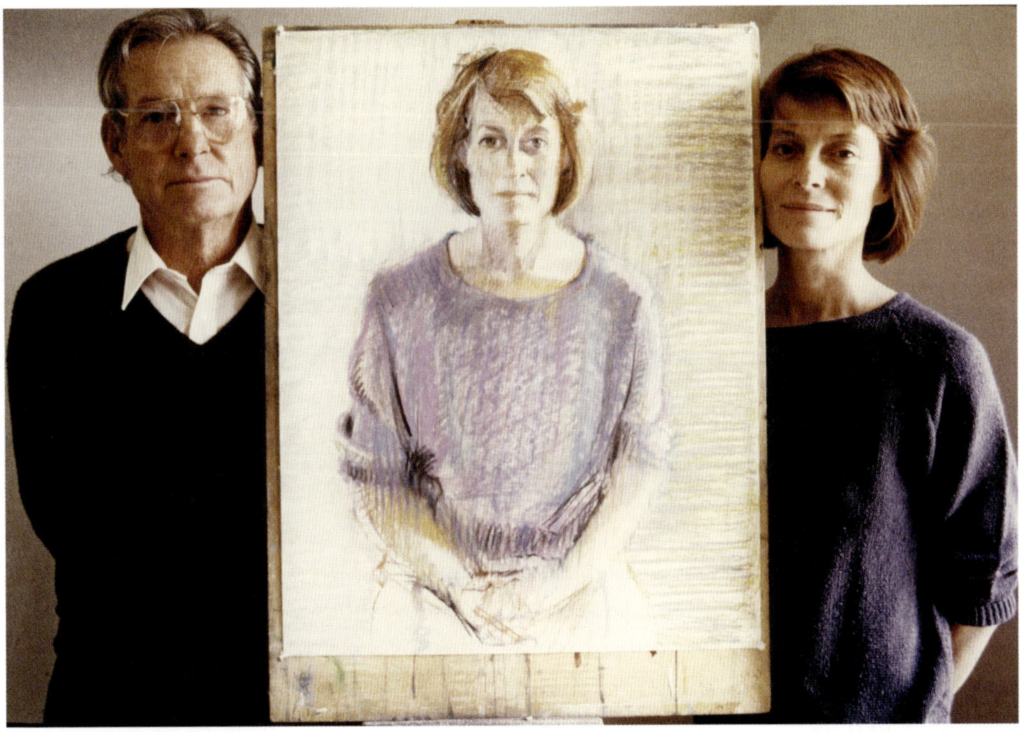

FIG. 2 Wayne Thiebaud and Twinka Thiebaud with *Untitled*, circa 1985. Collection of the Wayne Thiebaud Foundation.

and administrative support; Erin Aitali, who tracked loans and coordinated exhibition-related tasks; and Matthew Isble, who was responsible for the exhibition's installation. Brian Suhr was an integral member of the catalogue team, as he photographed and scanned many of the artworks and ephemera contained herein. We extend our appreciation to Hirmer Publishers for producing such a beautiful catalogue, their team including Elisabeth Rochau-Shalem, Senior Editor; Rainer Arnold, Project Manager; Michael Pilewski, Copy Editor; and Lucia Ott, Designer.

Most significantly, we are indebted to Twinka Thiebaud, who generously agreed to an exhibition of her life's work, much of which comes from her personal collection. We thank her for providing artistic and other support to the project. A skilled storyteller, Thiebaud enlivens the artwork and catalogue text with personal memories and cultural context. Not only did she help to conceptualize the framework for the exhibition, but she also opened her professional network and personal friendships to all involved.

LIAL A. JONES
Mort and Marcy Friedman Director & CEO
Crocker Art Museum

JAYME YAHR, PH.D.
Associate Curator
Crocker Art Museum

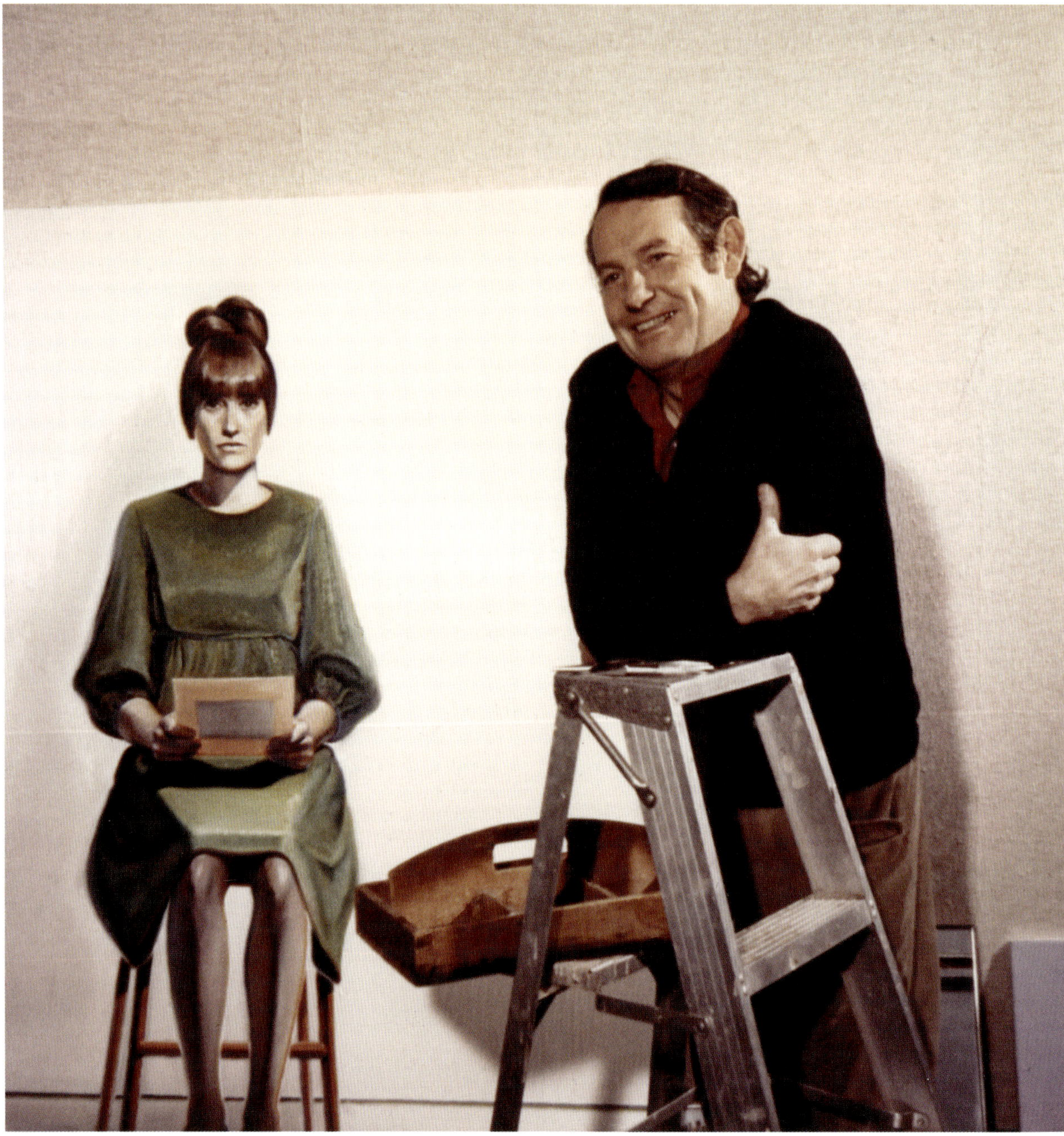

FIG. 3 Wayne Thiebaud with *Green Dress*, n.d. Courtesy of Twinka Thiebaud.

TWINKA BEGAN HER CAREER AS A MODEL PEEKING AT ME FROM UNDER A HOSPITAL MATERNITY BLANKET.

THANK YOU FOR OUR ENDURING PARTNERSHIP.

WITH ADMIRATION AND LOVE,
DAD

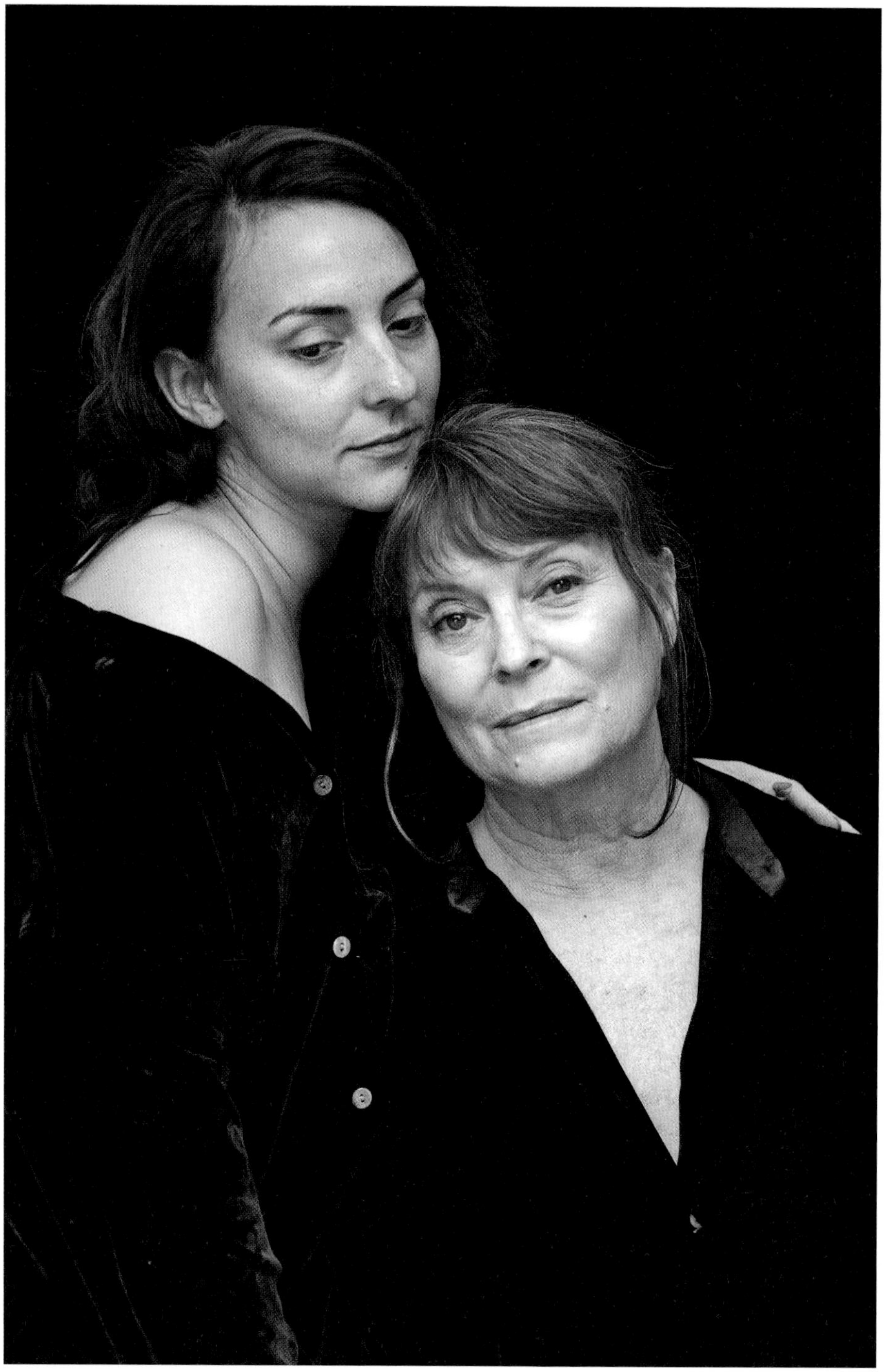

FIG. 4 Elizabeth Opalenik (American, born 1947), *Twinka with Sierra*, 2011. Archival pigment print, 13 ½ × 9 in. Collection of Elizabeth Opalenik.

DEDICATIONS AND THANKS

FOR MY FATHER, WHO LIT THE
FLAME AND PASSED ON THE TORCH.
AND FOR MY DAUGHTER,
SIERRA LE BARON MELLINGER,
WHO CARRIES IT FORWARD.

My gratitude goes out to the Crocker Art Museum and Scott Shields, Associate Director and Chief Curator, for this wonderful homecoming, and to Associate Curator Jayme Yahr, who kept the puzzle pieces together with kindness, good humor, and grace. Generous thanks to all the photographers and painters who found me a worthy subject. To those whose images remain in my collection but are not shown here, you encouraged me and helped me develop over the decades and are not forgotten. Special appreciation to my wonderful longtime collaborator, John Reiff Williams, and his wife Anarda, who lifted me up and helped me grow both as an artist's model and a human being. My friend Jessica Talisman worked tirelessly to keep this collection of images, and me, organized. Thank you. To my editor and close friend, Claire Sykes, who helped me find just the right words. Thank you also to my dear friend, photographer Lorijo Daniels, who helped me stay focused and in good physical shape with her yoga instruction and glowing positivity. Many thanks to Aline Smithson, who encouraged me to get my project completed while I could still enjoy it, and to literary agent Laurie Fox, an enthusiastic supporter from the beginning. A shout out to my sisters Jill Silva and Mallary Ann Thiebaud, who know what it's like to sit perfectly still, and to my sister Susannah Hardesty, who helped me stay on course. To Buffy Ford Stewart and Rose Beltrami, thank you for decades of sisterhood. To DeAnn Baker and DeAnn Prior, your hospitality, friendship, and generosity have been an immeasurable help to me and many other weary travelers; you are the best of the best. And, finally, thank you to the Wayne Thiebaud Foundation and to Colleen Casey for your assistance and contributions to the exhibition.

TWINKA THIEBAUD

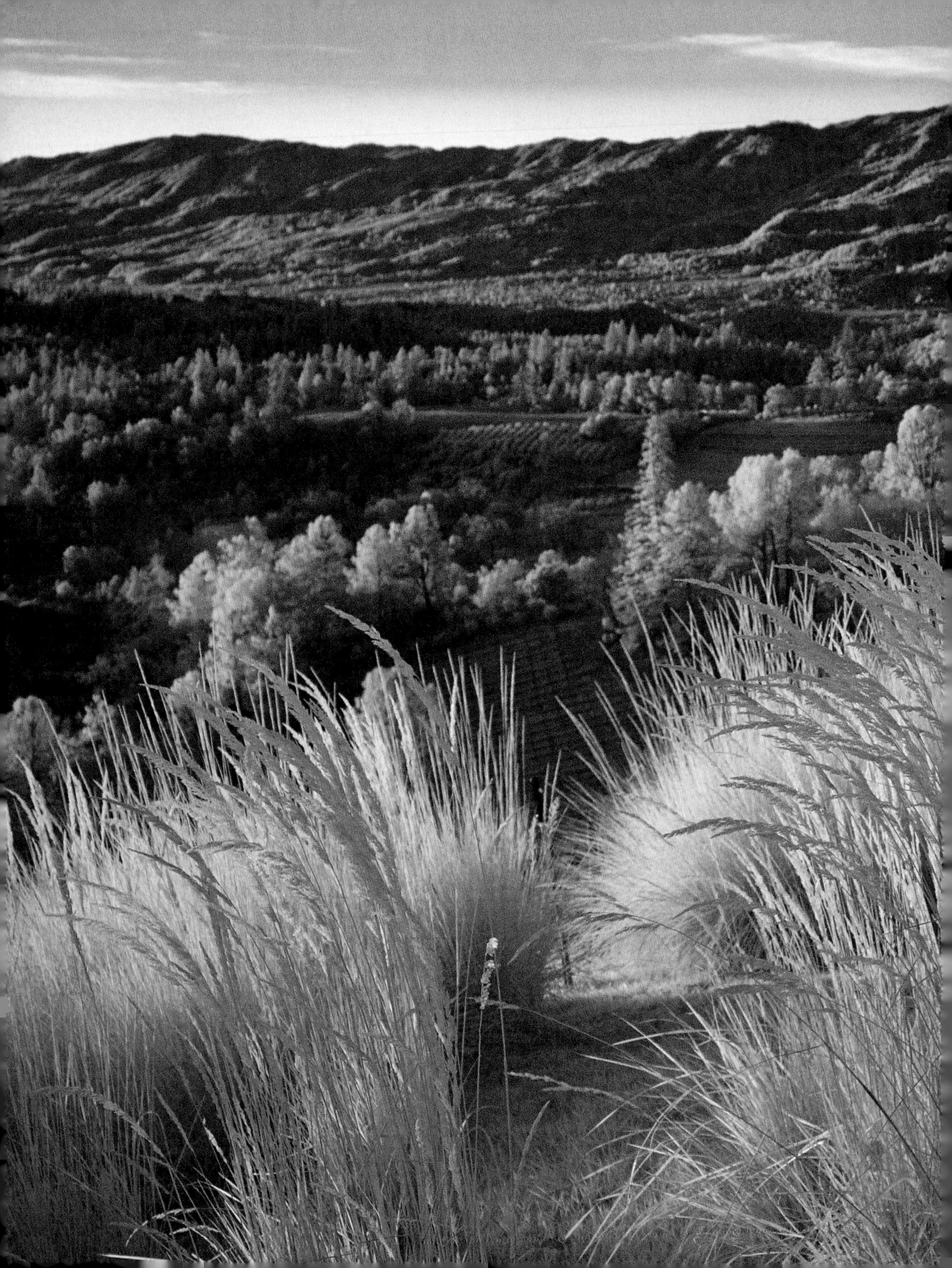

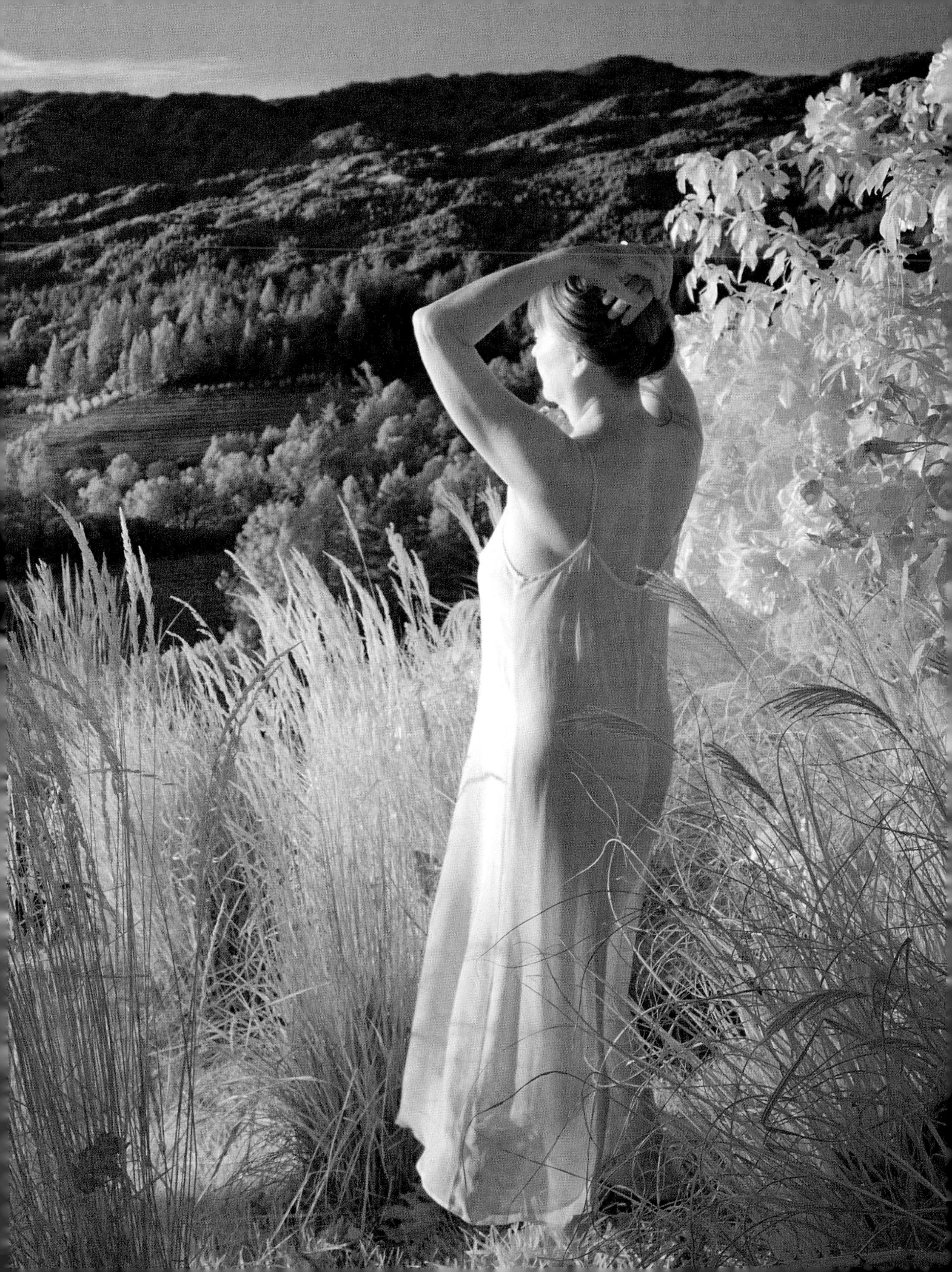

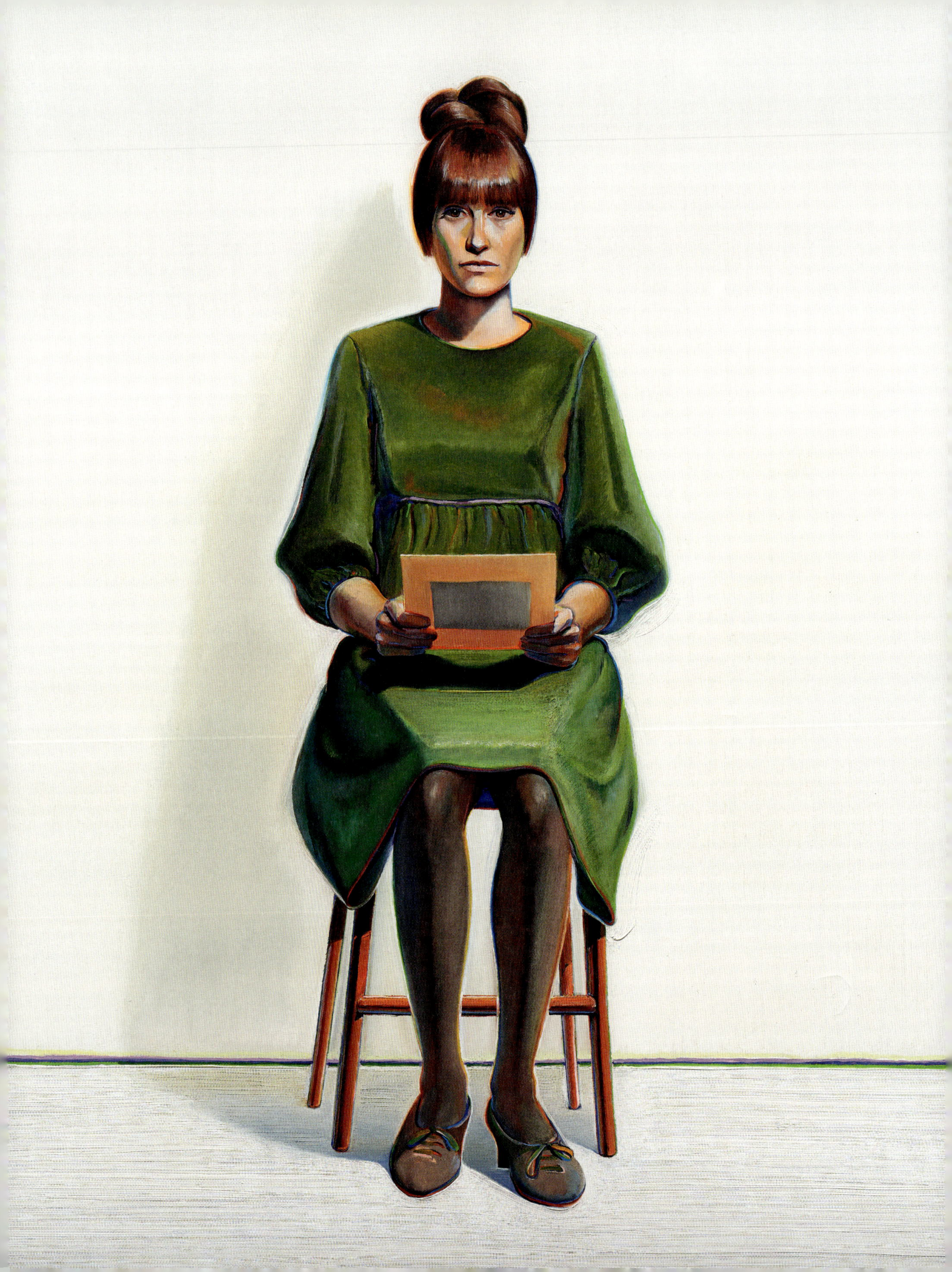

GAZING BACK: MY LIFE AS AN ARTIST'S MODEL

TWINKA THIEBAUD

BEGINNINGS

My earliest memory of my father centers on the way he studied me while scratching away on a piece of paper. Throughout my early childhood, if I was propped up on pillows reading a book or sick with a fever, there he would be, sitting on a chair at the end of the bed, carefully looking at me, completely immersed in his work (PL. 2). Under the spotlight of his gaze, I felt safe, comforted, and seen.

When the time came for me to pose for my first formal portrait with him, I was six. I wanted to be my dad's best model, especially after my ten-year-old sister had told me that posing was "very hard work." She had just returned from his painting studio with a serious look on her face. "You won't be able to sit still," she challenged. But I was determined to be great, to make him proud of me. Others had taken a turn in front of his easel, and I hoped to also see myself up on the wall as an image inside of a frame, hanging next to pictures of my mother and sister.

At the time, my father's studio was a windowless shack, a converted chicken coop in the backyard of a relative's house in Sacramento, California, where we lived while my dad was getting his master's degree. My dad was intent on making a space where he could work quietly and undisturbed while preparing for his first solo exhibition at the then-named E. B. Crocker Art Gallery (now Crocker Art Museum) in 1951: *Influences on a Young Painter–Wayne Thiebaud*. The studio was dark and stuffy, filled with the pungent odors of mold, dust, and turpentine. I had visited his makeshift studio a few times before my first modeling session, and during one visit I came out with bright-yellow paint in my hair and under my fingernails. Even in the dingy space, the delicious colors squeezed out

Wayne Thiebaud (American, 1920–2021), *Green Dress* (Detail), 1966/2017. Oil on canvas, 72 × 60 in. Collection of the Wayne Thiebaud Foundation.

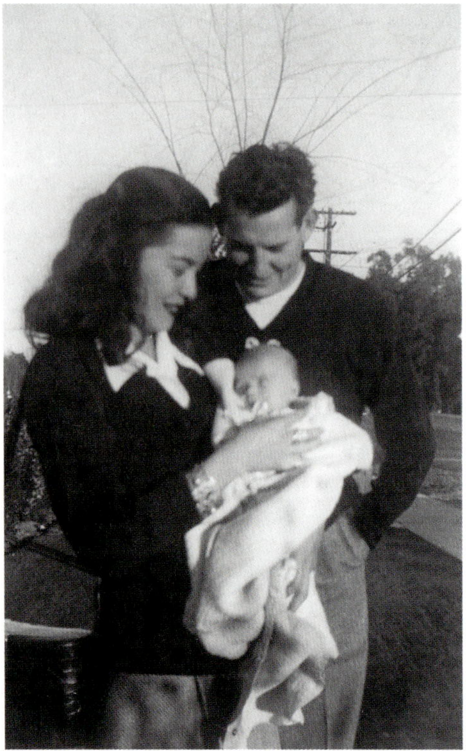

FIG. 5 Wayne and Patricia Thiebaud with baby Twinka. Courtesy of Twinka Thiebaud.

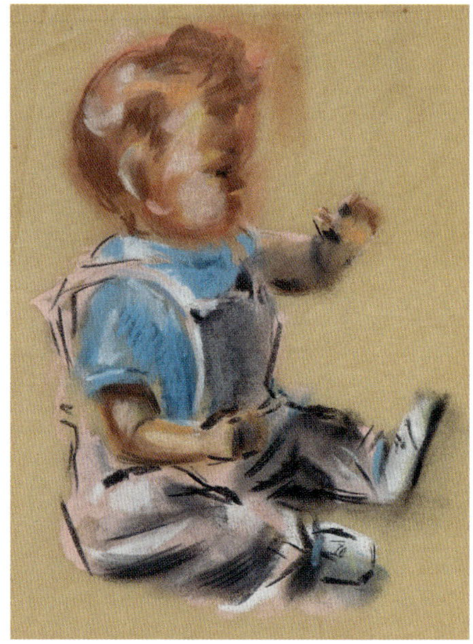

FIG. 6 Wayne Thiebaud (American, 1920–2021), *Untitled*, n.d. Pastel on paper, 6 ¼ × 4 ¾ in. Collection of Twinka Thiebaud.

onto his palette looked just like taffy, something sweet and tasty to eat.

My first effort at modeling did not go well. Dad was patient, but playing silent statue for more than a few minutes in that tight space with its strong smells felt like torture. He certainly did not pressure me to perform, but tried his best to cajole and humor me: "Just a few more minutes, please?" But his urging could not quell my misery. He eventually completed the portrait, mostly from memory, and I was certain I never wanted to model again.

The opening of my father's exhibition had our family buzzing with anticipation, and I soon forgot about my posing ordeal. I ran through the halls of the museum's gallery searching for the "me" inside a frame, and there it was, *Twinka*, looking back at me (FIG. 8). I was thrilled to be a part of his show. We all were. I stood by my picture, hoping to be recognized as the girl on the wall. Though few noticed me, I felt a part of something special that day.

The opening was also the first time I sensed my father was at the center of something significant and unique. His job had always been very different from the work of other fathers I knew, but here the rooms were filled with well-dressed people who had come to see his work. He had created all of the paintings on the walls, and he belonged to us. It was wonderful basking in the glow of his modest beginning.

Our family was also caught up in the whirlwind of Dad's enormous creative output. Beyond painting and teaching, he was designing theater sets, making public art, producing art-instructional films in our basement, and creating light spectacles for the city's music festival. Often, he asked us to help in some

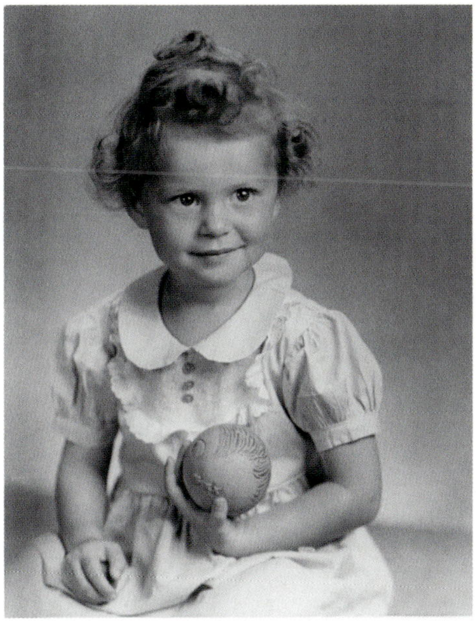

FIG. 7 Twinka Thiebaud, 1947. Courtesy of Twinka Thiebaud.

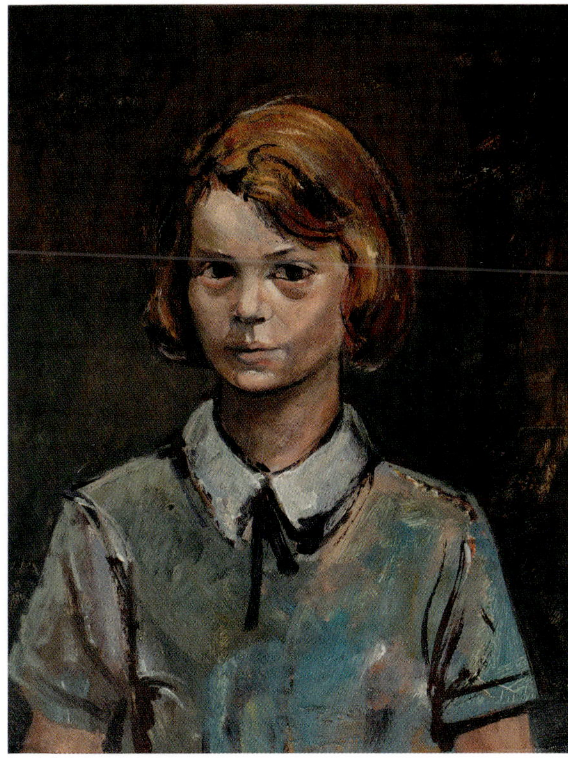

FIG. 8 Wayne Thiebaud (American, 1920–2021), *Twinka*, 1951. Oil on canvas board, 19 ⅝ × 15 ¾ in. Collection of Twinka Thiebaud.

capacity or, at the very least, we applauded his efforts from the audience. His confidence and willingness to dive into new endeavors made me feel self-assured and brave enough to try new things myself.

ASPIRATIONS

I was first inspired to become an actress when my dad started working on theater sets. He brought me with him when he was working, and it was thrilling to watch a play come together in rehearsals and see it culminate in the finished live performance.

In 1956–1957, my family spent a year in New York City while my father was on a sabbatical from teaching. During that time, my parents enrolled me in the Professional Children's School, which catered to children interested in the performing arts, though I was far from professional. I had performed in children's theater in California and my parents encouraged my acting ambitions. Private school was a significant expense for them, but they were concerned that I would struggle in New York's much larger public school system. My sixth-grade class consisted of just nine children, and it was the best year I had ever experienced as far as my education was concerned. I felt incredibly lucky. We were taken all over the city on interesting field trips—to the New York Stock Exchange, Statue of Liberty, American Museum of Natural History, Metropolitan Museum of Art, and the New York Public Library. The grand tour. I even learned to speak some French.

It was a gift and an inspiration for me to meet and befriend young actors, dancers, and singers. Among my sixth-grade classmates alone, there was a television whiz kid, a figure-skating champion, and a

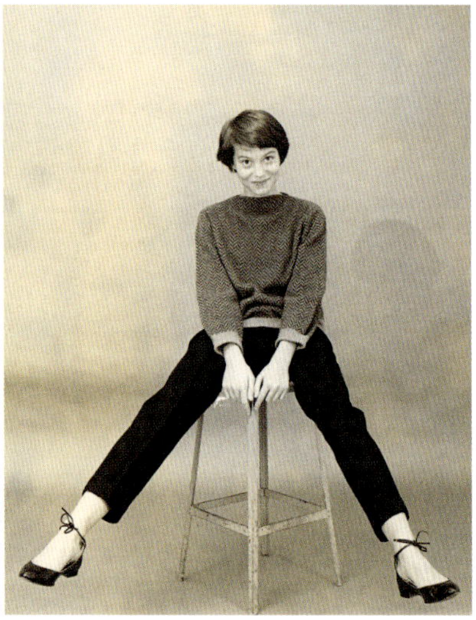

FIG. 9 Twinka Thiebaud, age 12, circa 1957, New York. Courtesy of Twinka Thiebaud.

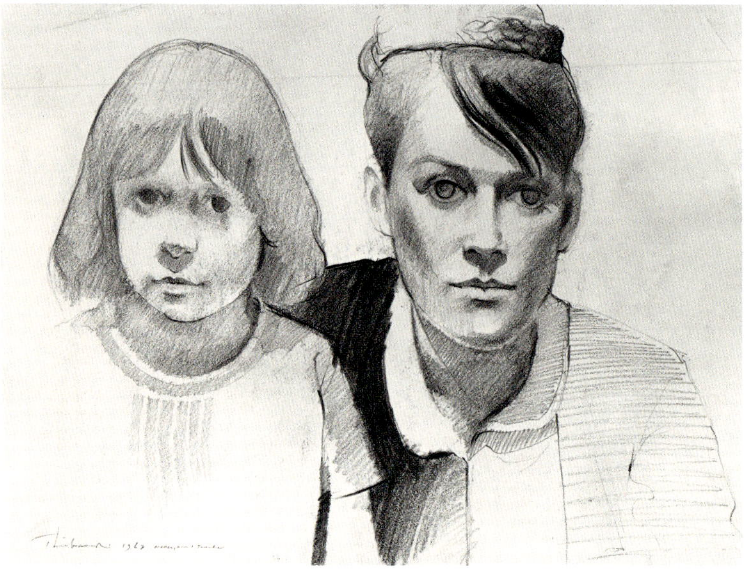

FIG. 10 Wayne Thiebaud (American, 1920–2021), *Mallary Ann and Twinka*, 1962. Graphite on paper, 24 × 18 in. Collection of Mallary Thiebaud.

working television actor whose older brother became the great character actor Christopher Walken. I wanted to be a professional like my friends at school, and their successes gave me a boost of confidence (FIG. 9).

One afternoon, I read a bulletin-board notice at school that was advertising tryouts for a Broadway show: "Looking for young actresses." When classes let out for the day, a classmate and I walked the long distance to the theater. There we found our way to the stage door and auditioned, but I did not get the part. I was twelve years old and fearless. My parents had no idea why I was so late coming home, but were not concerned. Living in the city, we had the freedom to roam and explore without constraints, and I often wandered the streets of New York, invigorated by the sights and sounds of the city.

I felt a deep sadness when we left it all behind. It had been such an enlivening year at school, and living in New York provided opportunities to indulge in my creativity. I saw numerous Broadway shows, went to tapings of popular TV programs, and learned to ice-skate at Rockefeller Center. New York City was my Wonderland, and the thought of returning to our quiet town in California worried me. The city had changed our family, including my parents. Rather than return to Sacramento, my mother decided to remain in New York to pursue opportunities in advertising and waved a bittersweet goodbye to us as we rode away in a taxi. Two years later, with all of us back in California, my parents separated. My sister and I moved to the San Francisco Bay Area with our mother, away from our dad, and seldom saw him except during school vacations. When our parents each remarried, this presented new challenges. We went to new schools, had to make new friends, and tried to find our place in new family structures. Before, our home had had an open-door policy and my dad's college students, fellow artists, and colleagues had often visited. My dad was always experimenting, learning, and expanding his knowledge and skills while inspiring others to do the same, and they became like brothers, sisters, aunties, and uncles to us. It was always lively and lots of fun when they were around. Now, the excitement and creative flow I had been so accustomed to was missing. It was as if a light switch had been turned off.

During my teenage years, I became a more patient model for Dad when he would ask me or my younger sister, Mallary, to sit for him (FIG. 10). He wanted to create a visual memory of our time together, and it was comforting to be alone with him after weeks or months of separation. I missed his drive and the animated, swirling energy of his students and fellow artists. To help me cope, the theater became a refuge. I attended workshops, traveled around with a teenage jazz band, played my guitar, and acted in school plays. Though I received an acting scholarship to San Francisco State College (now San Francisco State University) during my last year of high school, I decided to put college on the back burner. I was anxious to leave home and to discover what the world had in store for me (FIG. 11).

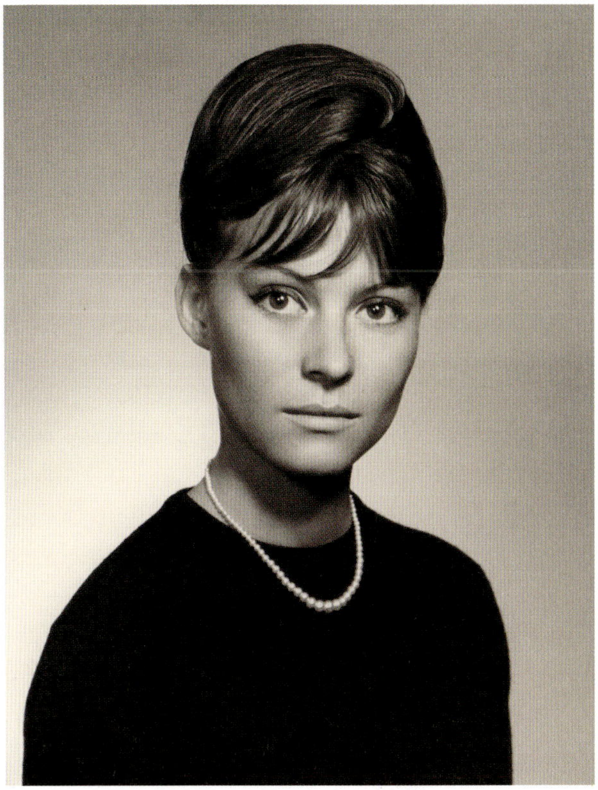

FIG. 11 Twinka Thiebaud, high school graduation photo, 1964. Courtesy of Twinka Thiebaud.

IDENTITIES

At eighteen, I was out on my own, working a series of odd jobs—shopgirl, file clerk, waitress, door-to-door encyclopedia salesperson, housekeeper, and cook. I sold vintage clothing at flea markets and designed and sold jewelry at craft fairs. When I had extra money, I took acting classes, which made me feel connected to my dream. I moved around a lot, struggled to get by, and, occasionally, my dad paid me to sit for one of his paintings. Then, one of his students, David King, who had become an art professor, invited me to pose for a life drawing class. The pay was better than working as a shopgirl, and modeling allowed me the flexibility to pursue my other interests. I steeled my nerves and dropped my robe and my inhibitions.

Of course, I had been exposed to artful depictions of the nude in every museum I had ever visited. And, as California kids, my friends and I thought little of shedding our clothes to swim in a private pool or to bask in the sun, tanning ourselves. We had little fear of the sun (my parents even believed it was healthy for me to be sunbathed as an infant), and I was a dedicated sun worshipper from an early age, just as comfortable in the nude as I was wearing clothes. Yet, posing naked in a room full of strangers was something unfamiliar.

Then came the women's liberation and counterculture movements. Gloria Steinem. Burn the bra!

The Beatles. Bob Dylan. Woodstock. The Summer of Love. Hippies and Haight-Ashbury. I was young, restless, and highly impressionable, and the intoxicating changes of the 1960s had a tremendous effect on me. Once bound up in tight girdles, utilitarian bras, and Ivy League fashion, my friends and I grew more comfortable adorning ourselves in feathers, beads, bells, colorful costumes, and body paint. Letting go of old inhibitions was a rite of passage, and I wanted to fit in. We were pushing the boundaries of identity expression, and nothing felt more liberating.

Working in art schools was very different from posing privately for my father in his quiet sanctuary or modeling for photographers. I was often booked at two or three schools in a single day, driving the freeways across Los Angeles to make my next session. There was nothing glamorous about the job of an artist's model. Often there was no comfortable place to change out of my street clothes, so I would get ready in a school bathroom. The changing rooms in art schools were generally small, dark, makeshift spaces with a thick layer of dust everywhere. The moment my bare feet touched the floor, they were coal-black. I tried to bring a little glamour to the endeavor by wearing a colorful vintage velvet robe or a pretty, patterned wrap. I found interesting pieces of clothing at thrift stores that might work for a certain pose, if that was the professor's wish.

With modeling, I never knew what to expect, other than that the job would entail sitting absolutely still for half an hour at a time. Trying to do that without the protective armor of clothing on a cold winter's day in a poorly heated room was especially difficult. Hard-backed chairs would press painfully against my body. It was nearly impossible to scratch an itch or stifle a sneeze brought on by the charcoal dust swirling about the room during an intense drawing session. At times, my limbs would get so numb that I could only feel pins and needles and needed help getting down from my perch.

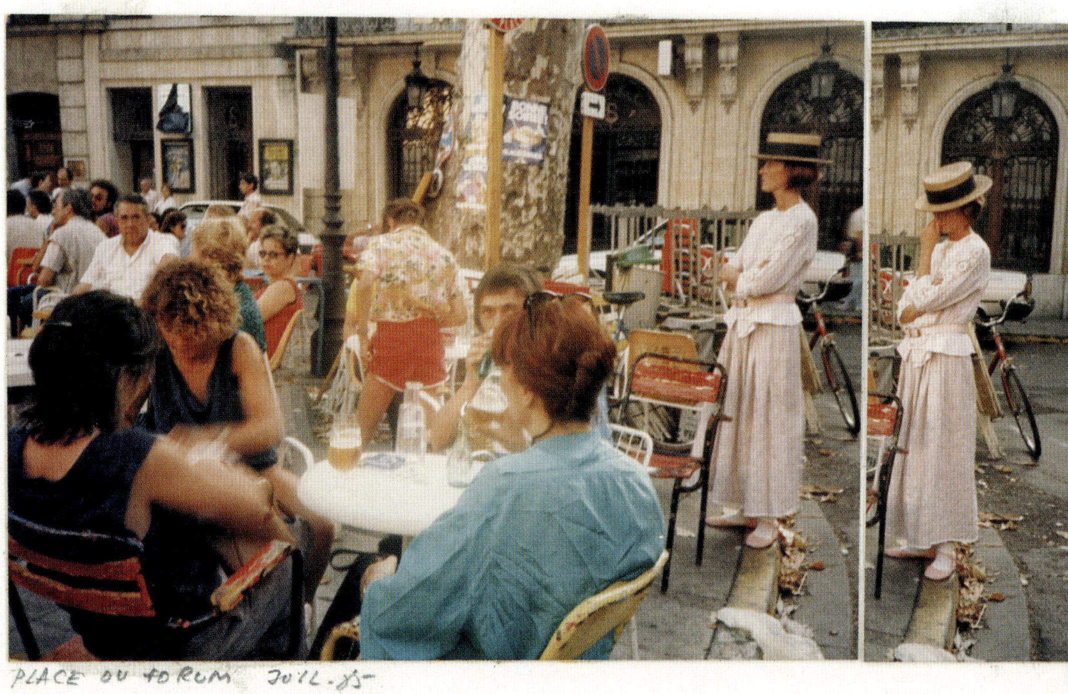

The mind could go a little mad sometimes from the tedium, but if music was allowed or I could hold a book and read, that was a plus. I always carried *The Complete Works of William Shakespeare* with me so I could memorize monologues. When the professor would turn away, I turned the page. There was one great advantage, though, and that was the free art education I received. I was learning a lot by overhearing the professors' instructions and sitting in during teachers' critiques of student work. I became curious about the possibilities of doing some drawing and painting of my own.

VIEWPOINTS

I had been working at art schools for a while when, in 1970, I met two photographers at a party in San Francisco. I always liked to dress theatrically. That night, I was wearing a hand-crocheted dress over a body stocking, adorned with a Superwoman belt I'd designed and had a friend make for me. Photographers Judy Dater and Jack Welpott were a couple then, working on a book of images from both the male and female perspectives. They admired my look and asked if I would pose for them. The project sounded intriguing. Judy and Jack preferred working with women in their own environments, so I invited them to come to my studio apartment, where I was photographed by each of them separately (PLS. 10 AND 11).

Not long after, Judy asked to photograph me again, this time at her home in Marin County. For inspiration, I brought some of my vintage clothing and a beautiful dress I had borrowed from a friend. Judy liked the delicate, translucent quality of the dress and wanted to photograph me in it, crouching at the base of a redwood tree in her backyard. She allowed me to experiment with the pose and settle into it, and when I raised my arm up to steady myself, that was it.

Posing for Judy felt very much like posing for my dad. She did a lot of looking; that is what painters did, too. She took time setting up the photograph with her

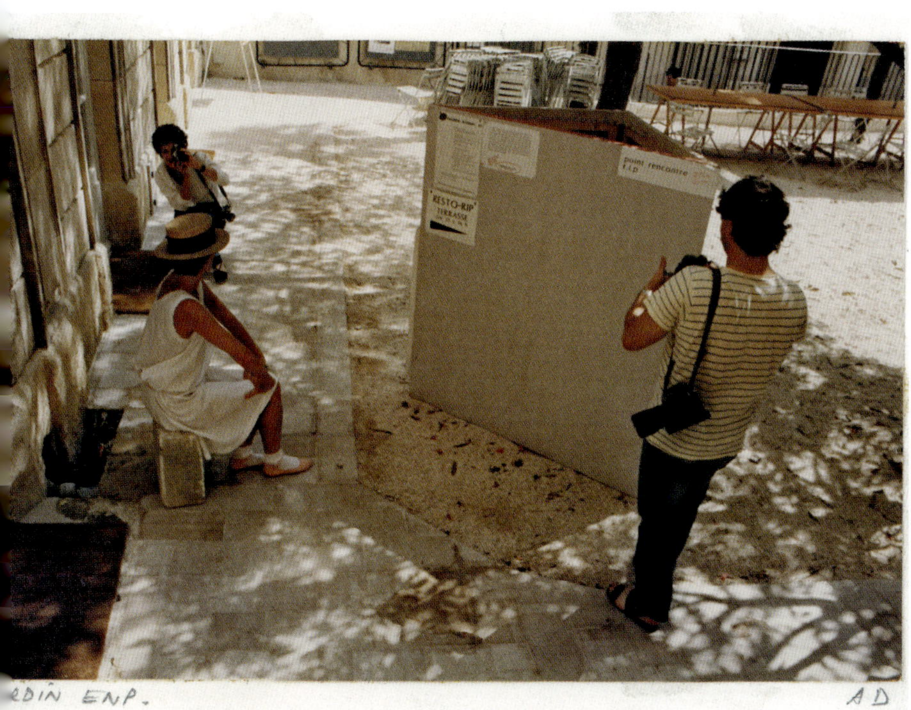

FIG. 12 Twinka Thiebaud posing in Arles, France, 1985. Courtesy of Twinka Thiebaud.

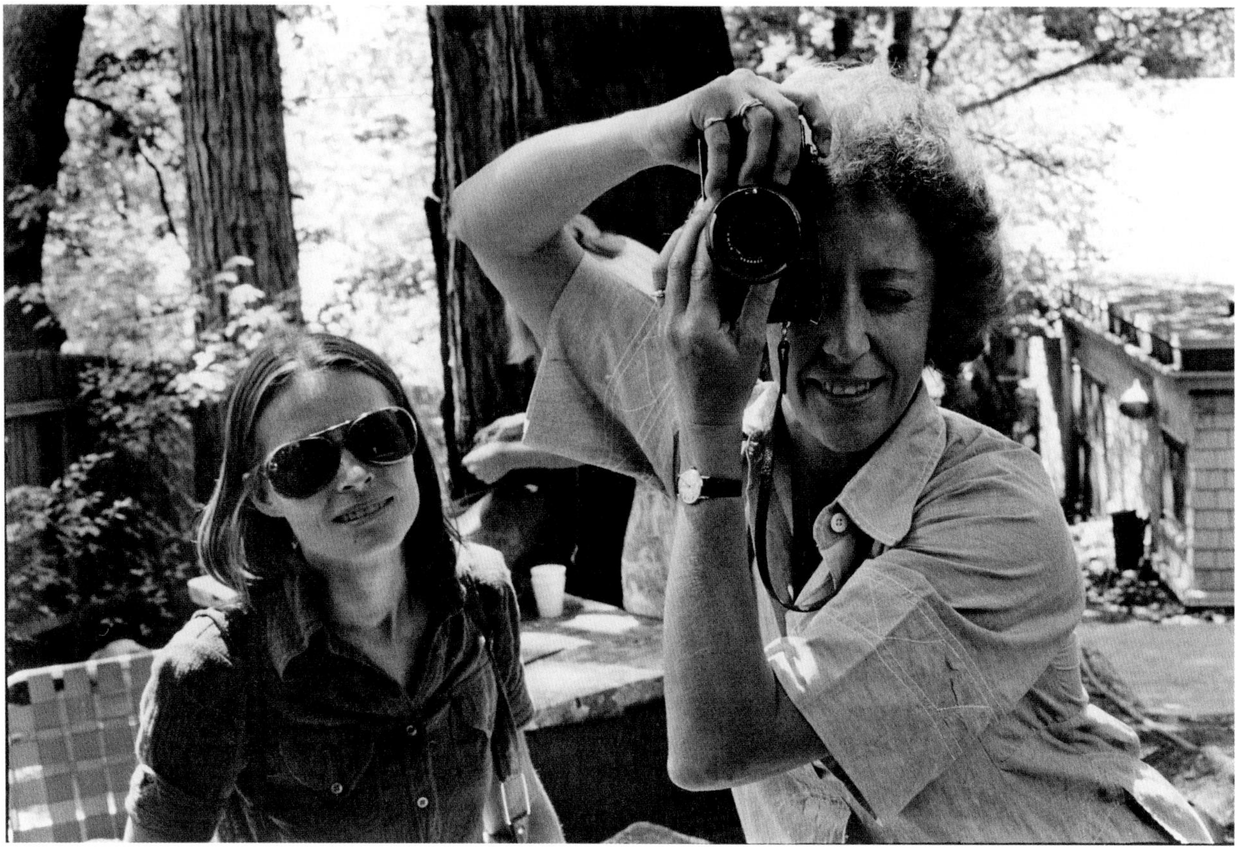

FIG. 13 Twinka Thiebaud and Eva Rubinstein in Yosemite, 1974. Courtesy of Twinka Thiebaud.

large-format camera, checking the meter, moving the camera slightly, getting under the black drape to look, and moving again, all while we talked about our personal lives. But while crouching in the same pose for so long, I got cold and stiff. My knees and hips ached, and I felt I could not hold the pose any longer. In her photo, *Twinka Thiebaud (Twinka and Tree)*, the stress can be seen in my wide-eyed stare (PL. 13). After we finished, Judy offered me a bowl of steaming borscht to warm my belly, one of the great perks of working in a person's home.

I did not know much then about the world of fine-art photography, since my museum experiences were mostly about looking at paintings. I owe Judy and Jack a great debt of gratitude for introducing me to both a new visual world and a new form of self-expression. I was grateful for their referrals and the invitations that opened doors for me to other photographers like Arnold Newman, Ralph Gibson, Mary Ellen Mark, Arthur Tress, Lucien Clergue, Eikoh Hosoe, and Robert Heinecken. That was the beginning of my career working with photographers, many of whom were and are dedicated, hardworking, and gifted individuals.

A few of the artists I worked with over the years were unreadable and seemingly disinterested in me as a person. They saw me simply as an object in their viewfinder, not as a fully fleshed-out human being. I was dumbstruck by the insensitive portrait photographer who tossed out directions like "Hold your breasts out to me" and "Lick your lips," as if I were a Playboy bunny. It unnerved and upset me. It was obvious he had never worked with a model before and had little regard for me as a person. That was my only distasteful experience in all the years of my career.

Some of the artists I worked with were generous, sharing their life stories and inviting me into their homes and studios where I met their families and got the chance to look at the art on their walls and books on their shelves. Forming relationships with artists was important to me, and their support, technical expertise, and artistic vision were vital in my quest to see how many faces I could manifest. If every picture tells a story, these were the people I relied on to help me tell mine.

While being offered more opportunities to express myself in photographs, I was still attempting to land auditions and film parts. I had met several Hollywood celebrities—Jack Nicholson, Warren Beatty, director Terrence Malick—and famous writers, like Anaïs Nin, Lawrence Durrell, and Erica Jong. They would come to dinner at the Pacific Palisades home of writer Henry Miller, whom I had met through my mother many years before, when she wrote a film treatment for a project based on his book *The Smile at the Foot of the Ladder*. I became fast friends with his daughter, Valentine, and she invited me to move into the Miller household as a paid caretaker to help her father, who was ailing after a significant stroke. I was Henry's live-in caretaker and cook for almost three years, from 1974 to 1977. He became a great friend, mentor, and surrogate grandfather.

The stories exchanged over Henry's dinner table with artists, writers, and friends were animated and inspiring. Being there and listening to captivating individuals reminded me so much of my early childhood, surrounded by interesting people engaged in fascinating work. But the glitter of Hollywood slowly began to fade when I was unable to land acting roles, and dealing with jaded, entitled, and pretentious personalities in the business was disheartening. When I left my job caring for Henry, I felt it was time to make some big changes. I was searching for my own artistic voice. I needed to find out what it felt like to stand in the shoes of an artist.

I began by writing a memoir of my time with Henry Miller, including those vibrant dinner conversations, titled, *What Doncha Know? about Henry Miller* (Eio Books, 2011). I also enrolled in college classes, studying art history, sculpture, drawing, and painting. In 1979, I gave birth as a single mother to a beautiful baby girl named Sierra. Needing a new, more financially secure way to support her, I went to work for a caterer and started a party-planning and private catering business a few years later.

I had not worked in front of a camera for several years following the birth of my daughter. Then, in 1986, while catering a wedding, I met photographer John Reiff Williams, who became my longtime collaborator, and a great friend, brother, and mentor to me and Sierra. He and his wife, Anarda, welcomed us into their home like a loving family. I can say, without reservation, he is one of the most thoughtful humans I know. I feel safe, seen, and held in his presence and in front of his camera. He has given me tremendous freedom to be seen—every aspect of me. And without Anarda's support, we would not have enjoyed "playing in the sandbox" as freely as we have for the past thirty-five years. The luxury of working together over a long period of time has been a great gift to us both. Bearing witness to one another's struggles and triumphs over the decades has added both texture and empathy to our work.

During our sessions, John does not direct me or impose his will; he gives me license to let out whatever feelings come up in me in the moment. If I am in an expansive or silly mood and feel like twisting my face into a bunch of distorted masks, he is there capturing every wrinkle, grimace, and gesture (PLS. 44–47). He has even turned me into a terrifying alien by combining and overlaying images to create something entirely new to add to my collection of pictures (PLS. 48 AND 49). We speak the same language and trust each other implicitly. I have even asked him to come to my bedside in the last stages of my life, if he so wishes, to make his final pictures of me into a poem.

EVOLUTIONS

I have also had the delight of working with wonderful women, and it gives me pleasure to see so much of their work represented here. I feel that women have a natural capacity to tap into one's vulnerabilities, weaknesses, and strengths. As I have aged and my body has changed over time, I feel comfort in the presence of another woman. Some men I have posed for in the past have come back to work with me later and want to Photoshop away my wrinkles, whereas women celebrate my courage to be seen as I grow, change, and evolve. The more recent images of me are not always "pretty," and that is okay. They are honest, and more than that, *human*. As the great Italian actress Anna Magnani once told a group of photographers: "Please don't retouch my wrinkles. It took me so long to earn them." And so it goes with me.

I have been asked if it hurts to see pictures of me as a young woman next to those that I posed for in my seventies. My answer is a resounding "No!" I do not cling to the pictures of a younger me like a security blanket. I think of them like shells I have outgrown or snakeskins I have shed along my path. All of the images are different aspects or facets of me, visual souvenirs as it were. Looking at them spread chronologically, I ask myself: "Is this image an honest reflection of who I was at the time the picture was captured? What was my state of mind? Where was I living? Was I in or out of love? What was I feeling about the photographer? Was I feeling comfortable in my skin or exposed and vulnerable?"

Every image evokes the circumstances of my life and my emotional state at that particular time. The pictures help me remember the details I might have otherwise forgotten. I can recall how and where I met most of my collaborators, the places where we worked together, and the hardships we endured to create those pictures. I remember the long, arduous road trips to reach locations where we could work undisturbed, contending with the harsh elements of scorching desert heat, the stinging cold of a bitterly windy beach, or a rainy mountaintop.

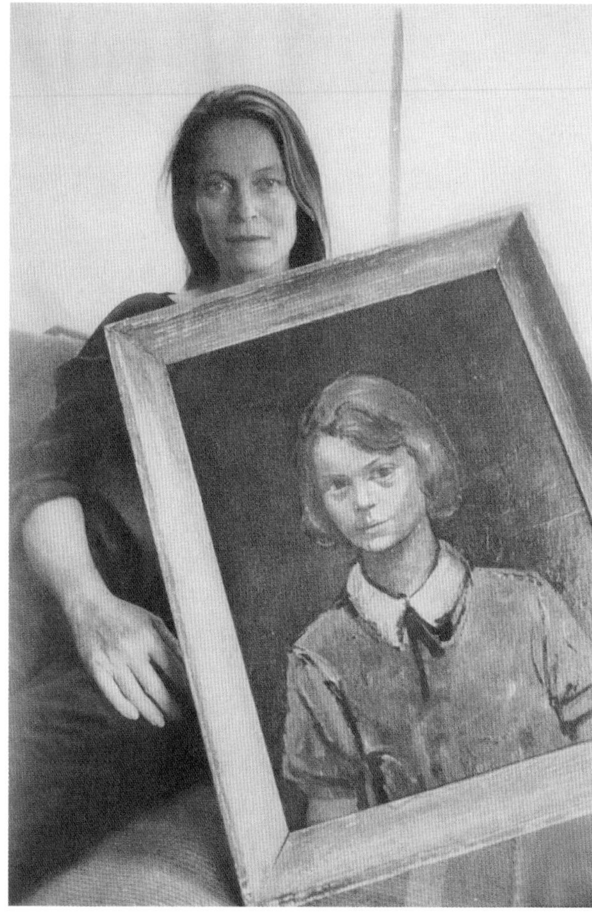

FIG. 14 Steven Josefsberg (American, born 1946), *Twinka*, 1989. Gum bichromate print, 18 × 12 in. Collection of Steven Josefsberg.

MEMORIES

I recall a shoot in the American Southwest with a photographer I affectionately nicknamed "The Maniac." Pete Saloutos had more energy than anyone I had ever worked with. He, his wife, Aleta, and I traveled to our shoot in an old Volkswagen bus, and as they slept in the back, I tried to sleep on a canvas sling suspended over the front seats. It was a long, miserable night. Before sunrise, we drove to a place that Pete was familiar with for its unique rock formations. We began hiking, hurrying to beat the sunrise. I was scrambling to keep up, skidding uneasily down steep slopes covered in hard, rolling pebbles. Then, lying on the cold, sharp rocks with my robe doubled up to pad my backside, I did my best to appear warm and relaxed while he took pictures. Later, he asked me to trek a very long way around a monstrous sand dune so I could keep my footprints out of the picture. The icy sand was bone-chilling. When we returned to the van, Aleta, an angel, tucked a warm quilt around my trembling frame and handed me a cup of steaming hot chocolate. Sadly, most of the images we made during that trip were lost, but the adventure is locked in my memory.

I have always felt more alive, more expansive, more animalistic out in nature. My muscles and bones can almost feel the poses as I remember gripping rocky ledges, wedging myself into granite crevices, hanging over icy waterfalls, and leaning into the bark of aromatic trees. The sheer physicality and sensuality of it all! I remember the way the light fell around me, the quiet concentration of the artist's gaze, and waiting, waiting, waiting for just the right moment for the click of the shutter. I hold these memories close, but I avoid clinging to the past. I am focused on the present. Who am I today? What stories do I have left to tell? And who will help me tell them?

This collection of images spans more than seventy years, from the life of a woman who happened to be the daughter of an artist and who kept choosing to be an artist's model. Portrayed in pencil, ink, charcoal, oil paint, pastel, acrylic, watercolor, and traditional and alternative photographic processes, many of these pictures will pass away, as I will one day. A few will live on after I am gone, a comforting thought, but to me, they are much more than images. As I look back through my many decades of work, I find connections to my family, childhood, and various stages of my life that form my story and at the same time are part of the larger art world. My father unwittingly set me on a path of self-discovery through the art of the pose, and most of all, this collection and exhibition are my love letter to him in return.

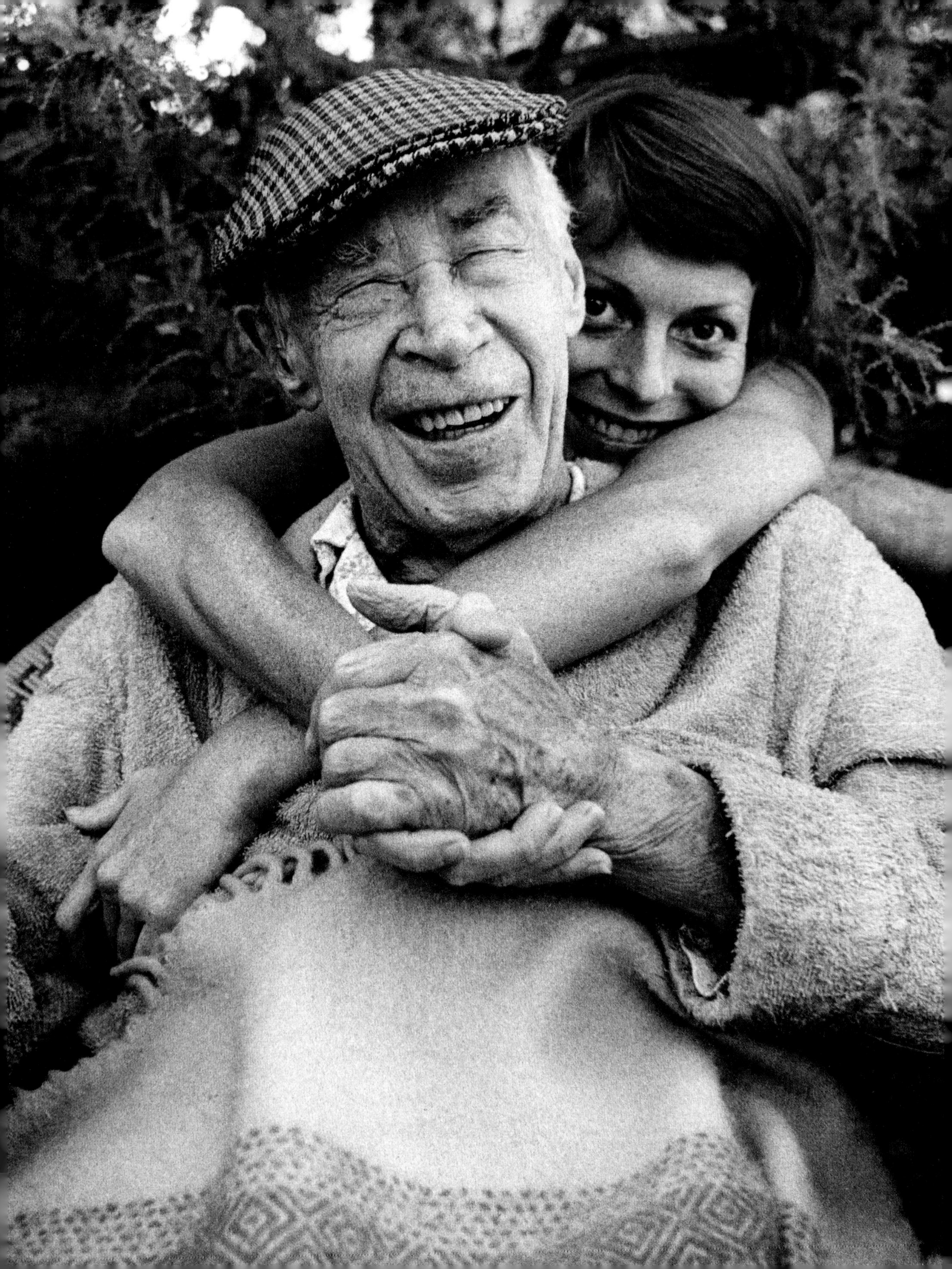

TWINKA: A MODEL FOR ALL TIME

HENRY MILLER

The name itself belongs to that of a celebrity! The single name always glorifies—like [Bruno] Caruso, [Dame Nellie] Melba, [Pablo] Picasso, The Duse [Eleonora Duse].

To begin with, let me say that I never owned a camera, never took a photo in my life, and, although I have had and still have some world-renowned photographers as friends, to wit: [Alfred] Stieglitz, Brassaï, Man Ray, and Wynn Bullock, photography itself is not of much interest to me. When I watch a good painter versus a bad painter at work, I am aware of the great difference of approach, but with photographers, good or bad, all I am aware of is the click of the shutter—like stepping on the accelerator. There must, of course, be something beyond this in the art of photography. Also, each person's work is different, unique. Wherein does the magic lie? I don't know and I don't care. All I care about is the difference between good and bad photographs, interesting and uninteresting subject matter.

In the case of Twinka [Thiebaud], the subject herself often appears in the nude. Sometimes the naked body itself is enough to guarantee interest in the model. Yet that alone is insufficient. When Twinka poses without clothes, she neither flings her sex in your face nor seeks to conceal it. She wears it openly, as one would a broach or an enlarged navel. One is aware of it but not disconcerted by it. She represents the primordial woman who is more closely allied to nature than man. At the same time there's something paradoxical about her. She is both the ultimate in sophistication and the indomitable female.

Among other things she knows how and what to wear. Some of her most inspired wardrobe may

Mary Ellen Mark (American, 1940–2015), *Henry Miller and Twinka Thiebaud* (Detail), 1975. Gelatin silver print, 7 ⅜ × 11 ⅞ in. Collection of Twinka Thiebaud.

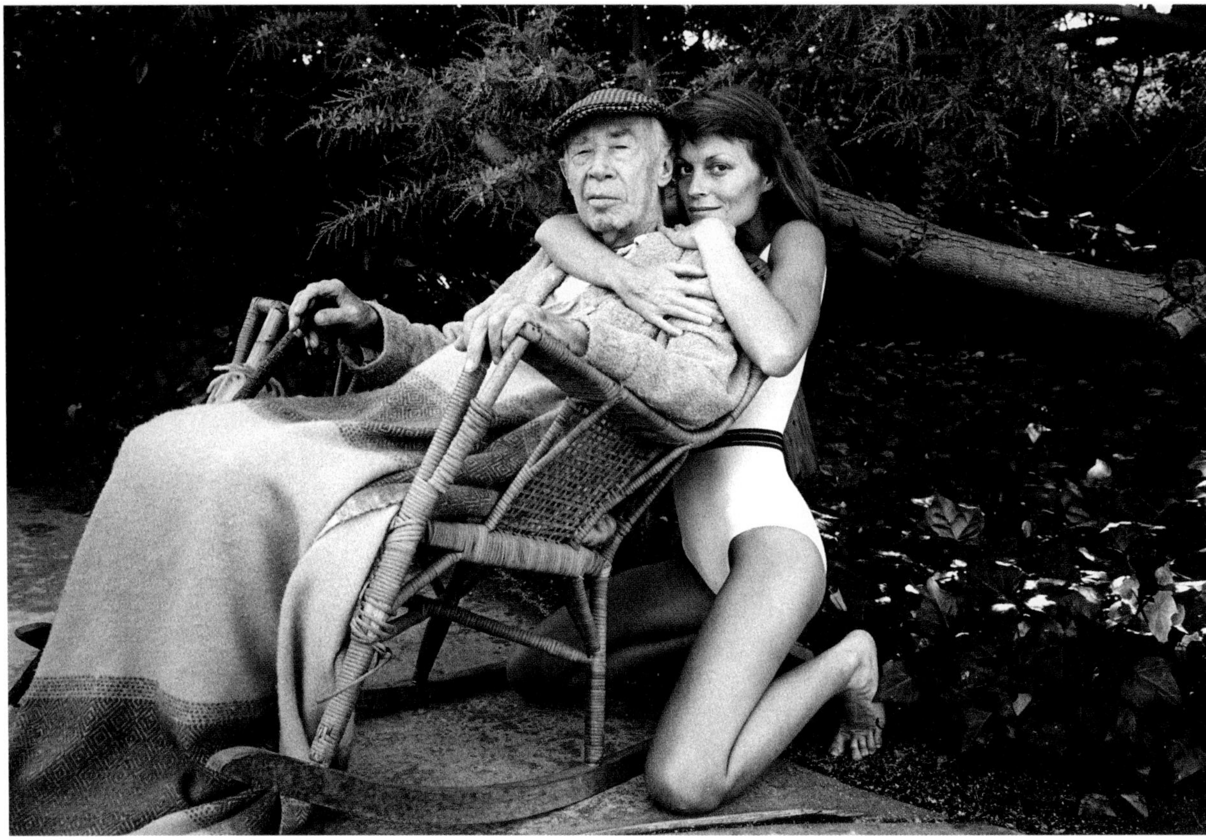

FIG. 15 Mary Ellen Mark (American, 1940–2015), *Henry Miller and Twinka, Pacific Palisades, Los Angeles*, 1975. Gelatin silver print, 7 7/8 × 11 7/8 in. Collection of Twinka Thiebaud.

have been found at the Salvation Army or St. Vincent de Paul's. In whatever is old-fashioned, out of date, she shines forth like a diadem. She is an Epiphany in rags.

Indeed, the thing which captivates the most perhaps, and immediately, are Twinka's eyes. They are the eyes of an inner being asserting its freedom. They can burn with the scorching heat of fury or simply melt one with their quiet rays of tender passion. If she were of another epoch, another land, one might find her on the façade of a Hindu temple, as one more disciple of the Goddess Kali.

But even the above-mentioned charms fail to explain Twinka's appeal for the artist. In a way, Twinka is something of a cross between an acrobat and an equilibrist. She was made to be a bareback rider in a [Georges] Seurat setting! She can assume the most difficult pose and maintain it indefinitely. Pitted against Nature's bare bones—desert, rock, cliff, etc.—she lets the animal in her loose. She can change her colors to match Nature's myriad designs as swiftly as the chameleon changes its hues to protect its life. The best in her cries out for the hungry, demanding eye of the camera.

The Twinka images herein collected represent years of work, years of struggle. Few people realize what it means to be a model—a good model. It doesn't mean holding one's body rigid while the shutter clicks, for example. Nor is it a matter of displaying one's physical charms. To be a model, for a painter or photographer, one has to create a rapport which inspires. One has to suggest more than one is. And although one's bones and muscles ache like fury, one must wear an air of intense interest and devotion. As a connoisseur of fine art once said to me, "Some of the greatest paintings of the world owe everything to the model." Certainly, when one thinks of [Pierre-Auguste] Renoir's wonderful females, one realizes the truth of such a statement.

In the end everything is highly personal—"subjective," we say. Twinka is the embodiment of the personal, the once only. For those who have eyes to see, I am certain she will give intense delight—and inspiration. – 10/27/1976

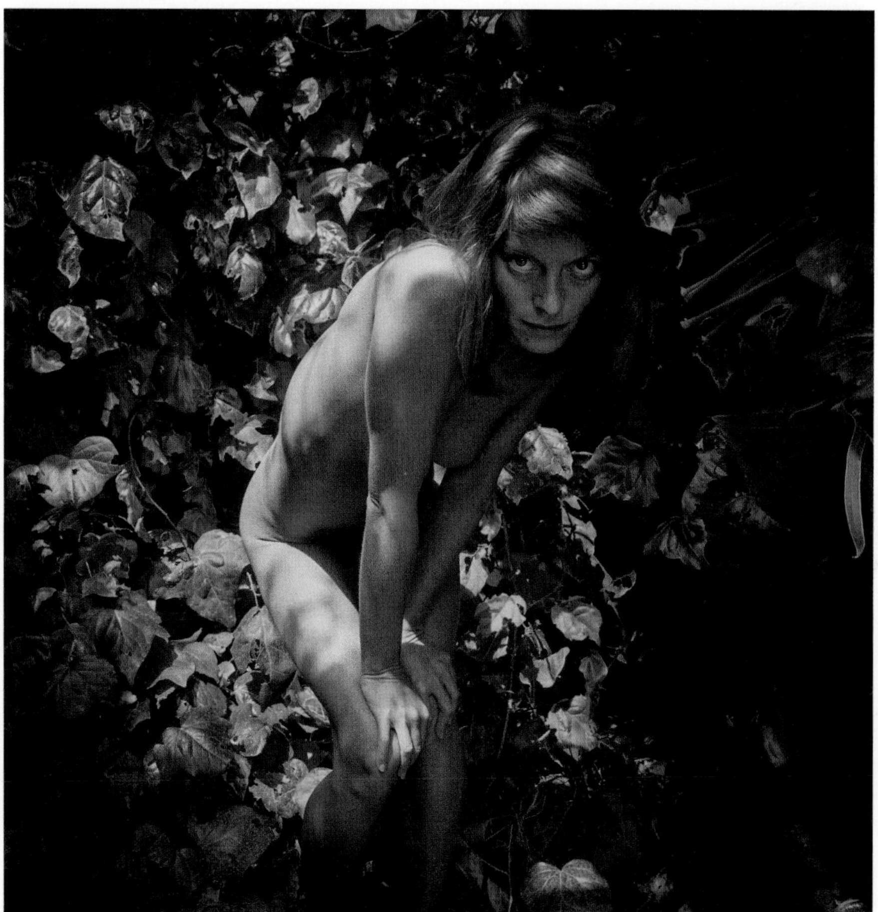

FIG. 16 R. Michael Walker (American, born 1950), *Twinka in Henry's Garden, Pacific Palisades, CA*, 1975. Gelatin silver print, 14 ⅝ × 14 ¼ in. Collection of Twinka Thiebaud.

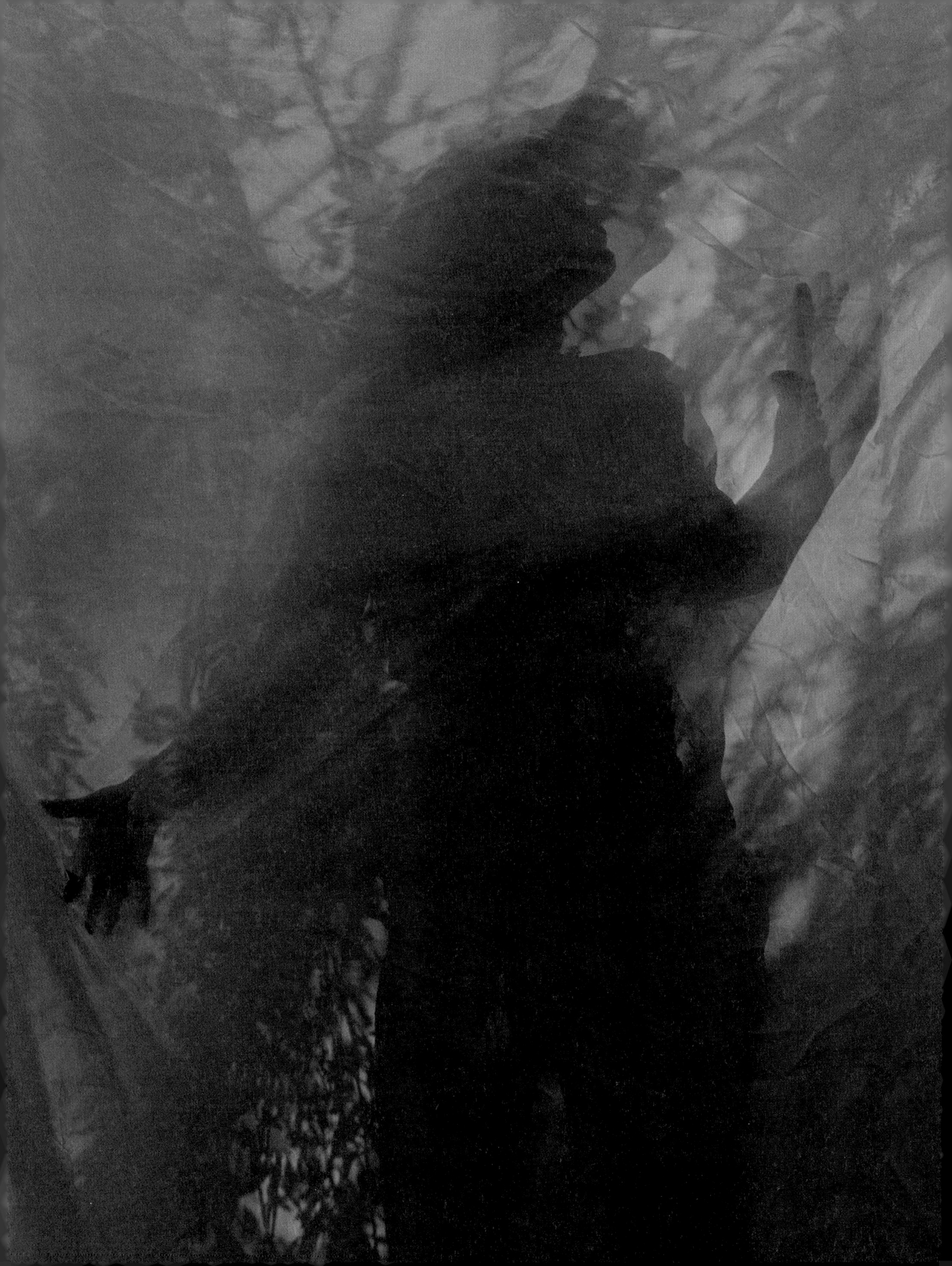

THE ART OF THE POSE: TWINKA THIEBAUD PAST, PRESENT, AND FUTURE

CLAIRE SYKES

In the fall of 2021, writer Claire Sykes met and spoke with close friend Twinka Thiebaud about her life and career as an artist's model. Together they talked with her longtime collaborator, photographer John Reiff Williams, and then Sykes interviewed photographer Judy Dater, both remotely. Here, Thiebaud, Williams, and Dater provide insightful views of the artist-model relationship, how, for them, it has shifted and deepened over time, and the enduring power of specific images and life experiences. Transcripts of the interview sessions were excerpted, edited, and combined for clarity.

CLAIRE SYKES: **Twinka, before we dive into your experiences as an artist's model, what is the story behind your name?**

TWINKA THIEBAUD: Twinka is my real name. It's on my birth certificate. It's not a nickname or a family name. My imaginative mother claimed she made it up. She said she wanted "an original," a name that "stood out." With my flaming-red hair and unusual name, I felt I was playing a starring role in my life. As a child, I got so used to people's attention, both in a good and a teasing way, that I coped by becoming the class clown, thriving on the laughter and applause of my peers.

CS: **What was it like growing up as the daughter of an artist?**

TT: I have many fond memories of those colorful and formative years in Sacramento [California]. I was never bored. As a young art professor, my dad [Wayne Thiebaud] was an inspiring figure to a legion of students, fellow artists, and colleagues, many of them

John Reiff Williams (American, born 1954), *Untitled (Twinka with Sheet 2)*, 2011. Archival pigment print, 16 ½ × 11 in. Collection of John Reiff Williams.

coming and going through our household. A group of students would show up unannounced on their way to the river for a picnic and they'd invite us kids to join them. And there were some lively parties with wonderful costumes. Dad was at the center, playing his guitar and singing old cowboy tunes, our beautiful mother dancing the hula and strumming her ukulele. There'd be music blaring from the record player, and someone would end up sitting down at Mom's pink piano. Friends crowded in the kitchen, taking turns making their specialties of homemade pizzas, checkerboard cakes, cowboy chili, or fudge. We kids always created a performance and were allowed to stay up late. Our parents knew how to celebrate life in the best ways.

I was creative as a child because I was observing my father as a creator, with so many different pursuits. He would play a classical tune on the piano by ear, so I thought I could play the piano, too. He played the guitar, so I took lessons. We had a potter's wheel in our basement and there were always art supplies, and he gave us art lessons. I wanted to be a ballerina or an actress after my dad started designing stage sets for local theater and college productions. He'd take me with him in the evenings to the college where he taught, and I'd watch him guide his students or other assistants in building and painting the sets. Or I'd go into the main theater and watch rehearsals. It just seemed completely natural to me to always be doing something creative.

CS: You really bring your creative childhood to life. What memories stand out to you most about modeling for your father?

TT: As a child, sitting still was really difficult. I wasn't a good subject and I thought posing wasn't for me. Later, it came to feel like I was sitting in a cell with a monk, watching him work in that deep, intense, and concentrated way. It was really kind of a dance, where he would look at me for long periods and then turn to the canvas, drawing with paint, squinting, moving back, moving forward, mixing paints. I knew I had to stay awake and stay present.

When I was seventeen, Dad began paying me a little to model for him. I got to his studio, and he said, "OK, you're going to lie down on the floor and pose there." This was for his painting *Supine Woman* (1963), which is in the permanent collection of the Crystal Bridges Museum of American Art (PL. 5). The cement floor was covered with cardboard and a white sheet. It was winter, I had on a long-sleeved white dress, black heels, and nylons, and I laid on the floor. It took about forty hours, six hours at a stretch. I distinctly remember the burning sensation of this little electric heater right next to my leg. We were cold, but my father was moving all around while looking at me, totally engrossed, so absorbed in his work.

I posed for him every so often while I was also modeling in art schools. At my father's studio, sometimes it was quiet, or there'd be classical music or a talk show on public radio. It could be mind-numbing to sit in a pose and my body would get stiff, so we'd stop to do stretching exercises together and move around (FIG. 17). Our break for lunch was always welcome, with Dad's navy bean soup and hearty bread and butter. We'd chat about my schoolwork, my acting classes and performing in school plays, and his latest endeavors, and visit with my stepmother and their kids.

CS: You were modeling for painting and drawing students at first. Then came the 1970s and the emergence of photography as an experimental art form in California. How did you start working with photographers?

TT: In the beginning, I didn't know much about fine-art photography. Then I met Judy Dater and Jack Welpott at a party in San Francisco in 1970, and not long after that they photographed me. From Judy, I eventually met and modeled for many famous photographers, and she invited me to pose at photography workshops. Others I met at art openings, or I'd see their work in a gallery or book and call them up. If we made a personal connection and felt compatible, we'd work together. I was paid a few times by

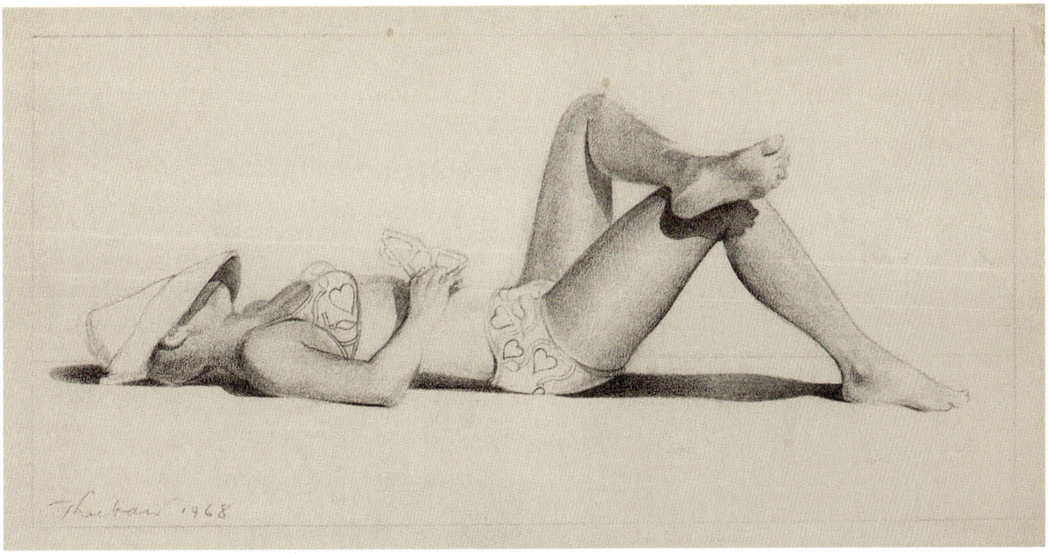

FIG. 17 Wayne Thiebaud (American, 1920–2021), *Untitled*, 1968. Pencil on paper, 6 × 12 in. Collection of Twinka Thiebaud.

photographers when I worked in art schools. Rather than payment, I preferred to have a photo from a modeling session and the signed rights to use it in a future book or exhibition that I was determined to have one day. I've certainly amassed a great collection of images along the way.

CS: What happened that day in 1974 at the Ansel Adams photography workshop in Yosemite National Park, "The Nude in the Landscape," to which Judy Dater had invited you, resulting in her iconic photo, *Imogen and Twinka at Yosemite*?

TT: A group of student photographers and several models, including me, arrived in a school bus, which dropped us off near Bridalveil Fall, far from the eyes of most hikers and tourists. As the group assembled, waiting for instruction, a few models suddenly dropped their robes and pandemonium broke loose, and I followed suit. My first impression was that many of these students hadn't ever worked with a nude model. It was like being in front of a firing squad full of irritable paparazzi shouting at one another and at the poor models. "Twinka! Over here!" "Get out of my way. I had her first!" "Put your arms up!" "No, I want them down!" yelled another. "Turn to your right!" "I don't want that pose," complained someone else.

I wasn't used to working in that kind of a frenzy. I noticed Judy and photographer Imogen Cunningham sitting quietly on a fallen tree in a clearing nearby, engaged in conversation. I put on my robe to escape the unruly crowd. As I walked closer, I heard Imogen say something like, "I don't know how anyone makes a photograph like that!" Judy thought it was time to demonstrate a better way to work with models. "Why don't the two of you go over and stand in front of that tree?" she requested. I leaned against the tree and shifted my body into different positions, and Imogen stood on the other side of it, looking at me. Judy gave us a few suggestions and then asked us to hold that pose.

As she took time adjusting her view camera and its settings, the squabbling students eventually took notice and joined us. They stood in a semicircle behind Judy, quietly observing her at work. After the demonstration, models and photographers were given time to work one-on-one, which made for a far more productive workshop. There are several images in my collection taken during that workshop at

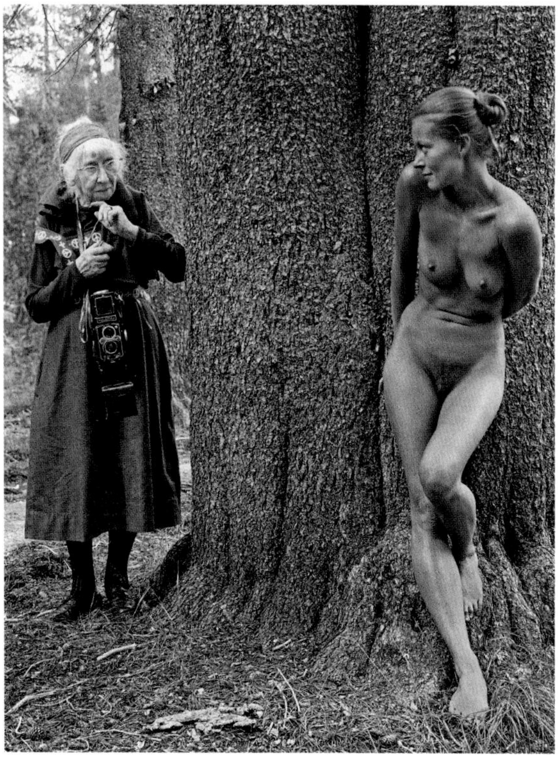

FIG. 18 Judy Dater (American, born 1941), *Imogen and Twinka at Yosemite*, 1974. Gelatin silver print, 9 ¼ × 7 ¼ in. Crocker Art Museum purchase with funds from the Shirley & Forrest Plant Fund, 2017.81.

magnificent Yosemite (FIG. 18). I love the photograph Judy took and am honored to have played a role in it. And the workshop catapulted me into posing for more photographers.

CS: Judy, as you look back on the resulting photograph, *Imogen and Twinka at Yosemite*, what do you think of it?

JUDY DATER: The photo is not really representative of the work I did at the time or have done since; it's a lot more light-hearted. And yet it has a pretty profound message, in that it's about youth and old age, and two women confronting that in each other, as crone and nymph, and all that the symbolism implies. But it didn't make me want to take more pictures like it. Most people who see that photo love it, though. It's a very popular image, and it's been reproduced more than any other photograph I've ever taken.

CS: How does the photograph you took four years earlier of Twinka crouched at the base of a redwood tree, *Twinka Thiebaud (Twinka and Tree)*, generally fit within the context of your work?

JD: I consider that a hallmark photograph of mine, and much more typical of the kinds of portraits I've taken. The photo is very confrontational (PL. 13). I am most interested in showing the interior soulfulness of a person, their mysterious and hidden side. In this photo, Twinka looks like a frightened creature, as if my camera and I came upon her suddenly and startled her. There is a lot of tension in the photograph, with her intense expression, her one hand clutching the tree and, to a lesser degree, her other hand grasping her knee. The gauzy, revealing dress adds a level of sexuality. There's a profound sense of something going on that's bigger than her. In that way, it's an edgier picture than *Imogen and Twinka at Yosemite*.

CS: Twinka, five years after the Yosemite workshop, you gave birth to your daughter, Sierra. How did modeling fit in with mothering, especially in the first decade of her life?

TT: I put my life as a model completely on the back burner. I never thought I'd have a child, but in my early thirties I was seeing someone eight years younger than me, and I got pregnant and gave birth. We didn't marry. I felt I was ready for the journey of motherhood, even though I was single. We shared some parenting duties, separately, and I needed to find a new, more lucrative form of work to support my girl.

I went to work for a caterer, and a year later I opened my own catering and party-planning business. We sent out lunches all over the Los Angeles area to commercial shoots and music-video productions. That's when I met, and eventually married, a video artist and documentary filmmaker, and soon I was catering for movie-industry clients and large weddings. I had a wonderful crew and it was great fun, more of a party for us in the kitchen. I had been thinking about posing again and was reevaluating what kind of work I was interested in doing with artists, because I didn't want to do any more "ethereal nudes in the landscape." I started delving more into photography and art, looking through books and going to exhibitions. And I began seeking out photographers who were open to collaborating with me.

CS: As you explored the visual possibilities of posing, whom did you find to be an inspiration for you in the world of artist's models?

TT: At the top of the list is Georgia O'Keeffe, perhaps the greatest of all artist's models. She often posed for her husband, Alfred Stieglitz. His photographs of her speak volumes about how the intimate connection between model and artist lends itself to the soul of an image. When I look at the pictures he made of her, I see the depth of their connection and the vulnerability and fragility of a marriage. She didn't pose for him to have her pictures shown; they were intended to be kept private. There's an awful lot to unpack in those photographs. I see a lot of love, struggle, pain, hard work, and extraordinary beauty in the humanness of the images. And no other model I know used their hands to convey emotion better than Georgia O'Keeffe.

CS: What would you say has been the guiding principle of your work as an artist's model?

TT: As I gained experience, I felt I should give something of my humanity to the process, that I'm not just a body. One doesn't do that by merely holding still. It's also about projecting one's energy and focus throughout a pose. My training in acting and dance has been invaluable for that. Overall, modeling, to me, has always been about the communication between me and the artist. It matters to me to participate in their creative process and inspire their best possible work.

CS: After you decided to reinvigorate your career as an artist's model, you began a decades-long collaboration with John Reiff Williams. John, what is your overall photography background?

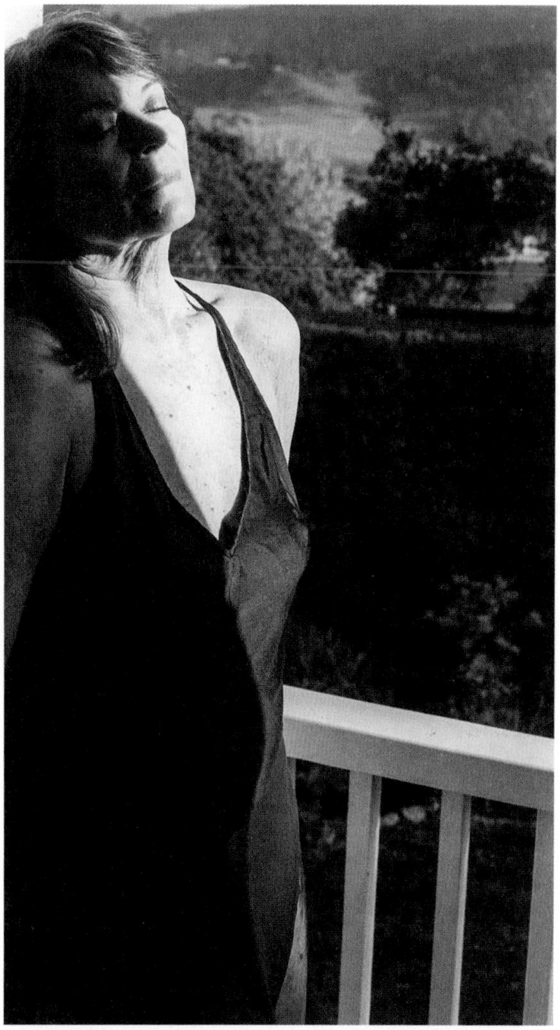

FIG. 19 Michelle Magdalena (American, born 1985), *Soulshine*, 2014. Gelatin silver print, 6 7/8 × 3 7/8 in. Collection of Twinka Thiebaud.

JOHN REIFF WILLIAMS: I earned an MFA from the University of Southern California. Earlier, I'd done two apprenticeships, one with Ruth Bernhard and one with Al Weber, the director of Ansel Adams's Yosemite workshop. For nearly fifty years, when not on assignment, I've continued fine-art photography on my own.

When Twinka and I met, in 1986, I was building my own commercial-photography business. At that point in my life, I was very comfortable photographing people—about one to three thousand images per month. The commercial work fed the fine art, in terms of a fluidity, fluency, and practice with the mechanics of the cameras, from 4×5 view cameras to medium formats to 35mm.

CS: John, I know that you met at a wedding where you were the photographer and Twinka, you were the caterer. How did you know that you wanted to collaborate as artists?

TT: I learned firsthand that while working huge catering events, there's a lot of pressure and you can be dealing with difficult personalities. Coordination between the crew and the photographer is critical. John was a dream to work with.

JRW: We developed an ease of working those events together, which made them a lot less stressful, more fluid, and formed the basis for how we both felt about each other's capacities and in each other's company. I loved working with Twinka. As time went on, our lives started to blend socially. I remember many visits and parties at her place in Santa Monica with friends and family. We knew who we were as people, working side by side.

When we worked together in the early years, the idea was just to make art. We weren't worried about whether or not the art went to market. That still isn't a driver in our reason to work together. Twinka and I were more interested in developing our relationship as real people with each other, throughout the full spectrum of friendship—from serious, trusting confidants to side-splitting, belly-laughing comic jokesters. Twinka is fast and very, very funny, as well as a woman full of feeling and willing to share the full arc of her humanity.

CS: What were the first images you made together, and how did you approach collaborating?

JRW: They were of Twinka and Sierra in Santa Monica, perhaps made casually, as I carried a camera nearly everywhere I went. So much of that situation was about establishing comfort for all of us.

TT: Getting to know the photographer and feeling relaxed with them in front of the camera is everything to me. Sierra was meeting John for the first time. Photographing us was a way to ease into our working relationship. It's always been about connection, communication, and building trust.

JRW: More and more, as time goes on, another photograph isn't going to change my life. To me, with photography, it's about opening to the subject. It's a give-and-take, a take with permission, respect. I don't take pictures. I give pictures. This suggests the development of a relationship with the person I'm photographing, which facilitates the narrative of the image. The narrative says something visual about emotion, time, place, and circumstance because, in meeting over the decades, Twinka and I both have been changing in those ways. With her, the act of making a photograph has always felt like sharing, and the "share" is the evidence captured in our collaborative process. Twinka is giving Twinka, and I'm giving me. The only purpose the camera has is to record that. After those first photos, things just happened organically. Twinka would come to where my wife, Anarda, and I lived. I would set up lights and drops in the apartment, working with the view camera, sculpting her with light. Her poses led the way to the questions of evocation, mood, and lighting design, concealing and revealing her form and gestures, and the emotional direction of a given setup. Everything was mutable.

CS: Is there a photo, or a series of photos, that you made early on in your collaboration that stands out to you?

JRW: What I call the *Funny Faces* (1987). The historical precedent for these images lies in the 1862 published photographs by Paul Tournachon [the son of famous French photographer Nadar] of the work of French neurologist [Guillaume-Benjamin-Amand] Duchenne de Boulogne. Duchenne believed that electrically stimulating facial muscles could help him understand human emotions and peer into people's souls.

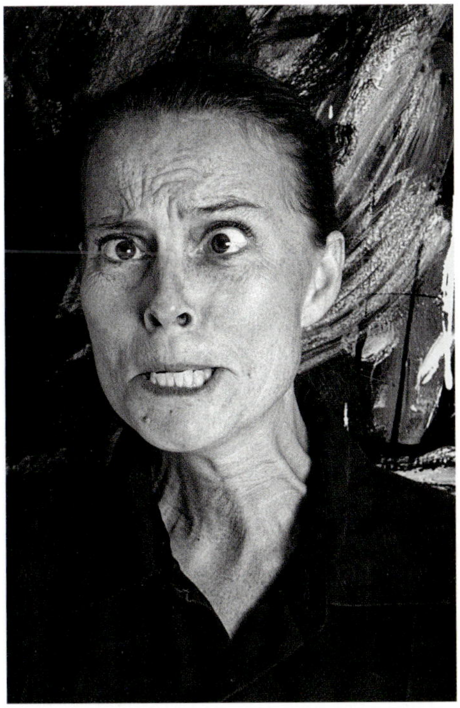

FIG. 20 John Reiff Williams (American, born 1954), *Untitled (Twinka with Eyes Crossed)*, from the *Funny Faces* series, 1987. Archival pigment print, 16 ½ × 11 in. Collection of John Reiff Williams.

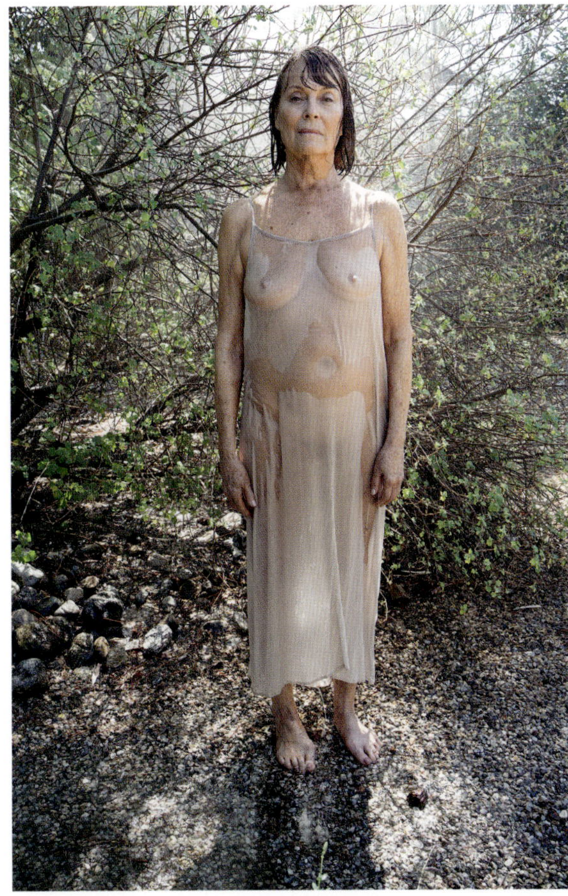

FIG. 21 John Reiff Williams (American, born 1954), *Untitled (Twinka in Wet Slip)*, 2013. Archival pigment print, 16 × 10 ⅝ in. Collection of Twinka Thiebaud.

Twinka and I were looking not so much for the gestural, but for who and where she was in that moment, as a being, a soul, a person. At the same time, Twinka's expressions were dependent on their temporality, yet they seemed like masks, not unlike those in [Japanese] Noh theater. I think that her ability to stretch and distort her face came out of her life. The expressions are narratives in themselves. Behind them lies the range of emotional capacity from a very real person playing as if she's in pain. The work is tender, revealing, explosive—and funny (FIG. 20).

CS: Twinka, you have such unbridled emotion in John's photo, *Twinka Crying* (1987). What was going on in your life at the time?

TT: I drove through a rainy night to work with John at his home, feeling anxious and distraught that my marriage was on the verge of a breakup. I tried to keep myself together when I walked in the door. He had a background set up, and his camera was pointed toward me. I looked at him and he asked, "So, how are you feeling?" and I just broke down in tears. I felt shattered (PL. 38).

CS: That same outward expression of human experience is visible in your work together decades later, especially in the 2013 photo of you, Twinka, in a see-through, soaking-wet slip. What are both of your thoughts on this image?

TT: I love the humanity of this portrait (FIG. 21). I was feeling the weight of my age and my body changing, and I wanted to be as emotionally naked as I could possibly be, and I think that shows.

JRW: I felt Twinka's vulnerability in her sharing of it. It was palpable. In this photo, there's no artifice, nothing faux, fake, false. It's raw. It's like she was plugged into the wall, a hundred and twenty volts of Twinka. The image speaks directly to the issues of the passing of youth and accepting the evidence of aging. Twinka embraces her physical changes and lets me in, and that's what makes her real and meaningful to me as a subject.

CS: Twinka and John, in working together over all these years, what has fed and impacted your collaboration and friendship?

JRW: The trust and depth of our work together, and our friendship, would not be possible without Anarda, to whom I've been married for forty years. My marriage has given me the capacity for the relationship that Twinka and I have. In Twinka, could I ask for a more open, sharing, vulnerable, loving, trusting artist, colleague, and friend? No.

TT: I know I wouldn't have begun this partnership with John if not for my then husband's blessing and John's generous partnership with Anarda. She has given us the freedom to enjoy one of the deepest relationships you can have with someone that has nothing to do with a love affair.

JRW: Twinka and I are the lucky ones, sustaining the thread, the continuity of our relationship over nearly four decades. That's a gift. We get the opportunity to share and witness a place where we own time together. This has afforded us extraordinary access into each other's lives, and that makes our collaboration all the richer for both of us.

CS: As I ruminate on the larger idea of past versus present in the collaboration between photographer and artist's model, I think of you, Judy, working with Twinka in the 1970s and revisiting your collaboration decades later with *Woman in a White Slip* (2014). What was it like to work with Twinka again, and what are your thoughts on the image?

JD: Twinka wanted photographers to rephotograph her as an older woman for a book she was working on, and asked me if I would like to do it, and of course I was interested. I wasn't quite sure how to start, but I wanted it to be a nude. She was in my studio, and I was trying different backgrounds, and nothing was working. She brought along a slip as a prop, so I asked her to put it on. That felt more right to me than when she was completely nude, and I got excited; I felt like something was happening. When I'm working, I'm just responding to what I'm seeing, and it's very visceral. That's what I was experiencing when she put the slip on. I liked the way it looked against the black background, the textures of silk and skin, and the quality of the light (FIG. 22). Those things simplified the picture and made it more graphic. I could concentrate more on Twinka's face and expression and who she was at that moment, as a person, an aging, very attractive woman, and not get hung up on looking at the naked body. It was concealing and revealing at the same time, showing an aspect of her sexuality, much like the 1970 photo of her at the base of the tree.

It is a mysterious and psychological image. I wanted the photograph to stand on its own, without the weight of the other photographs I had taken of Twinka years earlier. So I titled it *Woman in a White Slip*, because I didn't want people to immediately start making comparisons with Twinka of the [2014] moment to Twinka when she was much younger. What interested me was the soulful quality of a portrait of an older woman who's strong and tough, sturdy and together, not as a "here's Twinka and she's not twenty-four anymore".

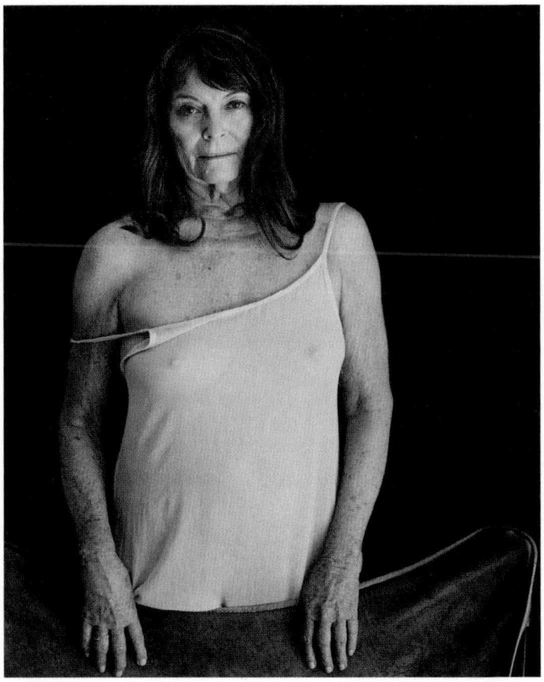

FIG. 22 Judy Dater (American, born 1941), *Woman in a White Slip*, 2014. Archival pigment print, 20 × 15 ⅞ in. Collection of Twinka Thiebaud.

CS: Judy, expanding on the then-and-now comparison, how do you view Twinka as an artist's model at this point in her life?

JD: I think it took a lot of courage—and trust—for her to want to pose for me forty years later. She had to be willing to let all the years of living and all the life experience show. She revealed to me that day as much as she could regarding the wind-tossed life that she and most of us have lived. She becomes a symbol, particularly for all strong, older women, not to be afraid to show who they are in the present moment. There stands Twinka in all her strength, dignity, and power, looking directly into the camera, confronting her anonymous viewers, and saying, "I'm OK."

CS: Twinka, along with Judy and John, you've inspired many photographers and other visual artists throughout the years. Aside from posing for them, how have you been creative?

TT: Since my forties, shortly after I started working with John, I've drawn and painted, mainly in oils, for pleasure. I've copied many contemporary masters' works, including my father's, to have a sense of how a painting comes together. Now I'm trying to find my own language in paint. I don't show my work. Also, in the last ten years, I've done interior design for my sister's home and my own. I find I really enjoy that. And I love to cook.

CS: I can personally attest to your beautiful home and your talent in the kitchen, Twinka. And I think I speak for everyone when I say that I hope you'll continue collaborating with artists. Is this your plan?

TT: Yes. John and I know we'll be working together again. And I'm open to collaborating with new photographers and visual artists. Also, there were artists I posed for that I felt, at the time, we didn't quite hit the mark, but if we worked together a second or third time, we might get to something really interesting. Each artist I've modeled for has brought out some aspect of who I am in their images. To me, the photos acknowledge the life of a human being who changes and ages—and hopefully always evolves.

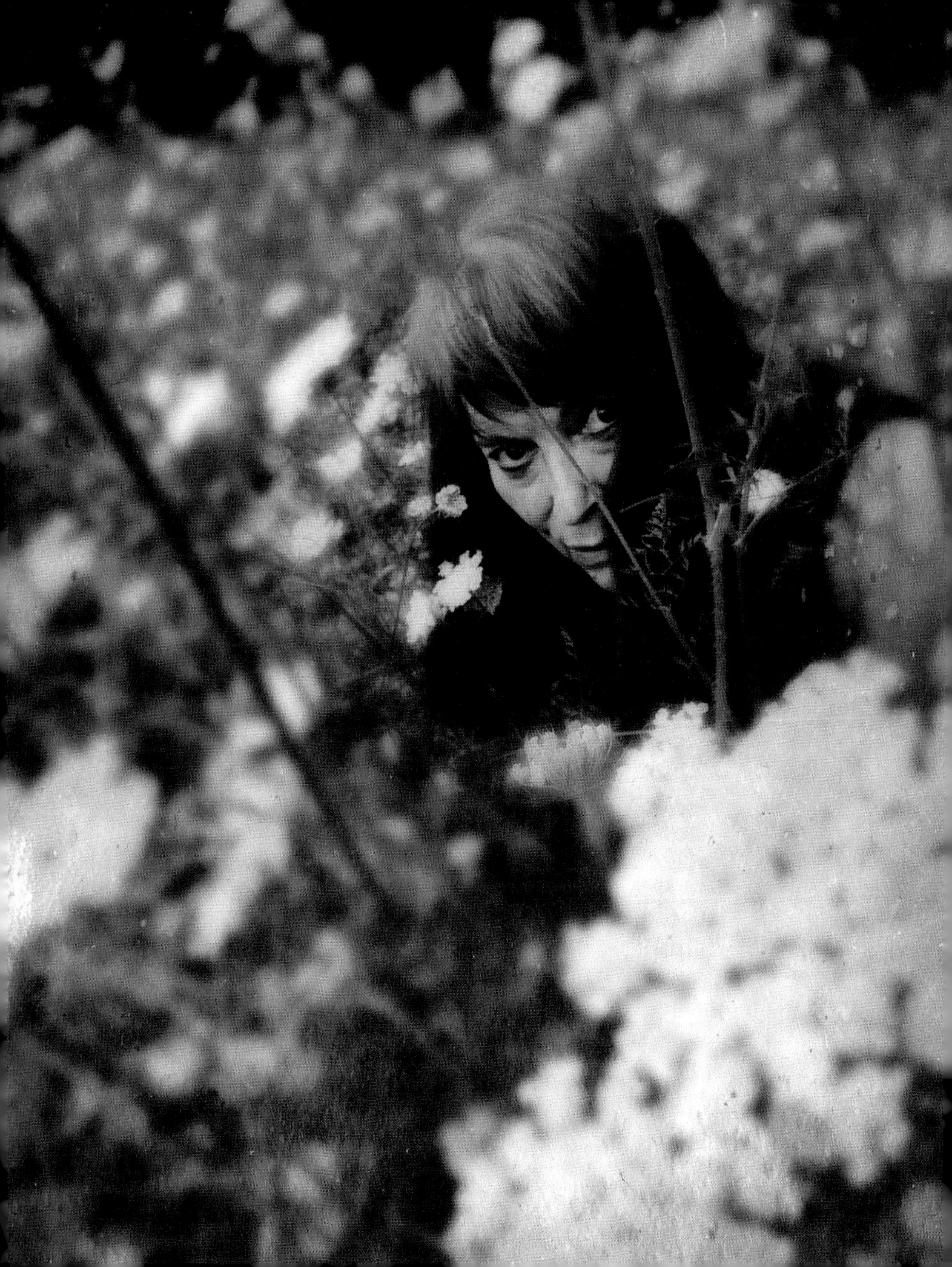

HUMAN NATURE: THE BODY/ENVIRONMENT RELATIONSHIP IN PHOTOGRAPHS OF TWINKA THIEBAUD

JAYME YAHR, PH.D.

AESTHETIC SENSIBILITY

Twinka Thiebaud's career as an artist's model is comprised of artistic experimentation and relationships that span three specific time periods in her life. Her role as a model began as a small, pony-tailed child, when she posed for many drawings and paintings by her father, renowned artist Wayne Thiebaud (1920–2021). These first efforts at being an artist's model were followed by a prolific second period of her career, the 1970s, during a time of significant cultural change in America. A third phase in the 2000s is defined by collaborative partnerships, many between Twinka Thiebaud and women artists, which bring her confidence to the forefront. Nestled within this timeline are important thematic threads that tie the artworks of these disparate periods together. The first is Thiebaud herself, an active partner in the creation of each image in this catalogue and the exhibition *Twinka Thiebaud and the Art of the Pose*. None of the artworks would exist without her presence and the physical and emotional awareness she brings to the creative process. The second is the environment. The relatability of the artworks, many of which are photographs, depends upon Thiebaud's relationship to the natural environment that surrounds her as she poses, including trees, water, rocks, sand, flowers, and leaves. Often, Thiebaud aligned, contorted, or expanded her physical presence within a natural environment to communicate the connection between body and earth. This body/environment relationship within a variety of physical spaces is at the core of her aesthetic sensibility. She enlivens and challenges her body to both be within, and become a part of, her surroundings, echoing French philosopher Maurice Merleau-Ponty's explanation of body/space confluence:

Lorijo Daniels (American, born 1965), *In the Lace* (Detail), 2020. Tintype, 7 × 5 ⅛ in. Collection of Twinka Thiebaud.

> Our body is not in space like things; it inhabits or haunts space. It applies itself to space like a hand to an instrument, and when we wish to move about we do not move the body as we move an object. We transport it without instruments as if by magic, since it is ours and because through it we have direct access to space. For us the body is much more than an instrument or a means; it is our expression in the world, the visible form of our intentions. Even our most secret affective movements, those most deeply tied to the humoral infrastructure, help to shape our perception of things.[1]

While an artist may capture the body in a photograph, painting, or drawing, Thiebaud's ability to communicate a feeling through her pose, such as fear, sorrow, surprise, or contentment, gives her larger agency in the creative process. This collaboration between Thiebaud and artist is what makes the artwork relatable and true to the human experience, in which actions are inextricable from place and time. The artist Mark Dion explained this relationship between perception, time, and nature, stating: "It's important that the category of nature is not something the field of science has a monopoly on—that everyone has a say in what gets to be nature, at a particular time, for a particular group of people. In order to motivate people to care about the natural world around us, one of our chief tools is an aesthetic sensibility."[2] Dion's words, in many ways, affirm what Thiebaud enacted as an artist's model from the 1970s onward, as she developed a relationship to nature that was visceral and related to a specific moment in time, often delineated only by her age when the work was created (FIG. 23).

While Thiebaud's presence is central to the works in the exhibition, her participation as a model can be further divided into her relationships with the environment and with artists. The artist of each work engaged Thiebaud through their own aesthetic sensibility, capturing her movements, expressions, and bodily relation to nature. The result is an image that communicates an artistic partnership in a singular moment. To summarize scholar Richard Shusterman,

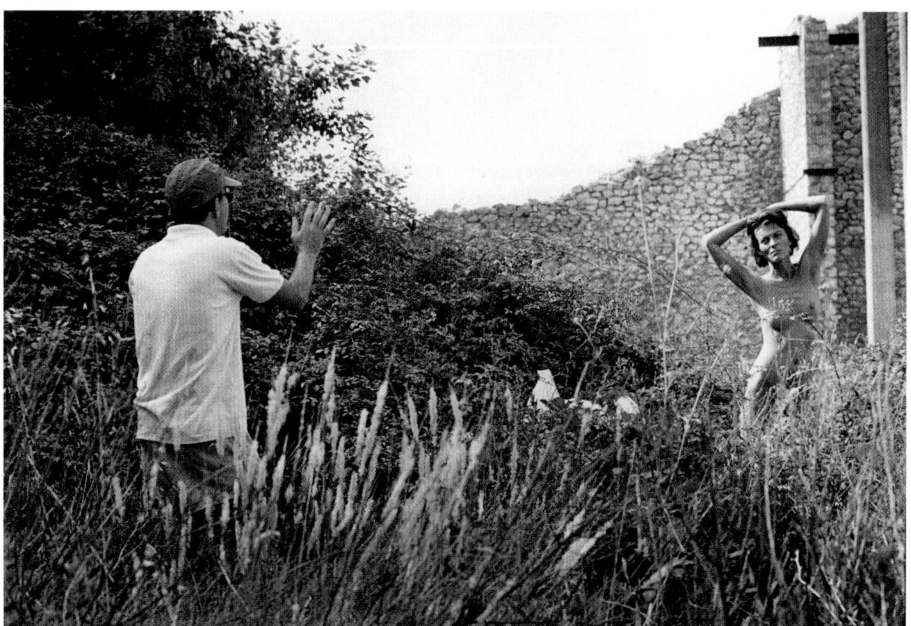

FIG. 23 Twinka Thiebaud posing, circa 1985. Collection of Twinka Thiebaud.

who has written about the importance of the photographic process, there is a web of elements that create value in a photograph, including the photographer, the camera, the subject, the subject's pose and styling, and the critical communication between the artist and subject. It is not only the final photograph that has value.[3] In the early years, Thiebaud primarily worked with her father, fine-tuning her ability to pose and work in partnership with an artist. When she embarked on a professional career as an artist's model in the 1970s, she worked with dozens of artists, honing her skills as a collaborator with photographers and students, including Judy Dater, Jack Welpott, Ralph Gibson, Arnold Newman, Pete Saloutos, Eikoh Hosoe, Robert Heinecken, and Eva Rubinstein.

A list of sites that includes the forests of Yosemite National Park, the California coast, the parks of Oregon, and the arid hills of Arizona and New Mexico runs parallel to this list of artists and defines a distinctly Western physical experience largely unassociated with cities or urban centers deemed artistic hubs at the time, such as New York City or Los Angeles. While it may have seemed a natural progression for Thiebaud to focus on urban scenes or move toward commercial work once her career was established, she took the opposite tack. Continuing to work as an artist's model throughout her career, Thiebaud established decades-long partnerships with photographers, including John Reiff Williams, who set the stage for experimentation and connection. Thiebaud's work with Lorijo Daniels, Elizabeth Opalenik, Aline Smithson, and Kim Campbell expands the ways in which a sense of identity changes with age. As her career became increasingly rooted in artistic partnerships, she gained poise and power and moved deeper into experimentation. Thiebaud's work within nature-based settings exemplifies her confidence as an artist's model; she pairs her body with her surrounding environment, which results in a series of emotionally resonant images that embody the concepts of place, memory, and experience. When taken together, the artworks in *Twinka Thiebaud and the Art of the Pose* represent Twinka Thiebaud's life and career, while simultaneously speaking to the possibilities and nuances of photographic, and often West Coast-based, experimentation over the course of seventy years.

1970s

> "Today everything exists to end in a photograph."[4]
> —Susan Sontag

The 1970s were a decade of change in the field of photography. Moving away from documentary photographs, artists experimented with mundane subjects, framing devices, off-kilter views, street photography, and snapshots. Although still tied to analog processes to create a photographic print, manipulation of the darkroom development process was a hallmark of the era.[5] Along with the advancement and refinement of color photography, cameras continued to change. Lighter and more portable, with faster shutter speeds, cameras became an essential tool for capturing everyday life, and were no longer bound only to the profession of photojournalist or portrait photographer. Publications emerged in the mid-20th century that created the backbone of art historical discourse related to photography's role in America. Robert Frank's *The Americans* (1958), Ed Ruscha's *Twentysix Gasoline Stations* (1963), John Szarkowski's *The Photographer's Eye* (1966), Susan Sontag's *On Photography* (1977), and Nan Goldin's *The Ballad of Sexual Dependency* (1986) represent a small cross-section of texts that address the photographer's eye, trends of the period, and the critical examination of photography as an art form that can both document and deceive.[6]

These texts, and many of the artists who produced them, helped to establish photography as a field of fine art and an art form that crossed socio-economic boundaries. Photography's emergence as an experimental artistic genre coincided with cultural and sociopolitical change in America, including such major events as the Kent State University shootings (1970), *Roe v. Wade* (1973), the Indian Self-Determination Act (1974), and the Vietnam War (1954–1975), but what makes Twinka Thiebaud's body of work particularly intriguing is its remove from any defining markers of urbanism, politics, or thematic constraints. Her works from the 1970s are tied together by an understanding of the changing role of photography and Thiebaud herself, rather than distinctive symbols, props, or trends of the period.

Two of the earliest works in the exhibition that explore Thiebaud's connection to nature without props or symbolism are Judy Dater's photographs *Twinka Thiebaud (Twinka and Tree)* (1970) (PL. 13) and *Imogen and Twinka at Yosemite* (1974) (PL. 16). Dater (born 1941) is a California-based photographer best known for portraits that are intimate, yet removed, and employ a contradictory set of characteristics that ask the viewer to both look and look away. As curator Gloria Williams Sander has explained with regard to Dater's aesthetic approach to photography, she has a "...keen ability to balance the facts recorded by the camera with a sensitivity to the humanity of her subjects, bringing an astute psychological focus to her portraits."[7] When Dater and then-partner Jack Welpott met Thiebaud at a party in 1970, it launched a successful collaboration that would be revisited in subsequent decades. In Dater's photograph, *Twinka Thiebaud (Twinka and Tree)* (PL. 13), Thiebaud's body position, expression of both determination and numbness, and intense focus on the viewer are juxtaposed with her sheer embellished gown. Here, fragility contrasts with the roughness of the tree trunk and the intensity of her pose. The contrasts also exemplify Dater's adherence to straight photography, a movement that does not allow for any manipulation of an image in the developing and printing processes.

Straight photography was championed by Group f/64, originally comprised of eleven photographers, including Edward and Brett Weston, Ansel Adams, and Imogen Cunningham. The group was based in San Francisco, California, and together, the photographers advocated for the use of aperture f/64 to create sharp focus, the use of a view camera, and the natural environment as muse. Dater aligned herself with f/64 photographers upon moving to San Francisco in the early 1960s. One of Dater's famous photographs, *Imogen and Twinka at Yosemite* (PL. 16), incorporates f/64 ideals while simultaneously framing numerous contrasts.[8] The first is Thiebaud's nude body against the old-growth tree and her bare feet against the pine needles and grass, smooth skin against rough bark. The second contrast is age and the comparison of emerging/established and young/old, defined by Thiebaud, then in her late twenties, and trailblazing photographer Imogen Cunningham, then in her early nineties. The third and fourth contrasts stem from the second. Thiebaud's body, at once a part of nature and in contrast with it, stands in opposition to Cunningham's completely covered body. Although the two figures look at one another, there is a distinction between Cunningham's direct gaze and the lifting of her hand to signal an element of surprise, and Thiebaud's slight smirk, a note of humor in the scene that mirrors the demure inward movement of her shoulders.

While the moment of physical closeness in *Imogen and Twinka at Yosemite* gives way to emotional closeness between two subjects, the photograph's framing is provided by the Yosemite landscape and is an element of Dater's aesthetic sensibility, which was first established in the 1970s. Rebecca Solnit posits in *As Eve Said to the Serpent: On Landscape, Gender, and Art* that Dater's contribution to the California-based photography movement of the 1970s and 1980s was an eschewal of typical "rules" related to depictions of the landscape. She explains: "Judy Dater, like many other women entering the landscape, seemed to have arrived without the usual guidelines: that landscape is separate from portraiture, that the photographer belongs behind the camera, that wilderness is impersonal, that the nude woman is aligned with or a metaphor for nature."[9]

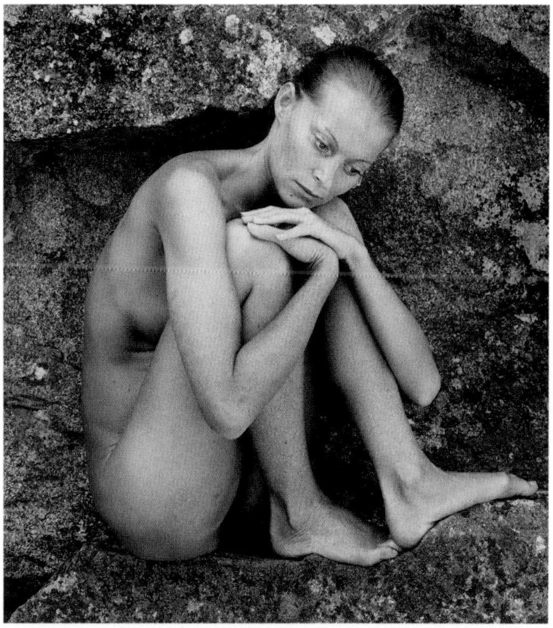

FIG. 25 Chris Johnson (American, born 1948), *Twinka*, 1974. Gelatin silver print, 8 ¼ × 7 ⅝ in. Collection of Twinka Thiebaud.

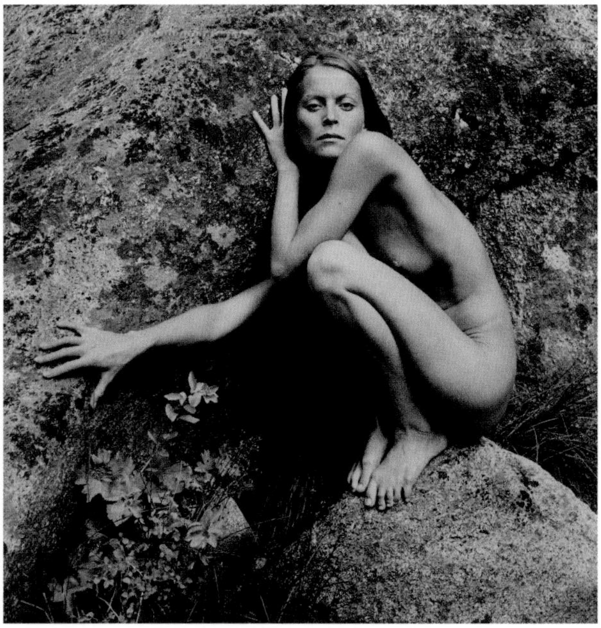

FIG. 24 Ron Jacomini (American, born 1941), *Twinka*, 1974. Gelatin silver print, 9 ⅝ × 9 ½ in. Collection of Twinka Thiebaud.

Imogen and Twinka at Yosemite serves as a prime example of Solnit's argument. In the photograph, landscape and portraiture are intertwined without the trappings of easily recognizable Yosemite landmarks, a photographer is a subject, the wilderness is personal, and the nude woman does not stand purely as a metaphor for nature.[10]

In considering Thiebaud's career as an artist's model with the body/nature relationship as a framework, 1974 is a pivotal year. In addition to Dater, Thiebaud worked with photographers Pete Saloutos, Ron Jacomini, Chris Johnson, Eva Rubinstein, and R. Michael Walker. Many of the photographs produced during that year parallel visual elements in Dater's work and stem from the same Yosemite-based workshop that produced *Imogen and Twinka at Yosemite*. American photographer Ron Jacomini's (born 1941) *Twinka* exaggerates the disparity between body and rock (FIG. 24). Thiebaud is crouched and contorted, hovering on a rock while extending her right arm across the rock's mossy surface. Her arm looks nearly detached from her body, and her expression is concentrated and engaged with her surroundings, rather than focused on the artist or viewer. Like Jacomini, Chris Johnson's (born 1948) photograph *Twinka* includes Thiebaud in a similarly crouched position against a rock face. The emotional disassociation from the camera is further evident in this work, as Thiebaud seems to physically retreat into thought (FIG. 25).

While the photographs by Jacomini and Johnson focus on the intensity of a crouching body, R. Michael Walker's (born 1950) *Twinka at Wawona/Yosemite National Park, CA* takes the opposite approach (PL. 17). Thiebaud's interaction with the landscape is visceral. She lies, extended, on large rocks lining a stream, with her arm crossed over her head. Similar to the disjointed arm in Jacomini's photograph, the bent arm in Walker's image provides a sense of exaggeration, stretching to meet the landscape's angles, while the view of Thiebaud from above further accentuates the amalgam of body and nature. This elongation of limbs is seen again in Pete Saloutos's (born 1947) photograph *Twinka Desert*, in which Thiebaud's body sinks into a sand- and rock-covered dune (FIG. 26). Any facial expression or engagement with the photographer is eliminated by the relationship between body and environment, a visual device also found in Polish-American photographer Eva Rubinstein's (born 1933) work *Twinka, Yosemite, 1974* (PL. 18). Thiebaud's torso, in shadow, confronts the viewer in the foreground of the scene with the only other indication of her body's positioning seen in the angled arm at left. Behind her lie the textured rocks that repeat throughout Twinka's career. Smooth, soft flesh against grainy, cold, and rough landscapes.

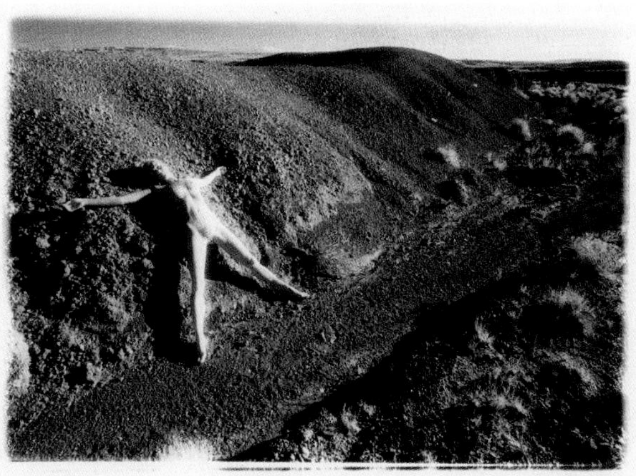

FIG. 26 Pete Saloutos (American, born 1947), *Twinka Desert*, 1974. Infrared black-and-white film, 6 ½ × 9 ½ in. Collection of Twinka Thiebaud.

BODY AS NATURE

While juxtapositions of Thiebaud and nature define much of 1974, there is a shift in the human/body interaction as the year ends and 1975 begins. Eikoh Hosoe (born 1933), a Japanese photographer best known for his experimental post-World War II images, provides the foundation for the visual shift in Thiebaud's work. Sitting cross-legged on a large, oblong rock with arms outstretched and hands on her knees, Thiebaud does not gaze at the camera or the viewer in *Twinka under the Tree Shadow, Yosemite* (FIG. 27). Instead, her eyes are closed, and her head is tilted back slightly in contemplation. Hosoe captures the aesthetic shift from body *in* nature to body *as* nature in the photograph by moving away from the depiction of a body positioned in contrast to or on top of a natural element. Instead, his work shows nature's imprint either through the ways that shadows from nearby plants fall across the body or a physical immersion of the body within natural forms. In this image, Thiebaud's body is what writer Claire Sabel described in relation to Hosoe's work as "unmediated" and "arresting terrain."[11] Shadows of leaves from nearby trees cascade across her arms and legs; her face is in partial darkness, her torso covered in fireworks made by pointed fronds and blades. A sense of physical depth is created within the scene by layers of rock, plants, and shadow. The throne-like rock just behind Thiebaud is almost completely shaded, the darkness like a mandorla that forms a frame around an iconographic figure.

Hosoe's approach to bodies in nature stems partially from his professional partnership with Tatsumi Hijikata (1928–1986), the founder of Ankoku Butoh. In 1969, Hosoe and Hijikata published the photo book *Kamaitachi*. The images in the book were taken between 1965 and 1968 in numerous locations throughout Japan, including the prefectures of Akita and Shibamata and the neighborhood of Sugamo in Tokyo. Hosoe photographed Hijikata embodying the folkloric kamaitachi, weasel-like demons who haunt fields with a sickle. When describing the images, Hosoe explained that Hijikata's body was the vehicle for documenting his memories.[12] The locations Hosoe and Hijikata chose for the *Kamaitachi* images related directly to their experiences of trauma during World War II (1939–1945). Both artists were born in northern Japan. Hosoe's family fled to a rural village during the war as a deliberate act of survival, which in turn was an act of displacement. The utilization of kamaitachi to express a traumatic, but also expressive, association with nature is exemplified in *Kamaitachi #34* from 1968, an antecedent to the image of Thiebaud by Hosoe in its use of light and shadow as a visual device, and its adherence to the idea of body *as* nature (FIG. 28). Kamaitachi, as folkloric figures, are inseparable from nature. They are the physical embodiment of cutting winds and are said to sweep through fields and leave gashes on the bodies of unsuspecting farmers. *Kamaitachi #34* introduces the weasel-like demon to viewers in human form, immersed in the fields. The figure is hidden within the grasses, prepared to move with the winds.

Similar to Hosoe's *Kamaitachi* series, in which body and nature are entangled, *Twinka under the Tree Shadow, Yosemite* visualizes how human body and nature can become one, as nature imprints on the body and vice versa. The image also implies, especially through the mandorla, an underlying connection to larger concepts of religion, culture, and identity that might not immediately be visible. Hosoe explains that truth in photography does not always mean that a photograph is an exact documentation of life, noting, "The camera is generally assumed to be unable to depict that which is not visible to the eye, and yet the photographer who wields it well can depict what lies unseen in his memory."[13] The visual aesthetic of seen/unseen is a Hosoe hallmark that follows the thread of contrasts and contradictions found in Thiebaud's work of the 1970s.

Hosoe does not typically reference specific places or recognizable landmarks in his photographs. Rather, the sense of place and time noted in his images stems from emotional sites and states of being. He uses the body to project calm, fear, anger, and mindfulness in ways that require his models/collaborators to be fully present and reveal their inner selves. The emotions that are evoked in such images as *Kamaitachi #34* and *Twinka under the Tree Shadow, Yosemite* are linked to history through physical experience. Hosoe does not use photography to document specific sites of historical trauma. Instead, his images reference survival in the face of, or in the aftermath of, trauma. Survival, in his works, can be seen in living bodies. In this vein, Linda Nochlin posits, "...the corporeal eye, the visceral eye—all eyes are located not merely in bodies but in historically specific bodies and can thus be viewed within a history of representation and a history of practices, a social history..."[14] that bonds artist and model, and by extension, artist with model and viewer. Hosoe's photographs, including their engagement with dualities such as salvation/displacement, light/dark, and past/present, provide the theoretical foundation for Thiebaud's later work and allow for critical inquiry into and redefinition of the body/nature relationship to artist and viewer.

Three images from 1975 provide evidence of Thiebaud's growing confidence as an artist's model and visually suggest deliberate interaction with the natural world. Much like Hosoe, Lucien Clergue's (1934–2014) work was influenced by bodies in movement and the trauma and changing global landscape brought about by World War II. Clergue's *Twinka at Pebble Beach, Monterey, CA (Falling Sand)* (PL. 31), one in a series of Thiebaud lying in various poses on a sandy California beach, eliminates the contrast between body and nature in many of the same ways as Hosoe's photograph of Thiebaud subsumed by leafy shadows. Just a portion of Thiebaud's legs, torso, and right arm are visible within the image by Clergue. The viewer is unable to register emotion through her face or discern a recognizable setting, which evokes a sense of immediacy. The falling grains of sand that slip through Thiebaud's fingers move across her body and pool, creating areas of light and shade. The sand becomes part of her skin, drapery that reveals and conceals.

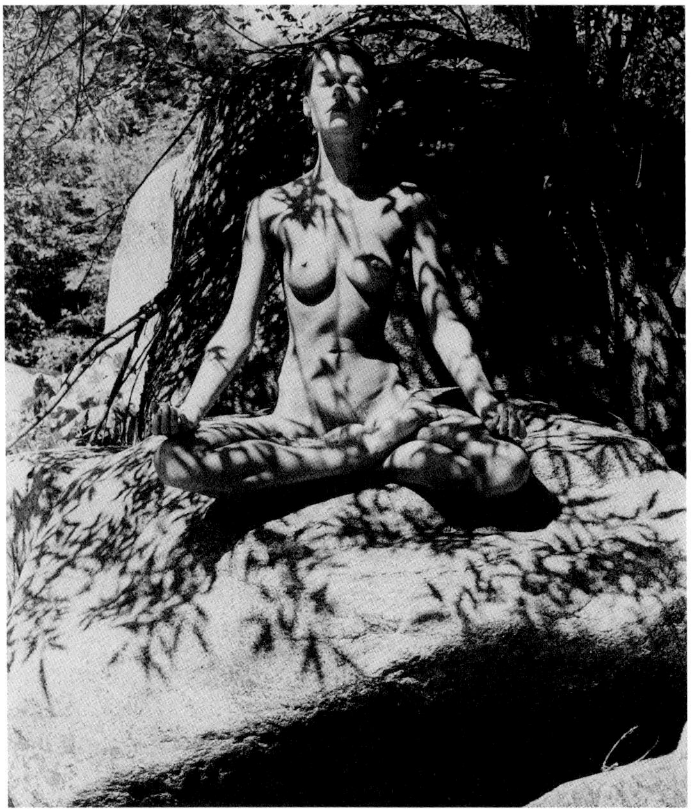

FIG. 27 Eikoh Hosoe (Japanese, born 1933), *Twinka under the Tree Shadow, Yosemite*, 1975. Gelatin silver print, 12 ½ × 10 ¾ in. Collection of Twinka Thiebaud.

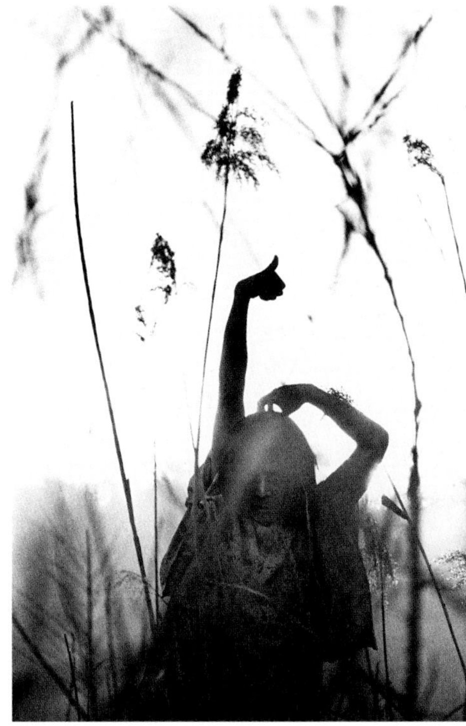

FIG. 28 Eikoh Hosoe (Japanese, born 1933), *Kamaitachi #34*, 1968. Gelatin silver print, 16 ⅝ × 10 ¾ in. SFMOMA, Collection of the Sack Photographic Trust. Photograph by Don Ross.

PLACE

As evidenced by Clergue's series of sand-based imagery, location is not a perfunctory element of 1970s photographs depicting Thiebaud. California turned steadfastly toward environmental causes and saw a surge in conservation-focused environmental organizations during the decade, including California Trout, which was incorporated in 1971; the Catalina Island Conservancy, created in 1972; TreePeople, founded in 1973; and California Conservation Corps, established in 1976.[15] Furthermore, the word "ecology" became prominent during that period, and the first Earth Day took place in the spring of 1970. The state's landscape, whether coastline, forest, or expansive desert, became a site of conversation, a physical thing to embrace in a lifelong relationship. Yosemite National Park, located in California's Sierra

Nevada mountains, is a site that many photographers featured in the exhibition, including Judy Dater, Ron Jacomini, Eva Rubinstein, and R. Michael Walker, have returned to repeatedly. Each artist embraced a lifelong relationship with the many natural and varied environments within the park. Although known for mammoth rock faces such as Half Dome and waterfalls like Bridalveil Fall and Vernal Fall, Yosemite also holds meadows, mountains, and wooded areas. Each of these wilderness zones reflects the varied landscape of California as a whole and provides a counterpoint to the urban development that swept, and continues to sweep, the major cities of the state, including San Diego, Los Angeles, and San Francisco.

Turning again to Pete Saloutos's work, the photograph *Twinka on Fallen Tree* (1974) references nature through trees, meadows, and scale (PL. 20). Saloutos positions the viewer above Thiebaud, looking down at her bare body intertwined with a fallen tree, a nurse log that serves in the role of ecological facilitator, offering "...seedlings shade, nutrients, water and protection from disease and pathogens, thus nurturing and making way for the new generation."[16] Contorted in multiple angles, her head askew, Thiebaud has become a different version of herself, a body that will age but can protect, much like the twisted bark on the nurse log below. The light and shade found in Saloutos's image are most striking in the contrast between Thiebaud's body (light) and the surrounding landscape (shade). This is not the only image in which the effect of light/shade is essential to the work's core theme and visual drama. Larry Keenan Jr.'s (1943–2012) photograph *Untitled* from 1975, taken from a high vantage point, eliminates Thiebaud's facial expression, as her head is nearly tucked behind her body and tilted up toward the sun at an angle that renders her emotion unreadable. Her left leg crosses her right, and her arms extend outward to stake a claim on the rock; she is again an embodiment of contrasts, at once rendered immobile and poised to emerge from the scene with a burst of energy (PL. 23).

PHOTOGRAPHIC EXPERIMENTATION

Although inexpensive digital cameras and photo-editing software were over a decade away from becoming mass-marketed consumer products, photographic manipulation was not new in the mid-1970s. The development of a negative was its own creative process for many artists. Beginning as early as the 1840s, photographers colored, scratched, and spliced negatives to create a new image. These early manipulation processes remained prevalent in the 1970s and are still used by photographers today. Two artists known for experimentation who worked with Thiebaud in 1975 include R. Michael Walker and Robert Heinecken (1931–2006). Walker's untitled, dream-like photograph portrays Thiebaud as a creature emerging from a jungle of leaves, her head much larger than the multiple superimposed bodies. She appears frog-like and otherworldly, yet her expression remains readable, serious, and skeptical (PL. 25).

The use of repetition as a visual tool is also found in Heinecken's *Space/Time Metamorphosis #1* from 1975. Thiebaud is depicted four times in four different poses within the work. The central figure is seen on her side, propped up on her elbow, looking directly at the viewer, while a second body lies below her. A third body, arms outstretched and looking away from the viewer, hovers above the first as if part of the rock face behind her. A fourth body, comprised of head and upper torso, looks directly at the first (FIG. 29).

Heinecken was a self-described "documentarian" of "manufactured experience" and preferred the descriptors "paraphotographer" and "photographist" to "photographer."[17] Based in Los Angeles, Heinecken founded the photography department at the University of California, Los Angeles and spent much of the 1960s rebelling against straight photography as championed by Group f/64, creating purposefully blurred imagery that lacked distinct contrast. It was also during this decade that his series of puzzle-like images of nude women emerged. Idealized bodies were cut up, reviewed, and rearranged. As his career progressed, he continued in this mode of experi-

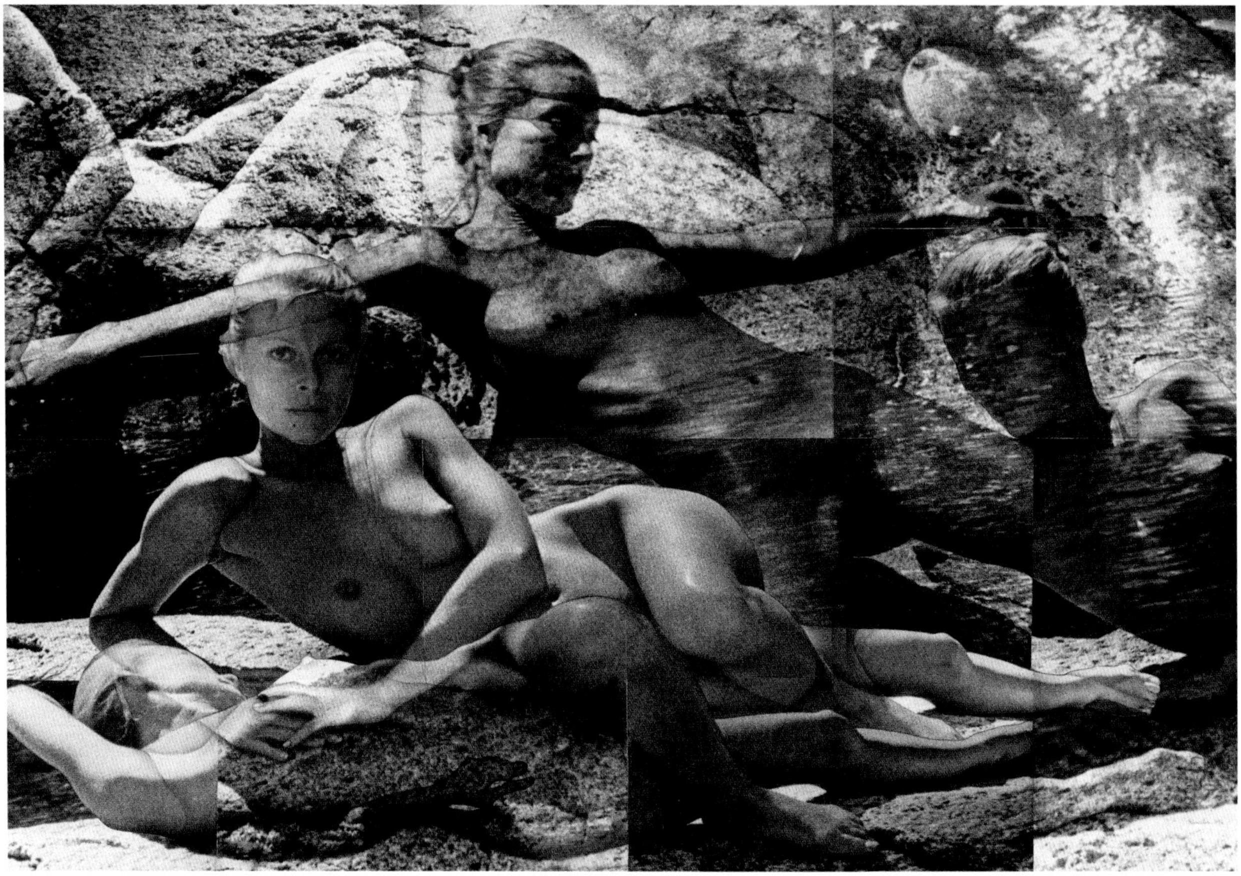

FIG. 29 Robert Heinecken (American, 1931–2006), *Space/Time Metamorphosis #1*, 1975. Gelatin silver emulsion on fabric with drawing, 42 × 62 in. The Museum of Fine Arts, Houston, The Target Collection of American Photography, museum purchase funded by Target Stores and the National Endowment for the Arts, 76.274. © The Museum of Fine Arts, Houston; Thomas R. DuBrock.

mentation and manipulation, moving to photograms in the second half of the 1960s. Photograms are made without a camera; an object is placed on light-sensitive paper and then directly exposed to light. The result is an image that appears to be comprised of negative shadows. The jarring, often strained, and difficult-to-read photograms are an extension of Heinecken's larger aesthetic questions: Can images mean many things at once? How does the proliferation of images in American culture contribute to idealism and consumerism? *Are You Rea* (1964–1968), one of his most famous series of photograms, addresses these questions through the haunting imagery of sexualized women in advertisements, images of somber interiors, and the process of photogram creation, which advocates for overlapping imagery and precipitates jarring or clashing themes (FIG. 30).

Photograms led Heinecken to experiment with photomontage at the start of the 1970s, as the medium allowed for greater alteration by the artist's hand. Generating a photomontage, like creating a photogram, is a camera-less process. Multiple photographs are combined into a new work through cutting, folding, overlapping, or rearranging. Heinecken's eschewal of any traditional photographic processes or tools was viewed as part of the counterculture at a time when many photographers were steadfast in their use of viewfinder cameras and documenting of California's landscape. Cutting, rearranging, and combining was the antithesis of the straight photography movement and set Heinecken far apart from other photographers whom Thiebaud worked with in the same decade. Art historian Matthew Biro has argued that "Heinecken's art thrived on contradiction, confrontation, and strategic shifts in medium and subject position"; his creative process was dependent on recognizing the photograph as both a representation of consumer culture and a commodity unto itself.[18] Heinecken described the appropriation of mass media in his work, including the repetitive use of bodies and branded images as "...the most important vehicle by which we gain information," noting that mass media is a "kind of quasi-nature."[19] The proliferation of images that define mass media were, to Heinecken, a combination of natural forms and natural settings (bodies and/or environments) and mediated images that held a specific purpose, either to sell a project or illustrate a specific point. Mass media cannot be purely equivalent to nature in Heinecken's world. Alternatively, mass media takes images of nature and then disrupts them through layers of overlap, rearrangement, and dislocation from their original purpose or intent.

The correlation between mass media as dependent upon images, and nature as malleable and devoid of any sense of place, ties back to Mark Dion's view of nature, where "everyone has a say in what gets to be nature, at a particular time, for a particular group of people."[20] Turning again to *Space/Time Metamorphosis #1*, the image exemplifies both Biro's and Dion's arguments. The work follows Heinecken's shifts in medium, his adherence to confrontation and contradiction, and his disinterest in formal documentation. The multiple Thiebaud bodies found within the image confront each other and the viewer, body parts overlap, and there is a disinterest in utilizing straight photography to document a specific time and place. The contradiction in the scene comes from the contrast of body against rock and from multiple identities that visually exist on top of one another. Nature, represented here in layers, is a product of

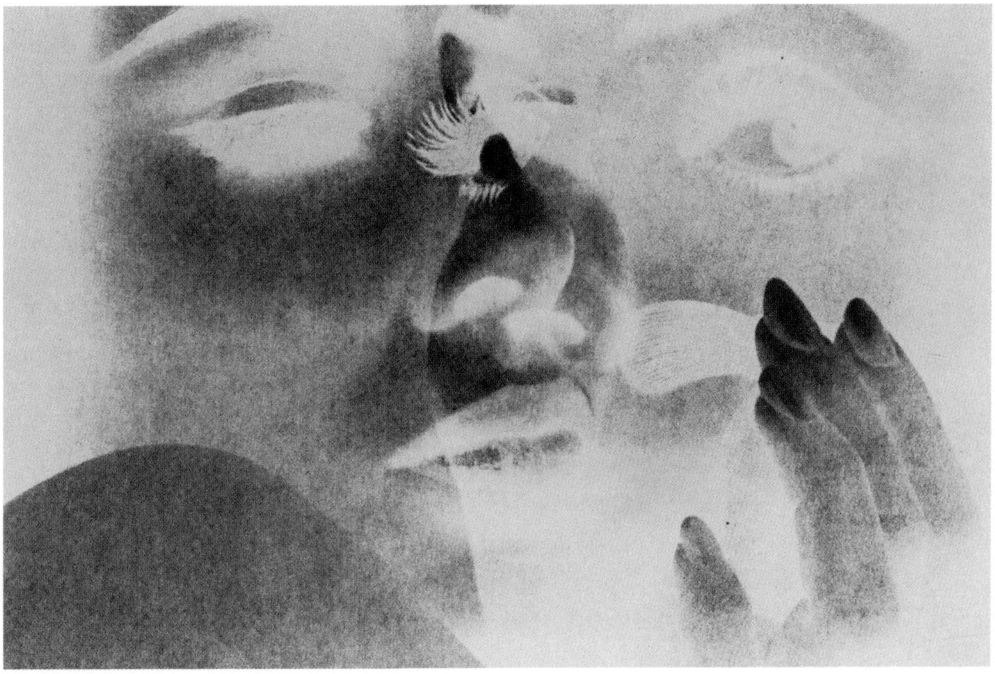

FIG. 30 Robert Heinecken (American, 1931–2006), *Are You Rea #2*, 1964–1968. Lithograph, 6 5⁄16 × 9 5⁄8 in. MoMA, Mr. and Mrs. Clark Winter Fund, 193.1991.2.

Heinecken's own making, rather than a result of clicks of the shutter by photographers most interested in capturing the scene directly in front of them.

2000s

> "There is indeed something omnivorous about the act of photography. It offers a way of responding to everything about everything."[21]
>
> —Lucy Lippard

While the 1970s marked the beginning of Thiebaud's professional career as an artist's model and the emergence of body/nature as a theme, the 2000s mark a period of growth and maturity centered on strengthening and deepening collaborations. As Thiebaud notes in her essay in this catalogue, she found the 2000s to be a period of examination: of her age, body, and relationships.[22]

Longtime collaborator John Reiff Williams's (born 1954) work from 2011 and 2013 positions Thiebaud in two distinct relationships with nature. In his photograph *Untitled (Twinka Reflection)* from 2011, Thiebaud is seen behind a glass window, separated in space from the viewer by the reflection of tree branches (PL. 58). Depth of space is conflated, and the viewer is asked to question whether Thiebaud is in front of or behind the trees or positioned in the middle of a park with greenery enveloping her body. The lack of eye contact with the artist or the viewer evokes a sense of thoughtfulness, but also a sense of isolation interestingly not found in many of the 1970s photographs.

As a counterpoint to the 2011 photograph, Williams's 2013 image of Thiebaud in a wet slip projects confidence and power, while steadfastly asking the viewer to look resolutely at the body/nature connection (FIG. 21). There is no impediment to the viewer's gaze, no window or shadow to hide Thiebaud's body. Similar to earlier photographs, Thiebaud's bare feet contrast with the rocks on which she stands. The branches and leaves of the trees and shrubs surround her body and provide a framework for visually reading the image as a step into a new phase of growth. Thiebaud does not hide her body, no matter her age, in any given image, and is firm in her understanding of her corporeal self. The professional relationship that she developed with Williams over many decades made these images—near visual opposites of each other—possible. Williams's series of photographs found in this volume speak directly to what scholar Ulrike Schneider has described as a "serial strategy" that includes "creating series of individual pictures to using sequences of photographs to represent the change and development of their subjects over time."[23] Working with Williams over the course of more than four decades, Thiebaud has provided the viewer a serial strategy in which her expressions change over time, her body ages, and she brings to the images a maturity and sense of power not seen in the early 1970s photographs.

Like Williams, photographer Elizabeth Opalenik (born 1947) encourages introspection by depicting reflections in water or vast expanses. Opalenik returns to the landscape as a time-tested subject while also looking for subtle ways to incorporate contemporary ideology. As historian Rachel McLean Sailor posits regarding photographs, "the habit of tracing the components of an image back to their historical roots is very much part of what it means to understand how contemporary images are conversant with myriad aspects of the past."[24] *Bird in Hand* (2011) is one of the few images in the exhibition that move beyond the landscape to incorporate fauna (PL. 54). Visible from the waist up and standing in a field of tall grasses, Thiebaud holds a dead bird in one hand while delicately lifting the other toward her shoulder. The photograph evokes Eikoh Hosoe's *Kamaitachi #34* (FIG. 28), in which a body has merged with nature, visible only behind tall reeds, a visual reflection of and on life and death.

Oppositely, Opalenik's *Twinka in Morning Light* (2011) gives credence to the idea that the natural world is bigger and more infinite than a singular body (FIG. 31). Thiebaud, standing with her back to the

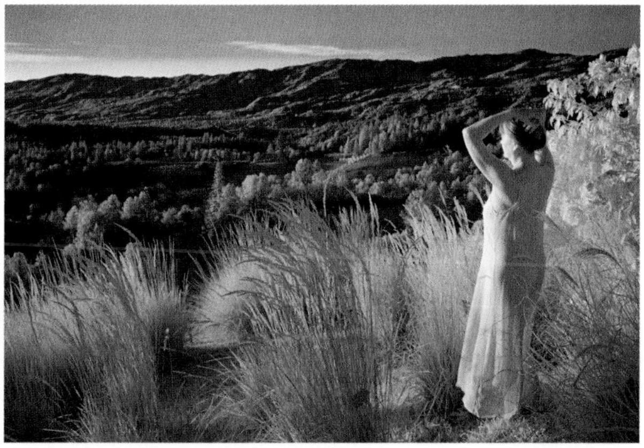

FIG. 31 Elizabeth Opalenik (American, born 1947), *Twinka in Morning Light*, 2011. Archival pigment print, 9 × 13 ½ in. Collection of Elizabeth Opalenik.

viewer at right, looks across an expansive landscape. The viewer, in return, looks at Thiebaud gazing across the landscape. The photograph is unique in its positioning; the viewer is behind Thiebaud and can replicate her pose in space. She is at once the artist's model and the viewer's model. So often in the artworks that comprise *Twinka Thiebaud and the Art of the Pose*, Thiebaud clearly enacts the role of model as artist, using her ability to contort or alter her body to meet the needs of the landscape. Here, the viewer is given the opportunity to absorb the vista as well and to participate in the creation of meaning with Thiebaud. The image brings the participatory nature of Thiebaud's body of work full circle, taking the message from artist to model to viewer.

The ways in which an environment changes, ages, matures, and provides fertile ground for new beginnings are a distinct aspect of the images created by American photographers Kathleen Malan-Thompson (born 1953), T. K. Thompson (born 1947), and Lorijo Daniels (born 1965). The environment becomes central to the meaning of the work, rather than a contrast between soft and hard or delicate and coarse, or a meditation on the body/nature paradigm. Images made in the later 2010s and early 2020s focus on nature as a distinct subject, using the smallness of the body and the body's secondary positioning against nature, or the use of facial expressions, rather than the full body in a particular pose, to engage the viewer.

Twinka at 65, created by Malan-Thompson in 2014, recognizes the landscape as a living thing, from the wishbone-like tree and grasses to the blossoms (PL. 72). The sense of movement in the landscape, Thiebaud's upward gaze, and the positioning of her hands form a triad of visual markers that lead a viewer in a circular motion through the image. Age is referenced through the body and in nature, while Malan-Thompson revisits the hallmark light/dark contrast created in the 1970s with an eye toward texture. This same focus on texture, age, and expression is palpable in Thompson's *Twinka* from the 2014 *Garden* series (PL. 68). The flower in Thiebaud's hair provides an association with spring and rebirth and is the central focus of the photograph. Calm, focused, and in profile, Thiebaud's face and shoulders live between two forms of nature in this work: the large flower in the foreground and the flora-covered garden wall behind her body. The image recalls John Reiff Williams's work from 2011 in which nature occupies multiple spaces within the scene, the human body being physically central within the work, but secondary to the context of the larger natural world.

As the 2010s stretched into the first two years of the 2020s, the emphasis on nature was amplified as a counterpoint to the global pandemic and to the new social, political, and economic events that defined the start of the decade. Lorijo Daniels's collaborative work with Thiebaud takes a decidedly 21st-century approach to compressing and concealing the body in nature while at the same time utilizing photographic processes from a century prior. Tintypes were a popular type of photograph in the later 1800s, as they were less expensive and lighter than daguerreotypes. To make a tintype, a thin iron plate is coated with a dark lacquer and a photographic emulsion is applied. This results in a positive image, and because tintypes are typically flat or dull, they are often hand-colored.

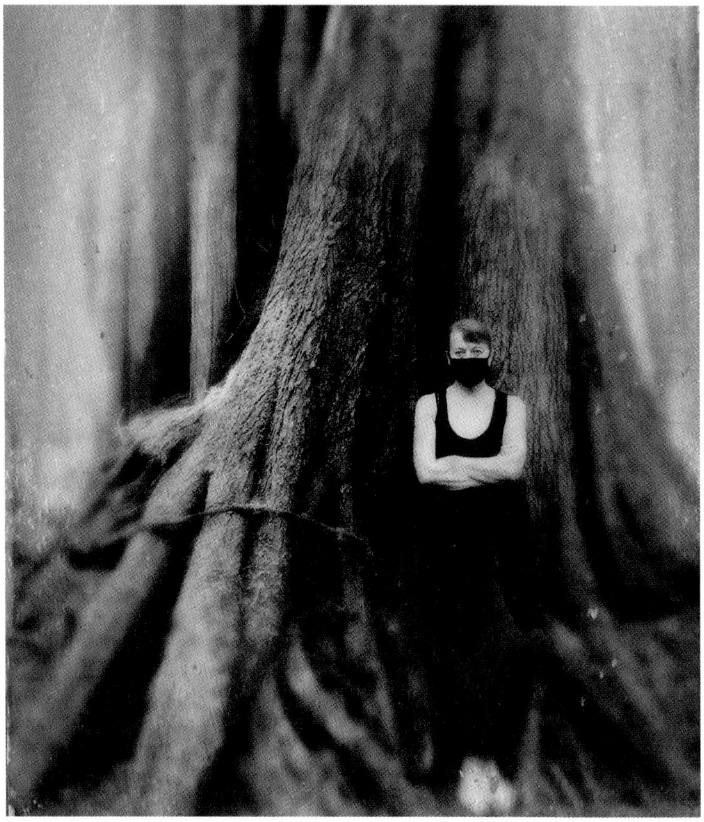

FIG. 32 Lorijo Daniels (American, born 1965), *You Name It*, 2020. Tintype, 5 ⅜ × 5 in. Collection of Twinka Thiebaud.

Two of Daniels's tintypes, *In the Lace* (2020) and *Double Allium* (2021), subvert the inherent flatness of the photographic medium by incorporating textures and unique perspectives (PLS. 82 AND 83). Furthermore, plants are used in each image as visual devices to obscure Thiebaud's body, much in the same way that the long reeds and grass obscure Tatsumi Hijikata's body in Eikoh Hosoe's *Kamaitachi #34* (FIG. 28). Partially hidden behind lace flowers in *In the Lace*, Thiebaud evokes the same intensity, directness, and skepticism found in the 1970s photographs by R. Michael Walker and Lucien Clergue. The central focus, which in prior decades was the whole nude body, is now the landscape's association with the bodily expression of an emotion or idea. In Thiebaud's early work, she is often juxtaposed with the landscape, either positioned as a counterpoint to the landscape or in the foreground of the scene with nature as a backdrop. In *Double Allium* and *In the Lace*, nature and body merge. Thiebaud's facial expressions mirror the landscape's textures and movements.

The hallmark of this third period of collaboration in Twinka Thiebaud's long career is Daniels's *You Name It* (2020) (FIG. 32). In addition to touching upon the key themes of body/nature and the expanded focus on the presence and power of the environment, Thiebaud's aesthetic sensibility is on full display. The image pays homage to Thiebaud's work with Judy Dater in Yosemite, the massive tree in both images standing for age and experience. *You Name It*, in subtle ways, is also a direct response to any Thiebaud image from a prior decade that may now, in hindsight, be seen as delicate or possess an air of uncertainty. Here, Thiebaud stands secure, arms and feet crossed, looking directly to the viewer, while her face mask serves as the only indication of a specific time and place. Her body positioning is especially interesting, given that the image was taken during a global pandemic defined by uncertainty and fear related to the body and geographical boundaries, and simultaneously a time of American political chaos. The idea of a photograph as a collaborative process between artist and model, and an ode to the multiple identities that any given person embodies over a lifetime, is explained by curator and writer Olivia Lahs-Gonzales as "...an exercise in balancing personal with socially constructed experiences. The outcome, an image of the sitter, is at once a substitute for the original, a fiction, a delineator, a commodity, and the object of the viewer's inquisitive gaze."[25] Daniels and Thiebaud created an image that requests the viewer look closely, particularly at the specific points in the photograph where the twisted roots of the imposing tree nearly overtake Thiebaud's legs and feet. Though her body is fully visible, the mask that Thiebaud wears obstructs her identity in a way unlike any other photograph in the exhibition. She is, without easy facial recognition or facial expression, a fiction, a representation of what Twinka Thiebaud, and by extension the viewer, might be or could be in a moment of powerful solitude within the social, economic, and political turmoil of the year 2020.

Daniels's deliberate mixing of a traditional photographic form with an intense focus on nature spins the old/new pairing, as does the use of a 19th-century photographic medium in a 21st-century context, and asks the viewer to question whether experimentation can be defined by looking at the past. When considered together, these three tintypes by Daniels are also an acknowledgment of photography's history, which was largely focused on landscape images or staid portraiture, and a sidestepping of digital processes that dominate the photographic landscape of the 21st century.

FUTURE TENSE

In returning to the participatory discussion addressed at the start of this essay, it is important to review the intertwined threads that run throughout Twinka Thiebaud's body of work, particularly photographs from the 1970s to the present. Thiebaud, as a collaborative artist's model, is the focus of each image, either subsumed by or in conversation with nature. Art Historian Katy Siegel, writing about art created after 1945, notes that "of the many relationships between present and past, a particularly important one is the way in which the meaning of a thing (an idea, an artwork, an essay, a person) changes over time as it exists in the world."[26] The changes over time that Siegel suggests relate to the diverse representations of Thiebaud's body, poses, facial expressions, confidence, and strength over the course of numerous decades. Yet it is not only the human body that provides meaning within the photographs discussed throughout this essay; rather, it is the shift in the importance, dominance, and relationship of nature to the human body that amplifies the light/dark, hard/soft, old/new, and past/present dichotomies. This shift can be seen in the 1970s, with each year connected to a different group of artists and environments. The jump between the 1970s and the 2000s, however, represents a larger change in Thiebaud's relationship with nature and deepened sense of self in relation to photographers and her own body.

Twinka Thiebaud and the Art of the Pose is not the end of the conversation about photographic experimentation, the environment in photographs, or Twinka Thiebaud's career. She continues to work as an artist's model and collaborator. The body/environment relationship will, no doubt, be amplified in future photographs that depict Thiebaud as photographers invest in new ways of thinking about the body in space, covered and uncovered.

1 Maurice Merleau-Ponty, "An Unpublished Text by Maurice Merleau-Ponty: A Prospectus of His Work," in *The Primacy of Perception: And Other Essays on Phenomenological Psychology, the Philosophy of Art, History and Politics*, ed. James M. Edie, trans. Arleen B. Dallery (Evanston, IL: Northwestern University Press, 1964), 5. See Mark Alice Durant, "Photography & Performance," *Aperture*, no. 199 (Summer 2010): 33.

2 Mark Dion, "Interview: Science and Aesthetics," Art21.org, https://art21.org/read/mark-dion-science-and-aesthetics/.

3 Richard Shusterman, "Photography as Performative Process," *The Journal of Aesthetics and Art Criticism* 70, no. 1 (Winter 2012): 68.

4 Susan Sontag, *On Photography* (New York: Picador, 1977), 24.

5 Analog processes rely on light-sensitive emulsions and chemical development to create a photographic print. The first consumer digital cameras and tools for digital manipulation did not emerge until the 1990s.

6 For further discussion related to the field of photography, its changes over time, and a critical examination of theory and ideology, see Victor Burgin, ed., *Thinking Photography* (London: Macmillan Education Ltd., 1982); Rosalind Krauss, "A Note on Photography and the Simulacral," *October* 31 (Winter 1984): 49–68; Naomi Rosenblum, *A World History of Photography* (New York: Abbeville, 1997); Vilém Flusser, *Towards a Philosophy of Photography* (London: Reaktion Books Ltd., 2000); Joan M. Schwartz and James R. Ryan, eds., *Picturing Place: Photography and the Geographical Imagination* (New York: Routledge, 2003); Mary Warner Marien, *Photography: A Cultural History*, 2nd ed. (London: Laurence King Publishing, 2006); James Elkins, ed., *Photography Theory* (London: Routledge, 2007); Fred Ritchin, *After Photography* (New York, W.W. Norton & Company, 2009); Jae Emerling, *Photography: History and Theory* (London: Routledge, 2011); Elspeth H. Brown and Thy Phu, eds., *Feeling Photography* (Durham, NC: Duke University Press, 2014); Liz Wells, ed., *Photography: A Critical Introduction* (London: Routledge, 2015).

7 Gloria Williams Sander, "Judy Dater and the Photographic Portrait," Norton Simon Museum, November 6, 2020, https://www.nortonsimon.org/learn/adults/impressions/judy-dater-and-the-photographic-portrait/.

8 Judith Fryer Davidov, *Women's Camera Work: Self/Body/Other in American Visual Culture* (Durham, NC: Duke University Press, 1998), 385.

9 Rebecca Solnit, *As Eve Said to the Serpent: On Landscape, Gender, and Art* (Athens, GA: University of Georgia Press, 2001), 8.

10 Judy Dater's *Imogen and Twinka at Yosemite* was created during an Ansel Adams photography workshop in Yosemite National Park in the Sierra Nevada mountains of California. The focus on bodies in the landscape is especially interesting considering that for Adams and many other members of Group f/64, the landscape *or* a body was typically the sole subject of a photograph, rather than the body *in* a landscape setting.

11 Claire Sabel, "Curated Body: 1959–1970. Eikoh Hosoe," *ArtAsiaPacific Magazine*, October 19, 2013, http://artasiapacific.com/Magazine/WebExclusives/CuratedBody19591970EikohHosoe.

12 Eikoh Hosoe, "Kamaitachi," in *Shashin Hosoe Eikoh no sekai* (Eikoh Hosoe Photographs, 1951–1988), Shashin Hosoe Eikoh no sekaiten jikko iinkai, 1988. See "Hosoe Eikoh ni kiku" (Interview with Eikoh Hosoe), *The Photo Image* 1 (1969).

13 Alex Merola, "Guts and Ghosts: The Radical Legacy of Japanese Photographer Eikoh Hosoe," *AnOther*, November 1, 2021, https://www.anothermag.com/art-photography/13692/guts-and-ghosts-the-radical-legacy-of-japanese-photographer-eikoh-hosoe.

14 Linda Nochlin, *Bathers, Bodies, Beauty: The Visceral Eye* (Cambridge, MA: Harvard University Press, 2006), 15.

15 Additional environment-focused organizations established in the 1970s include the Environmental Protection Agency (1970), an independent executive agency of the United States federal government (epa.gov); Greenpeace (1971), which was founded in Vancouver, Canada; the Arbor Day Foundation (1972); and The Trust for Public Land (1972), among many others globally.

16 Allie Wisniewski, "Nurse Logs: Healers of the Forest," *American Forests*, July 12, 2017, https://www.americanforests.org/blog/nurse-logs-healers-forest/.

17 Matthew Biro, "Reality Effects: The Art of Robert Heinecken," *ARTFORUM* 50, no. 2 (October 2011), https://www.artforum.com/print/201108/reality-effects-the-art-of-robert-heinecken-29044. See Robert Heinecken, *Are You Rea #18* (1968), Tate, https://www.tate.org.uk/art/artworks/heinecken-are-you-rea-18-p15114; Robert Heinecken, *#3*, from the "Are You Rea" portfolio, Museum of Contemporary Photography, https://www.mocp.org/detail.php?type=related&kv=11637&t=objects; Arthur Ou, "Robert Heinecken: Paraphotographer," *Aperture*, March 15, 2014, https://aperture.org/editorial/robert-heinecken-paraphotographer/.

18 Biro, "Reality Effects."

19 Robert Heinecken, *Robert Heinecken: Object Matter*, MoMA, https://www.moma.org/audio/playlist/177/2344. See Rebecca Morse, "Toward a Poetic Vision: Robert Heinecken's Ambition for Photography," *Aperture* no. 232 (Fall 2018): 72–77.

20 Dion, "Science and Aesthetics."

21 Lucy R. Lippard, "Brought to Light: Notes on Babies, Veils, War and Flowers," in *Defining Eye: Women Photographers of the 20th Century* (St. Louis, MO: The Saint Louis Art Museum, 1997), 131.

22 In addition to Twinka Thiebaud's essay in this catalogue, see "Twinka from 1951 to 2005 A.D.: Preview of a Work in Progress," *California* 11, no. 9 (September 1986): 81–83, in which Thiebaud discusses her career as an artist's model and notes that she tries "...to work with people who will help me bring forth all the various aspects of my personality, which may mean images that aren't so pleasant to look at—anxiety, craziness, stress."

23 Ulrike Schneider, "Serial Strategies in Portrait Photography: From Irving Penn to Hans-Peter Feldman," trans. George Frederick Takis, in *About Face* (San Francisco: Pier 24 Photography, 2014), 91.

24 Rachel McLean Sailor, "Western Landscape Photography: Then and Now," *Oregon Historical Quarterly* 116, no. 1 (Spring 2015): 107.

25 Olivia Lahs-Gonzales, "Defining Eye/Defining I," in *Defining Eye: Women Photographers of the 20th Century* (St. Louis, MO: The Saint Louis Art Museum, 1997), 35.

26 Katy Siegel, *Since '45: America and the Making of Contemporary Art* (London: Reaktion Books Ltd., 2011), 9. For further discussion of photography in relation to contemporary practice and postmodernism, see George Baker, "Photography's Expanded Field," *October* 114 (Autumn 2005): 120–140.

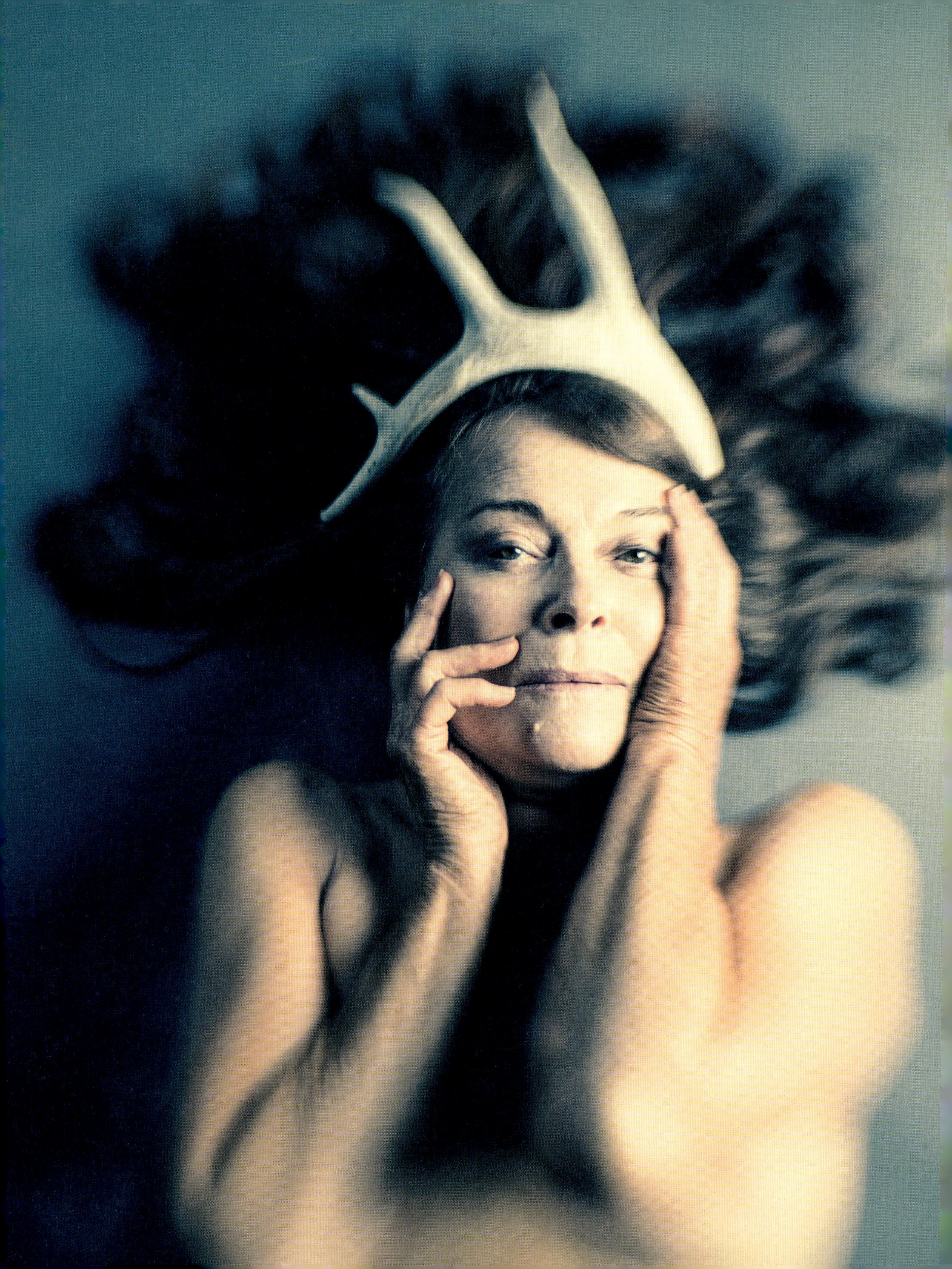

PLATES

Kim Campbell (American, born 1970), *Beguiling,* from the *Deep in Between* series, 2017. Archival pigment print on fiber paper, 15 × 10 in. Collection of Kim Campbell.

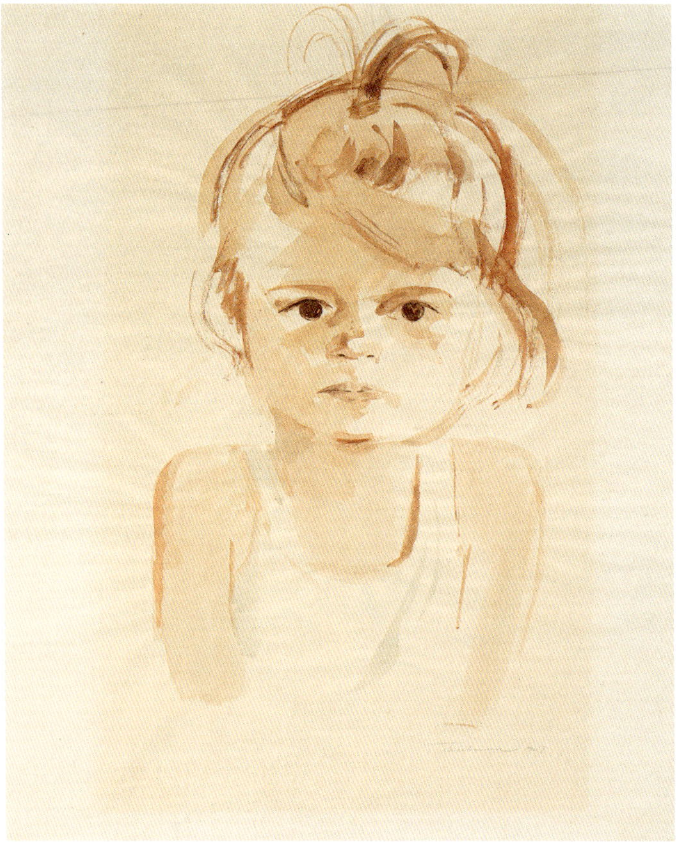

PL. 1 Wayne Thiebaud (American, 1920–2021), *Untitled*, 1948. Watercolor on newsprint paper, 17 ½ × 13 ¾ in. Collection of Twinka Thiebaud.

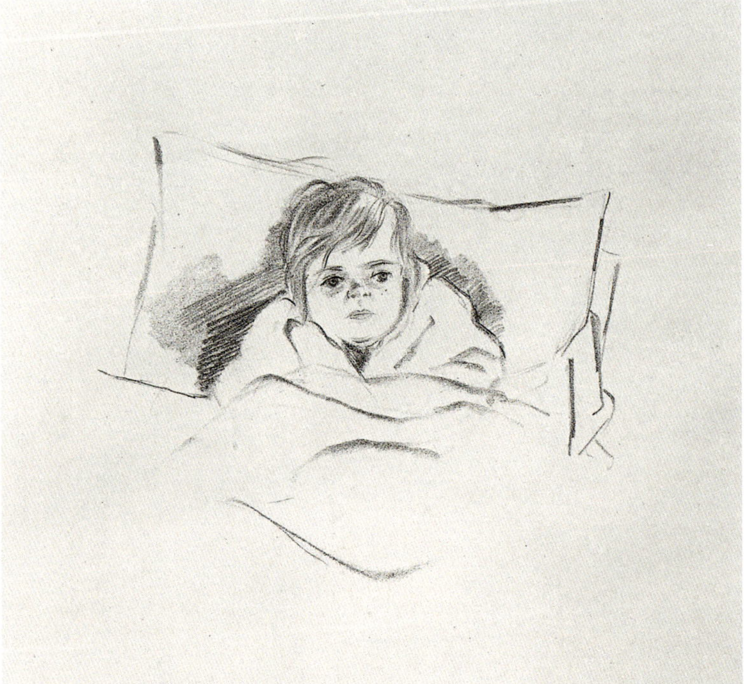

PL. 2 Wayne Thiebaud (American, 1920–2021), *Untitled*, 1949. Charcoal on paper, 11 ⅜ × 12 ⅜ in. Collection of Twinka Thiebaud.

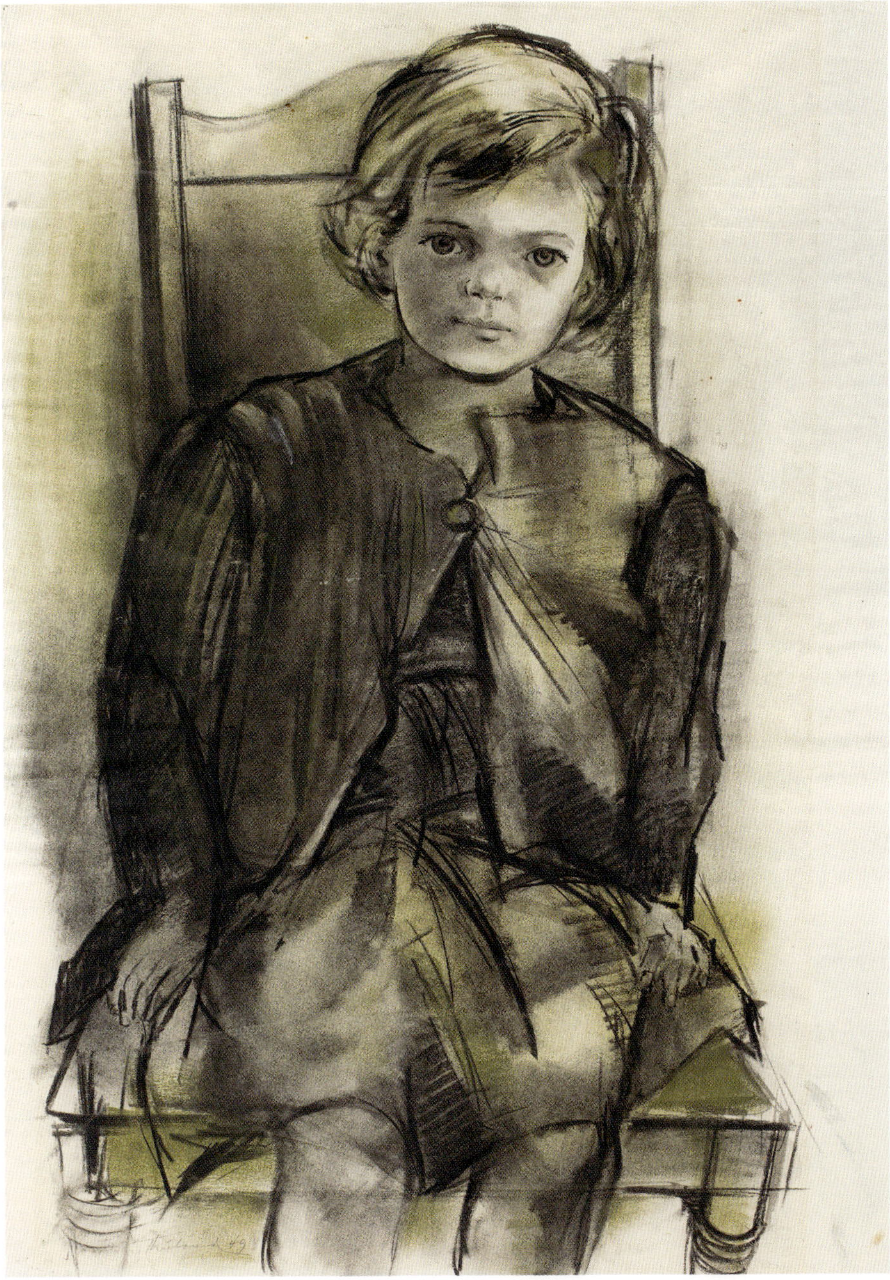

PL. 3 Wayne Thiebaud (American, 1920–2021), *Twinka Thiebaud, Age 4,* 1949. Charcoal on paper, 23 ⅛ × 16 ⅜ in. Collection of Twinka Thiebaud.

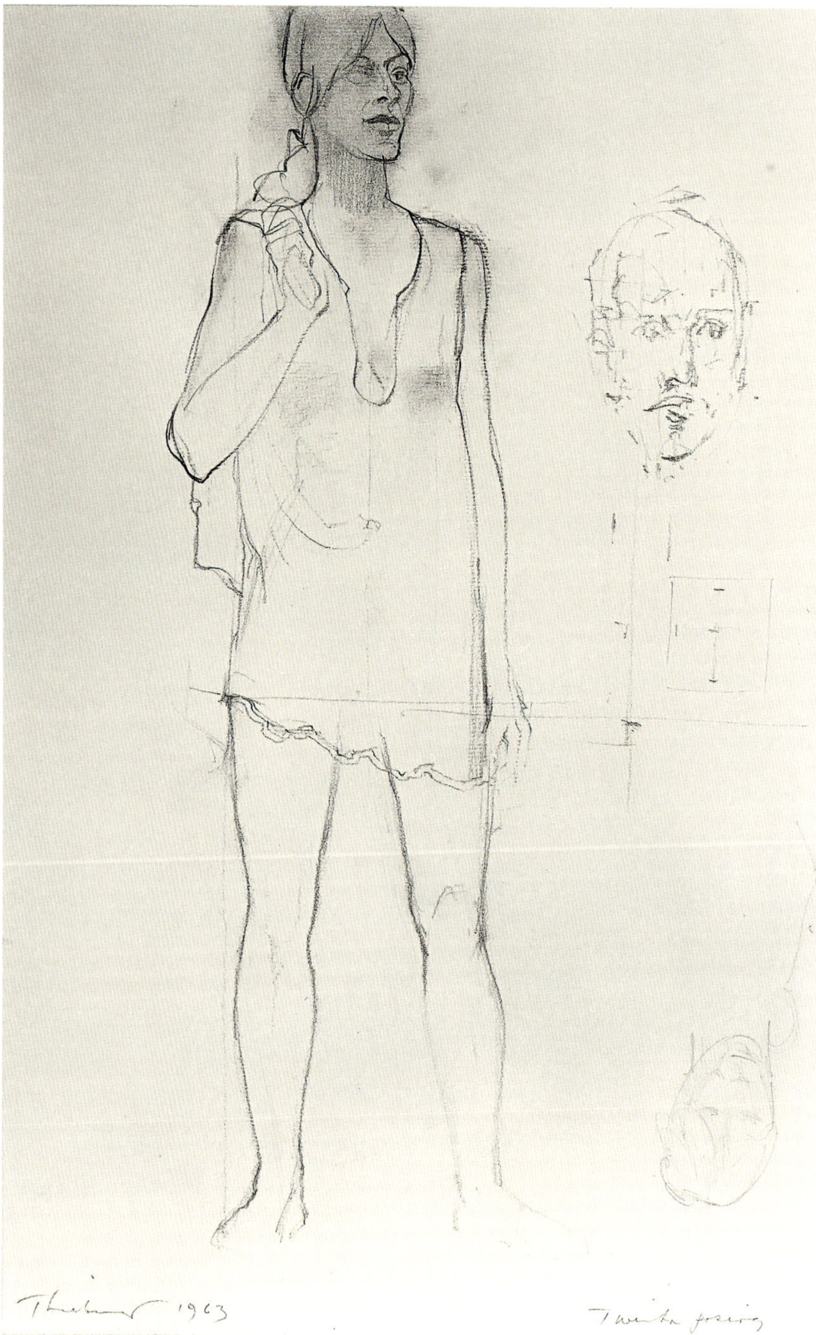

PL. 4 Wayne Thiebaud (American, 1920–2021), *Twinka Posing*, 1963. Pencil on paper, 17 ¾ × 11 ½ in. Collection of Twinka Thiebaud.

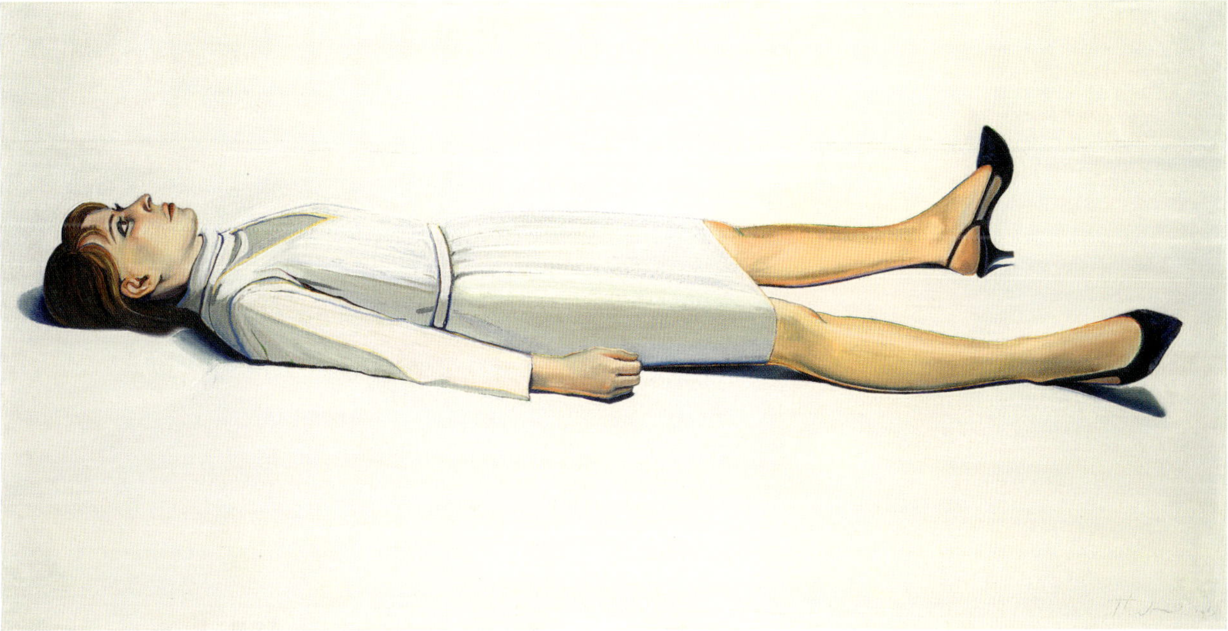

PL. 5 Wayne Thiebaud (American, 1920–2021), *Supine Woman*, 1963. Oil on canvas, 36 × 72 in. Crystal Bridges Museum of American Art, Bentonville, Arkansas, 2009.17. Photograph by Robert LaPrelle.

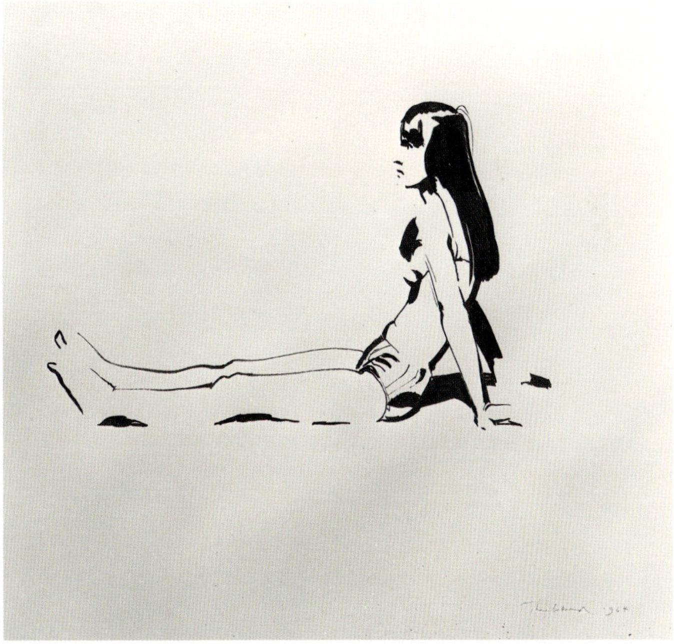

PL. 6 Wayne Thiebaud (American, 1920–2021), *Twinka Thiebaud*, 1964. Ink on paper, 14 × 17 in. Collection of Twinka Thiebaud.

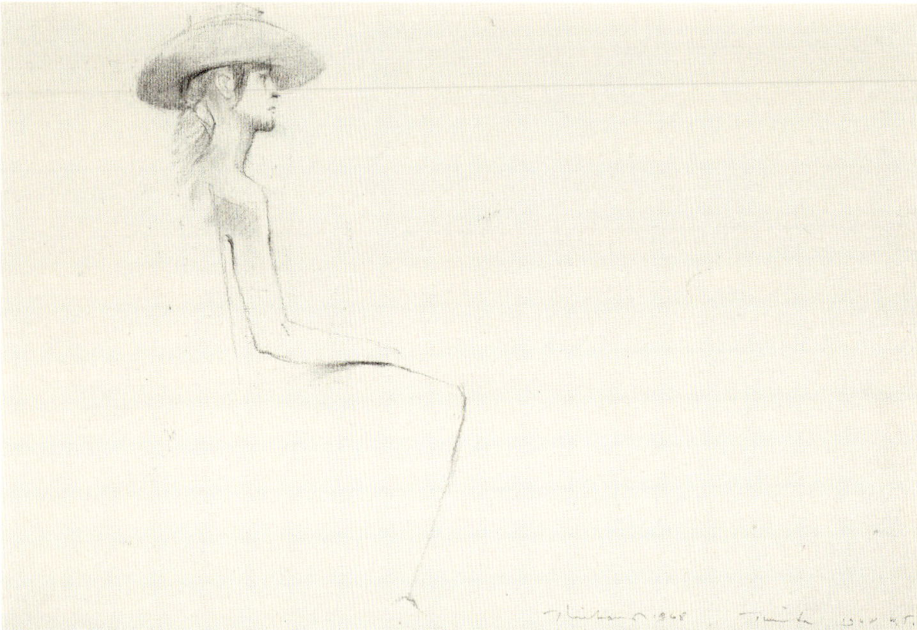

PL. 7 Wayne Thiebaud (American, 1920–2021), *Twinka (in Hat)*, 1968. Pencil on newsprint, 11 ¾ × 17 ½ in. Collection of Twinka Thiebaud.

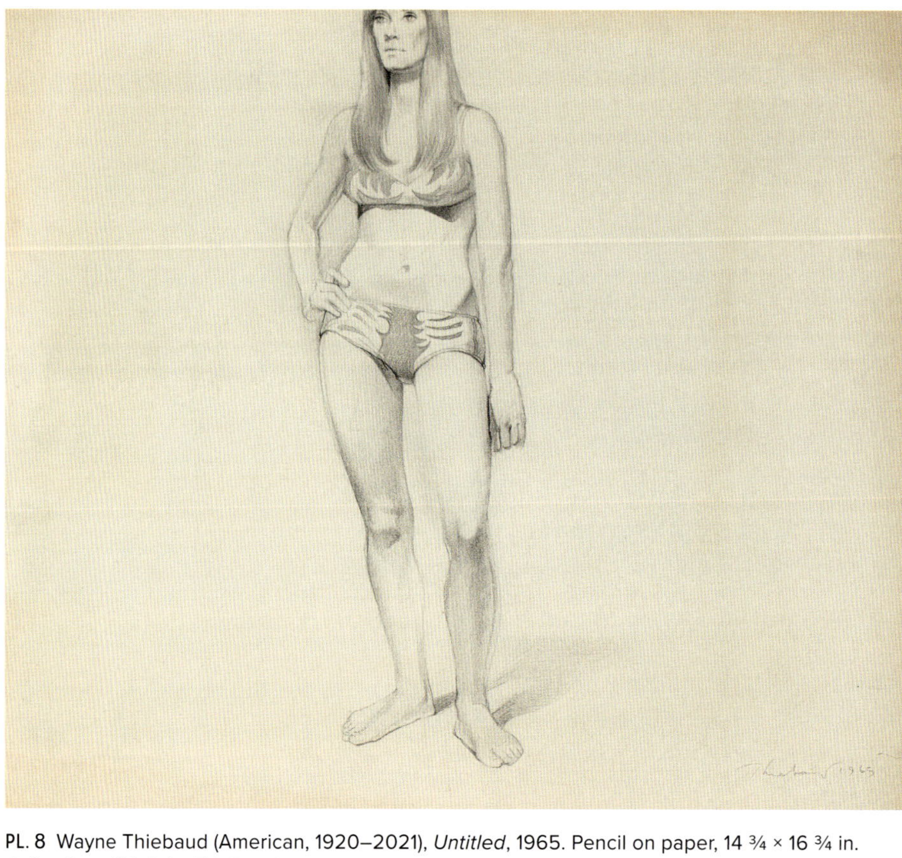

PL. 8 Wayne Thiebaud (American, 1920–2021), *Untitled*, 1965. Pencil on paper, 14 ¾ × 16 ¾ in. Collection of Twinka Thiebaud.

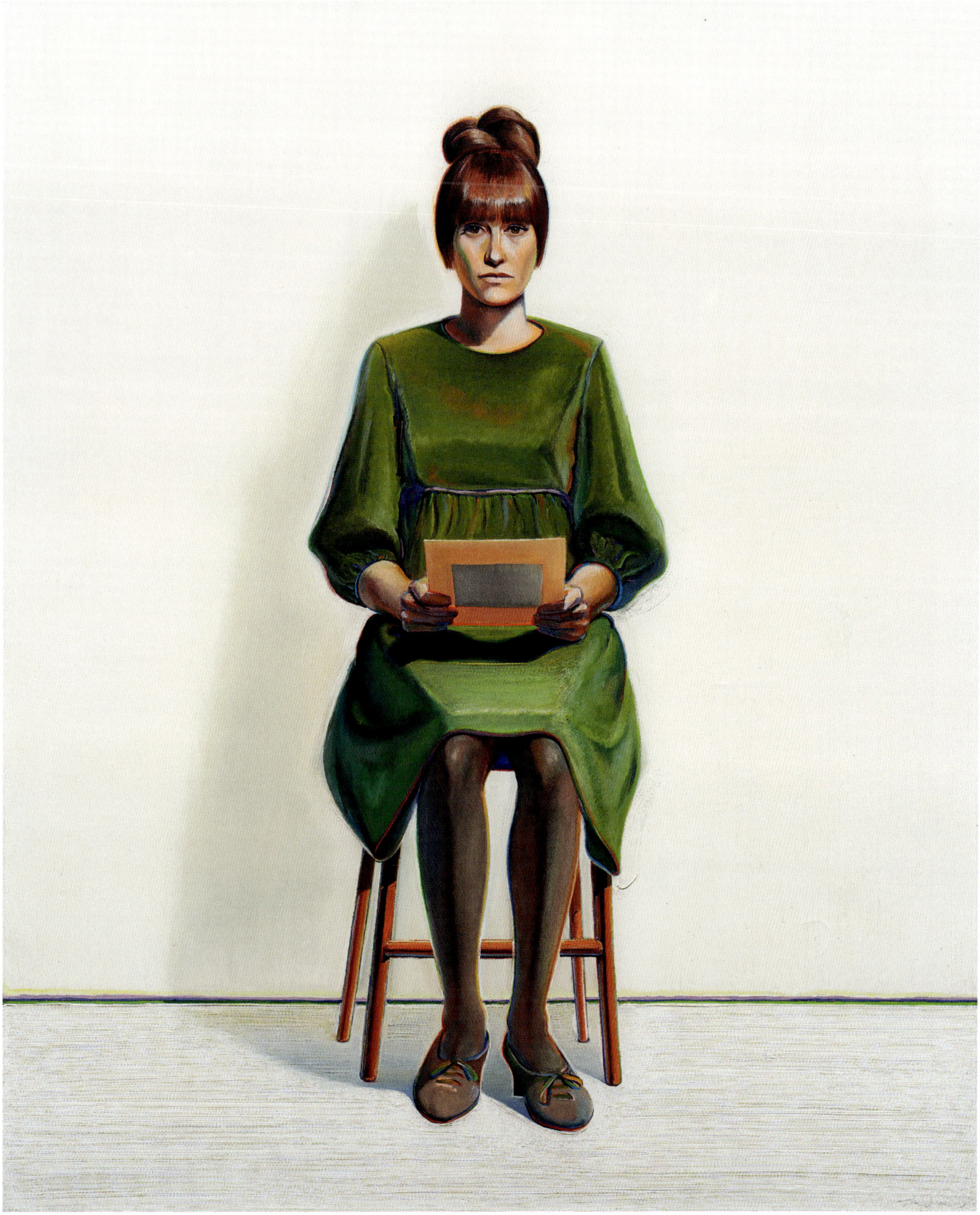

PL. 9 Wayne Thiebaud (American, 1920–2021), *Green Dress*, 1966/2017. Oil on canvas, 72 × 60 in. Collection of the Wayne Thiebaud Foundation.

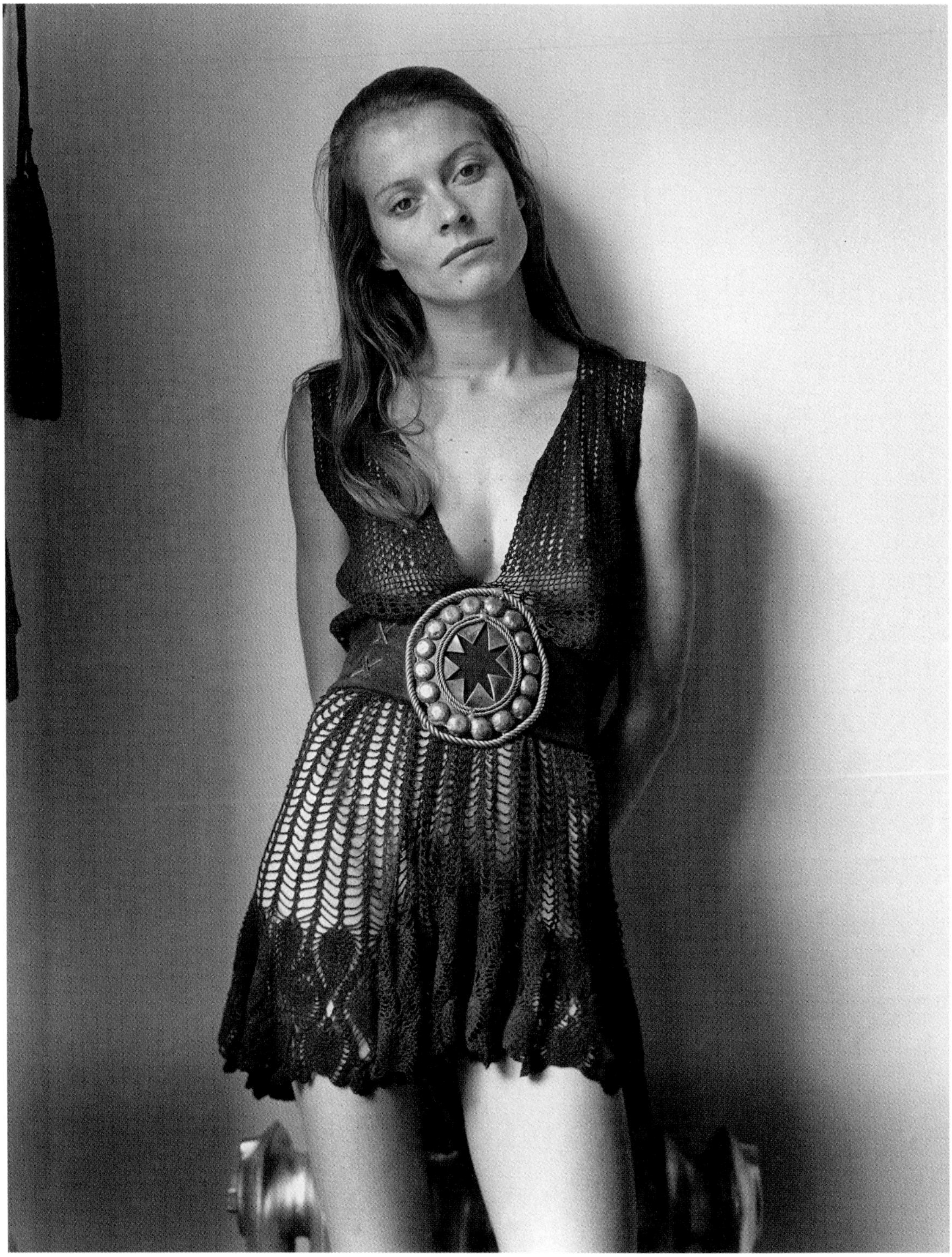

PL. 10 Jack Welpott (American, 1923–2007), *Twinka (Tilted Head),* 1970. Gelatin silver print, 9 ⅛ × 7 ¼ in. Collection of Twinka Thiebaud.

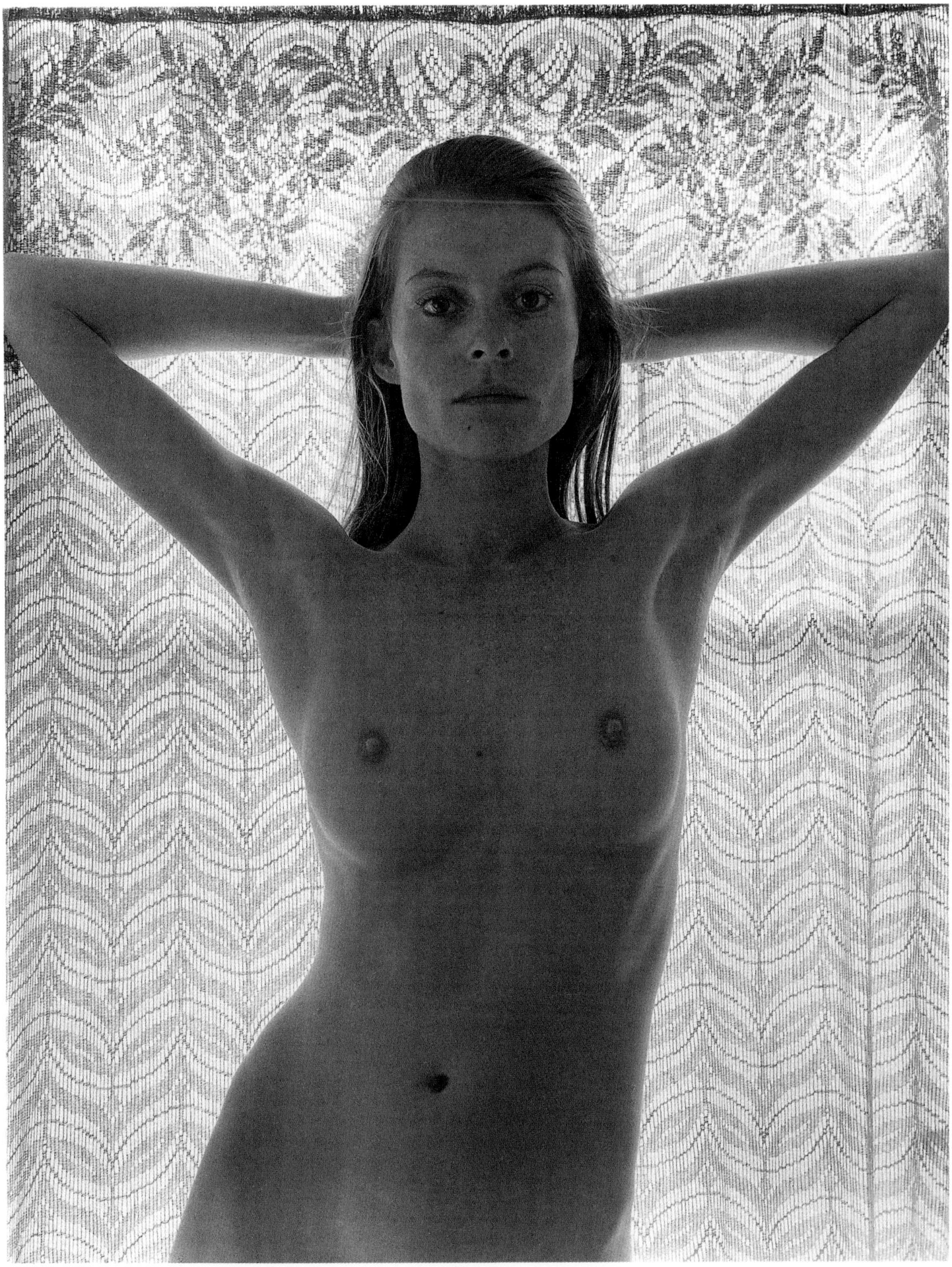

PL. 11 Judy Dater (American, born 1941), *Twinka and Lace Curtain*, 1970. Gelatin silver print, 13 ½ × 10 ⅜ in. Collection of Twinka Thiebaud.

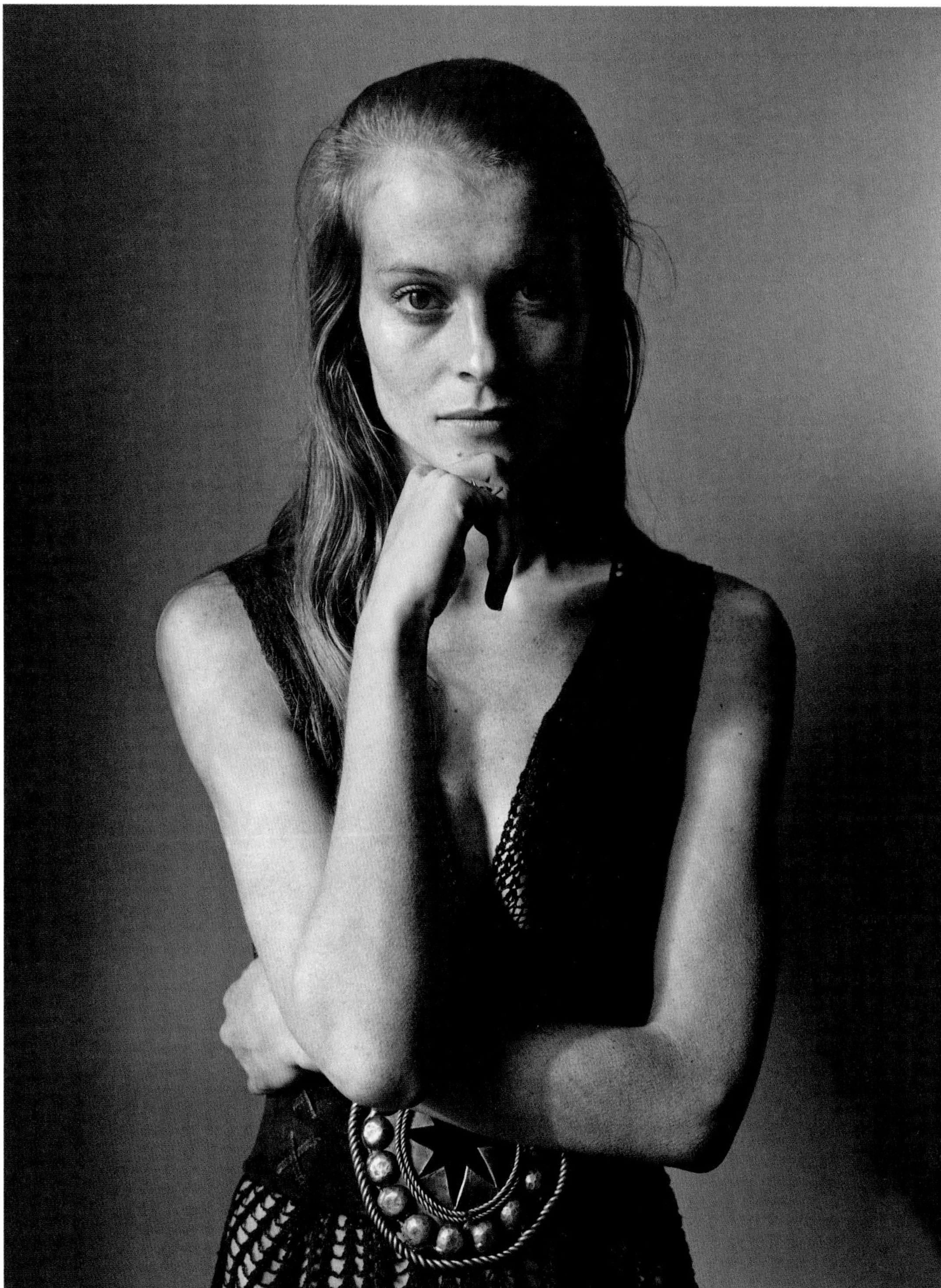

PL. 12 Jack Welpott (American, 1923–2007), *Twinka*, 1970. Gelatin silver print, 12 ½ × 8 ¾ in. Collection of Twinka Thiebaud.

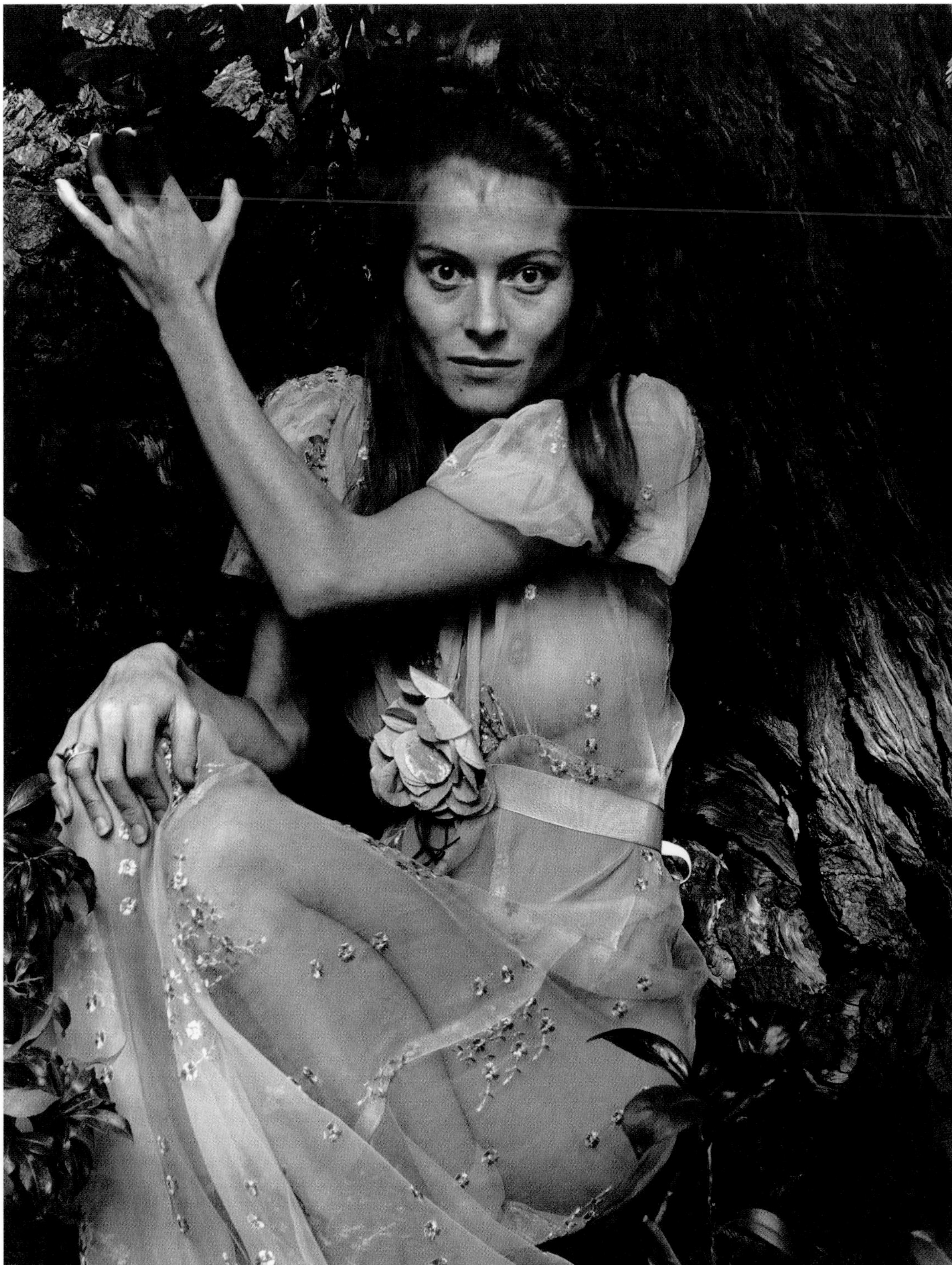

PL. 13 Judy Dater (American, born 1941), *Twinka Thiebaud (Twinka and Tree),* 1970. Gelatin silver print, 12 ⅞ × 10 in. Crocker Art Museum Purchase, 1978.2.4.

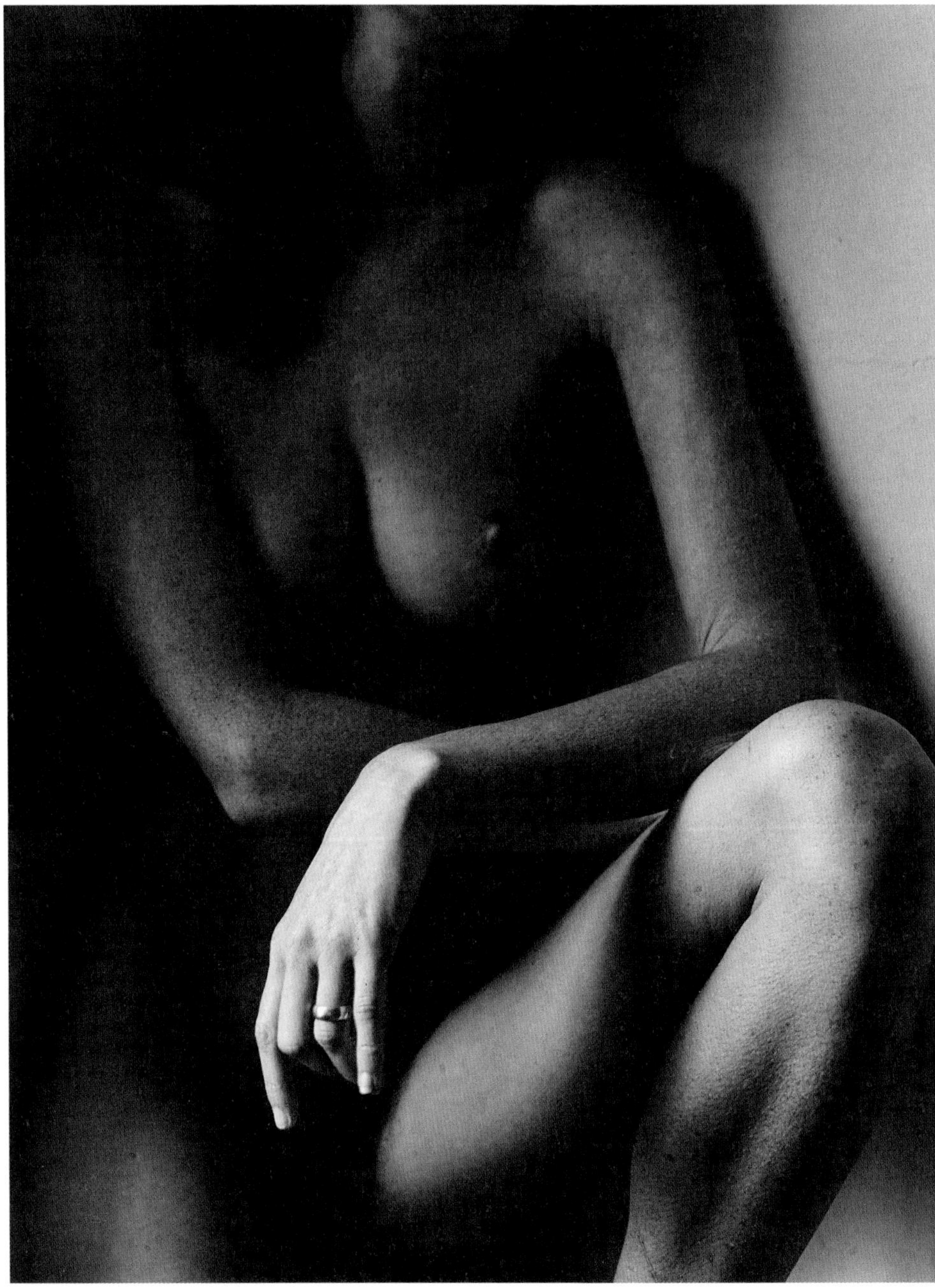

PL. 14 Jack Welpott (American, 1923–2007), *Twinka (Torso in Light/Dark Contrast),* 1970. Gelatin silver print, 9 ¼ × 7 ⅛ in. Collection of Twinka Thiebaud.

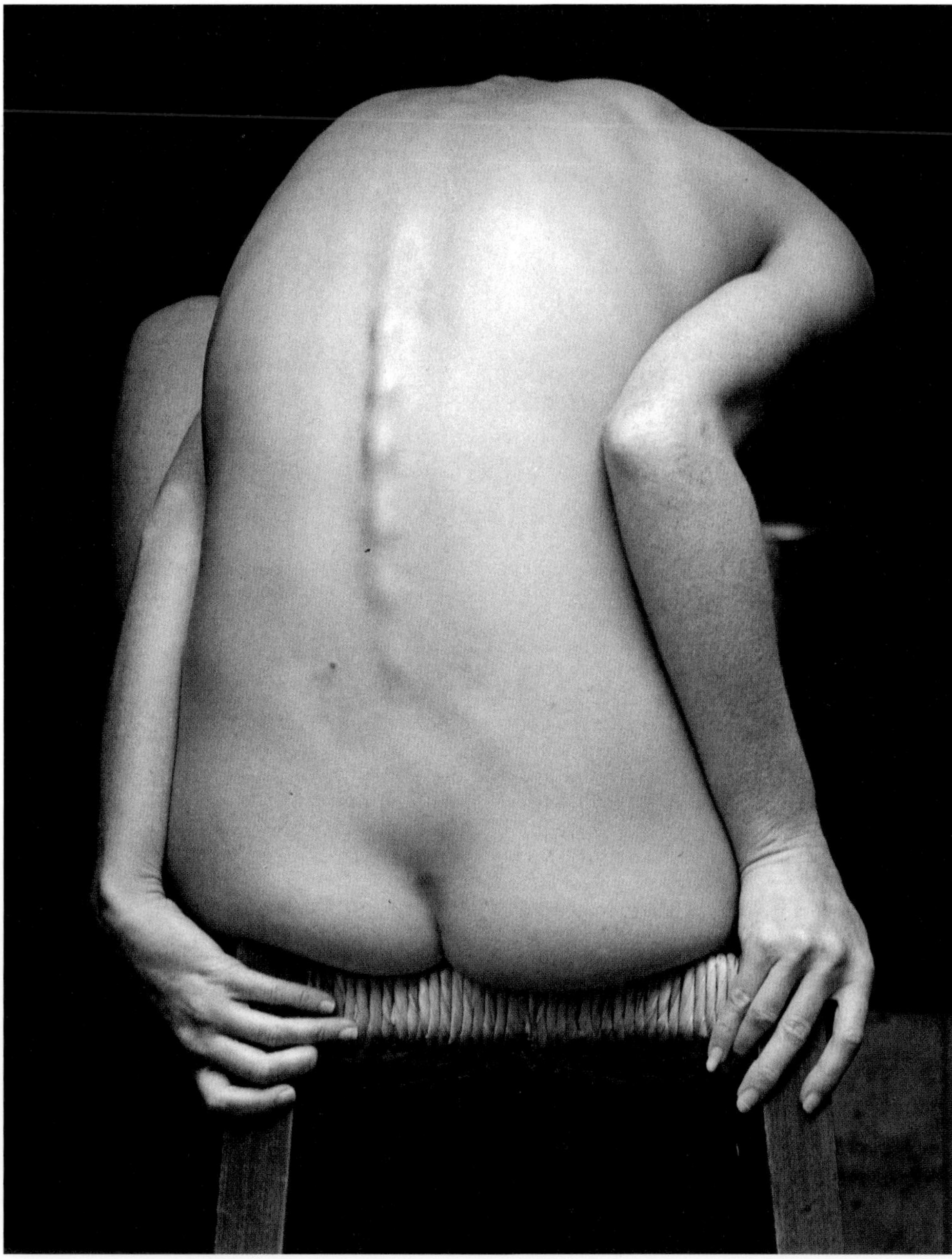

PL. 15 Jack Welpott (American, 1923–2007), *Untitled (Seated with Curving Spine)*, 1971. Gelatin silver print, 10 × 8 in. Collection of Twinka Thiebaud.

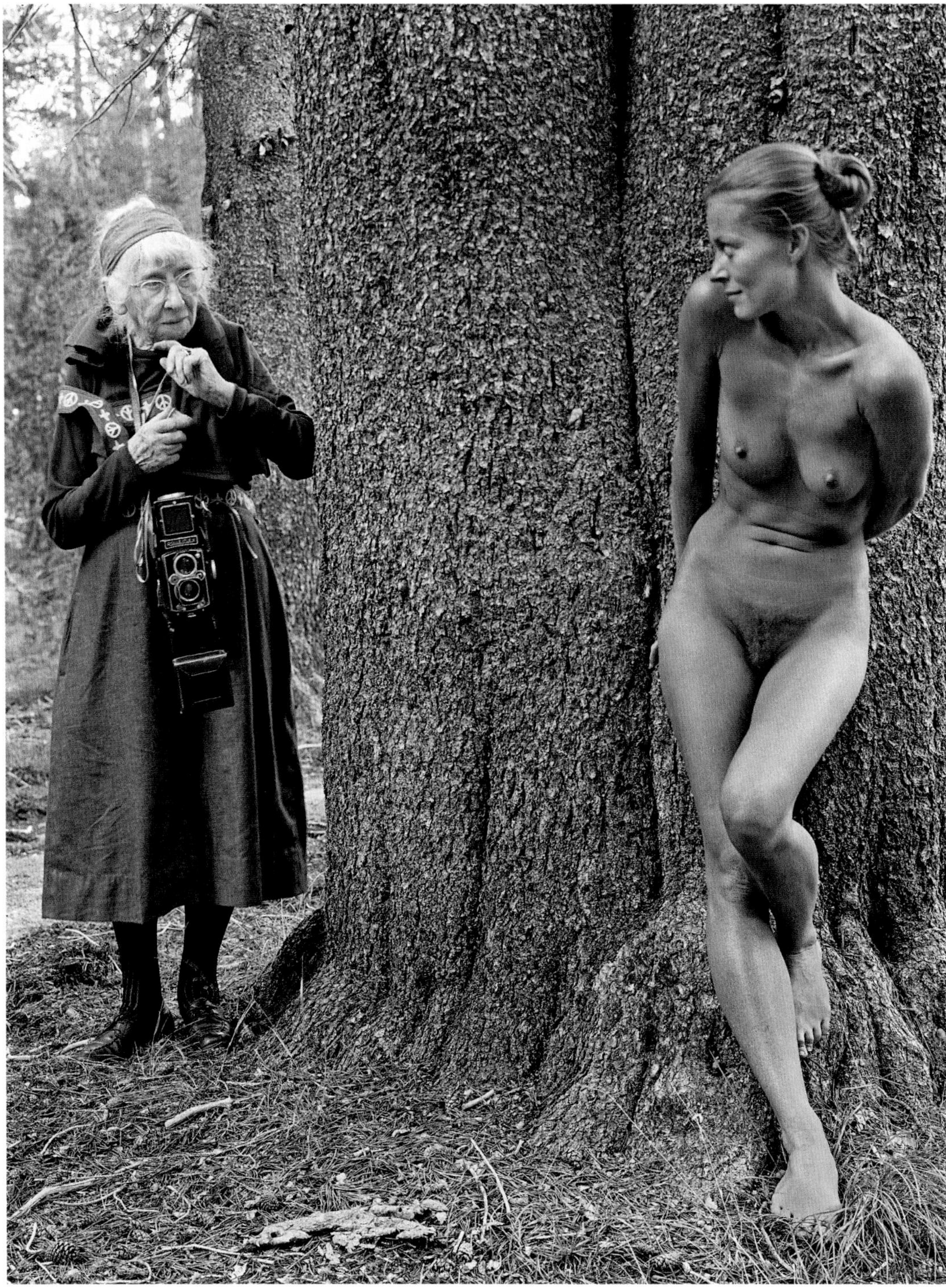

PL. 16 Judy Dater (American, born 1941), *Imogen and Twinka at Yosemite*, 1974. Gelatin silver print, 9 ¼ × 7 ¼ in. Crocker Art Museum purchase with funds from the Shirley & Forrest Plant Fund, 2017.81.

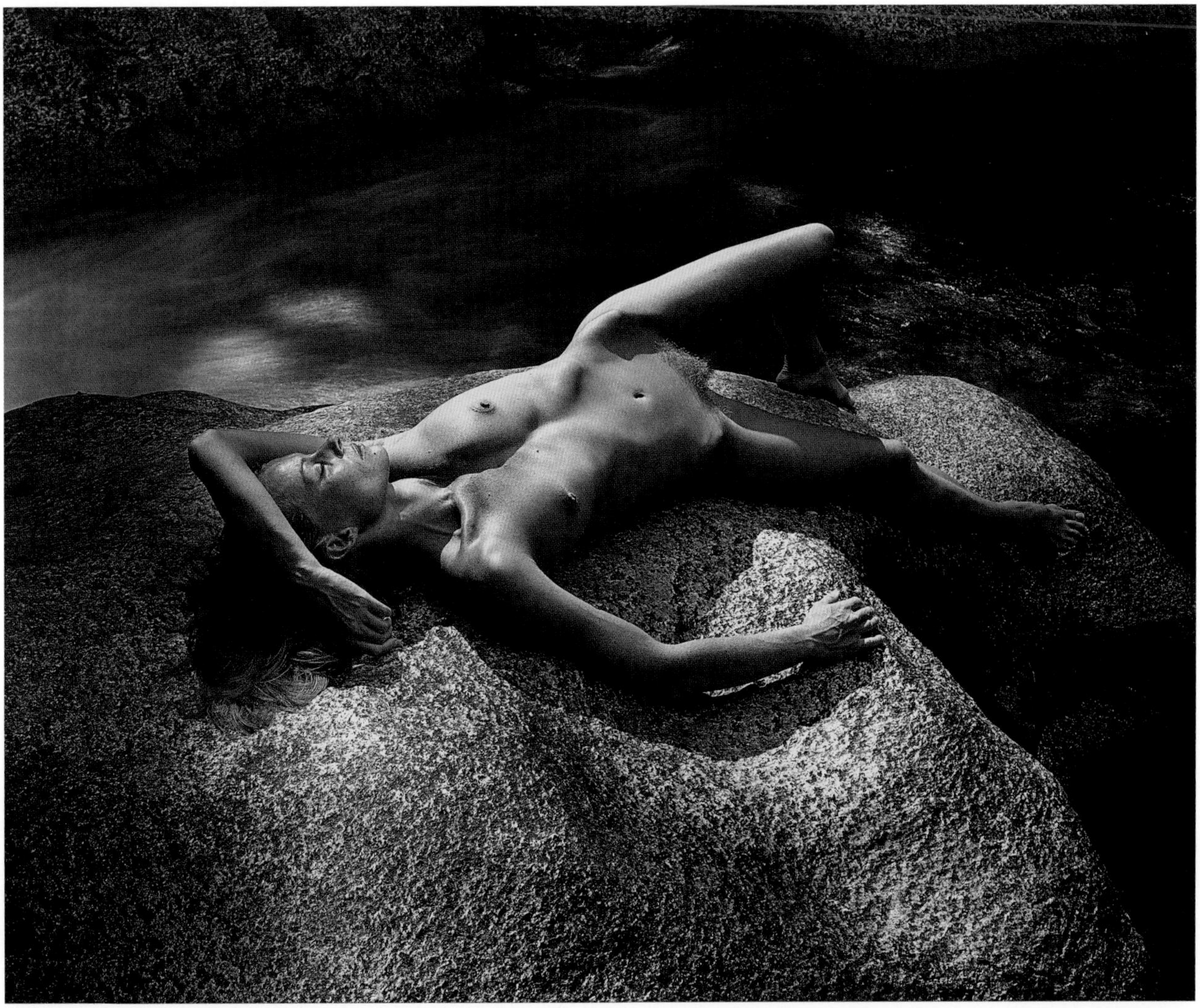

PL. 17 R. Michael Walker (American, born 1950), *Twinka at Wawona/Yosemite National Park, CA*, 1974. Archival inkjet print, 13 ⅝ × 17 ⅛ in. Collection of Twinka Thiebaud.

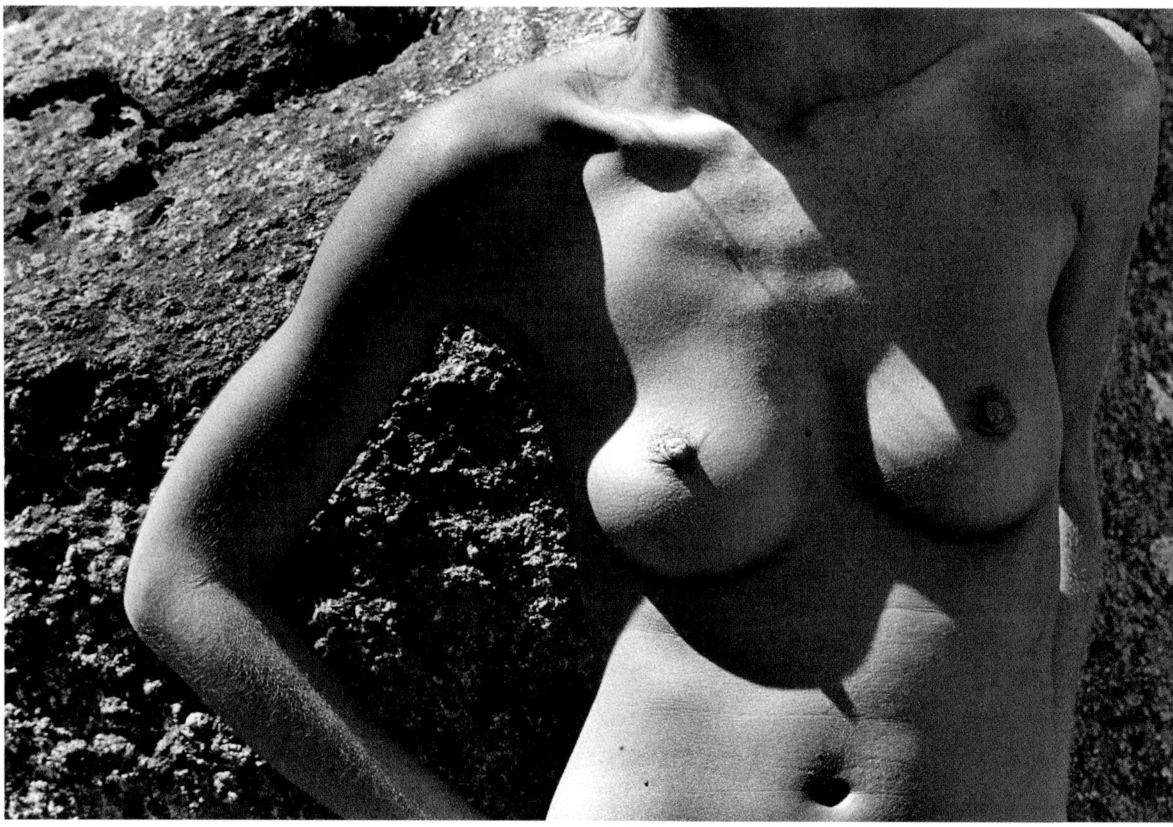

PL. 18 Eva Rubinstein (Polish-American, born Argentina, 1933), *Twinka, Yosemite, 1974*, 1974. Gelatin silver print, 5 ½ × 8 ⅛ in. Collection of Twinka Thiebaud.

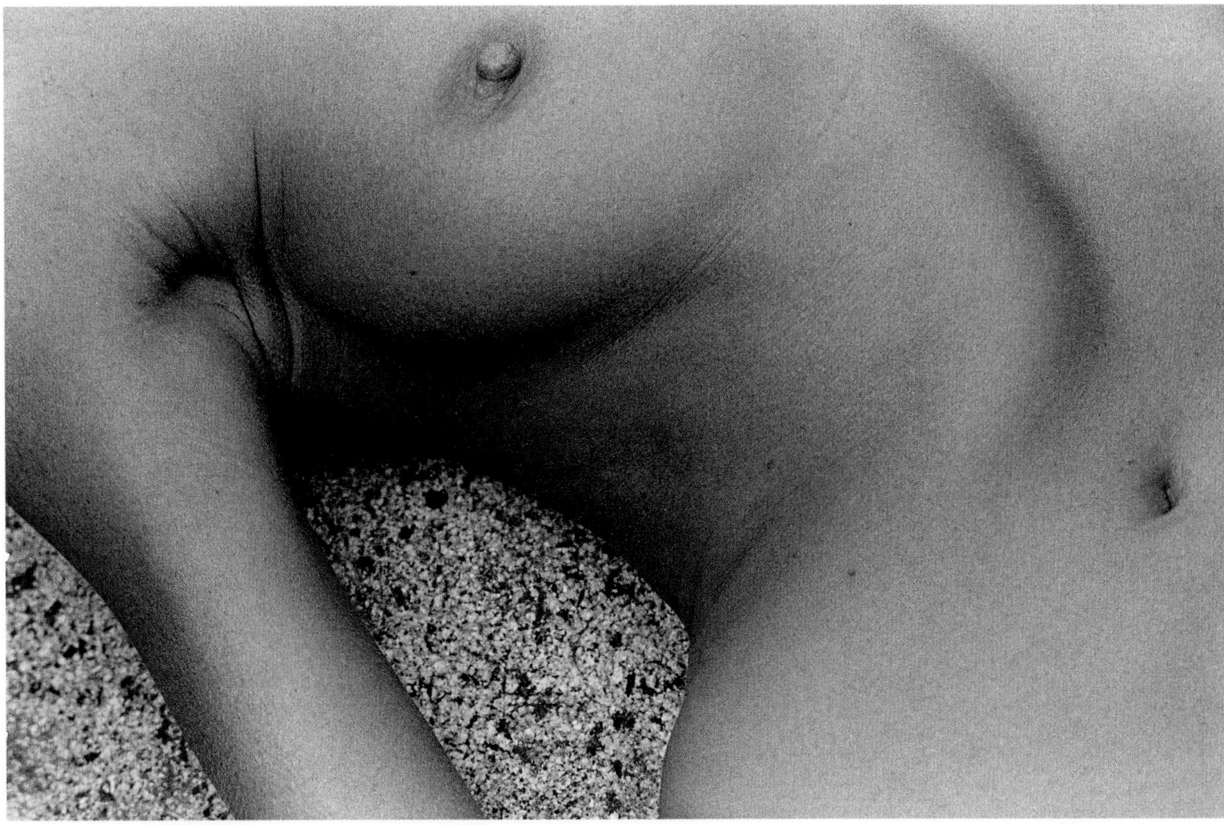

PL. 19 Eva Rubinstein (Polish-American, born Argentina, 1933), *Twinka on Rocks, Yosemite, 1974*, 1974. Gelatin silver print, 5 ½ × 8 7⁄16 in. Collection of Twinka Thiebaud.

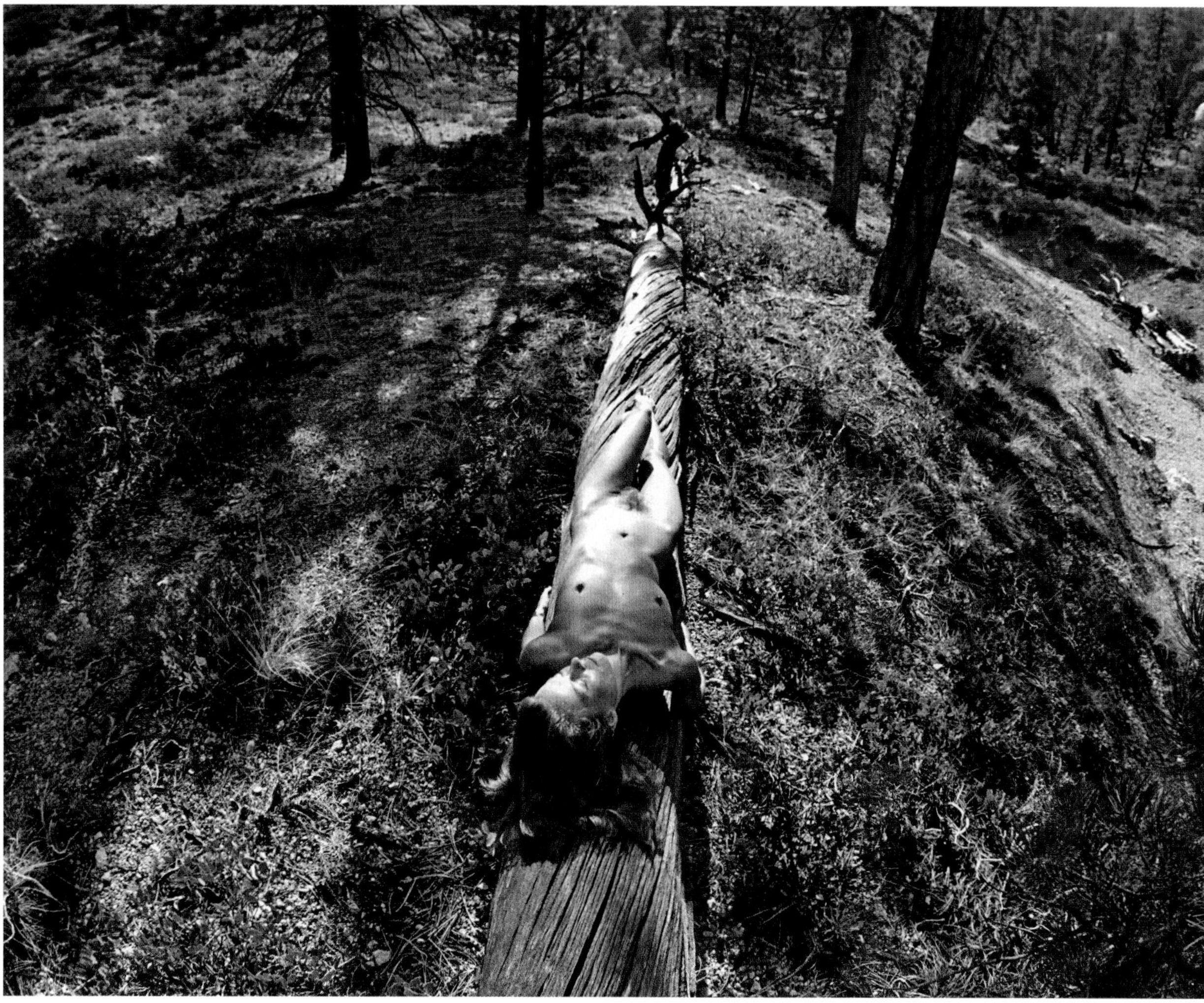

PL. 20 Pete Saloutos (American, born 1947), *Twinka on Fallen Tree*, 1974. Gelatin silver print, 8 × 10 in. Collection of Twinka Thiebaud.

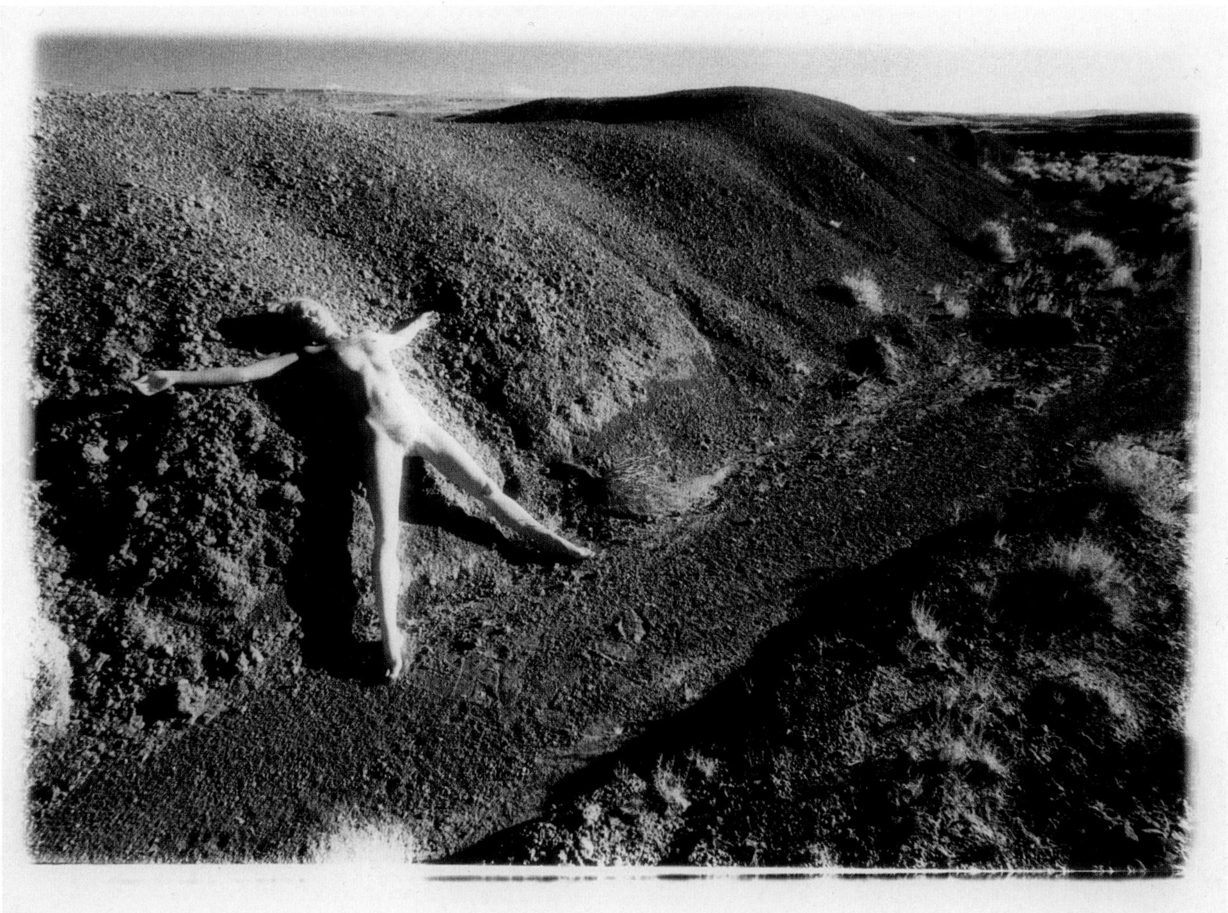

PL. 21 Pete Saloutos (American, born 1947), *Twinka Desert*, 1974. Infrared black-and-white film, 6 ½ × 9 ½ in. Collection of Twinka Thiebaud.

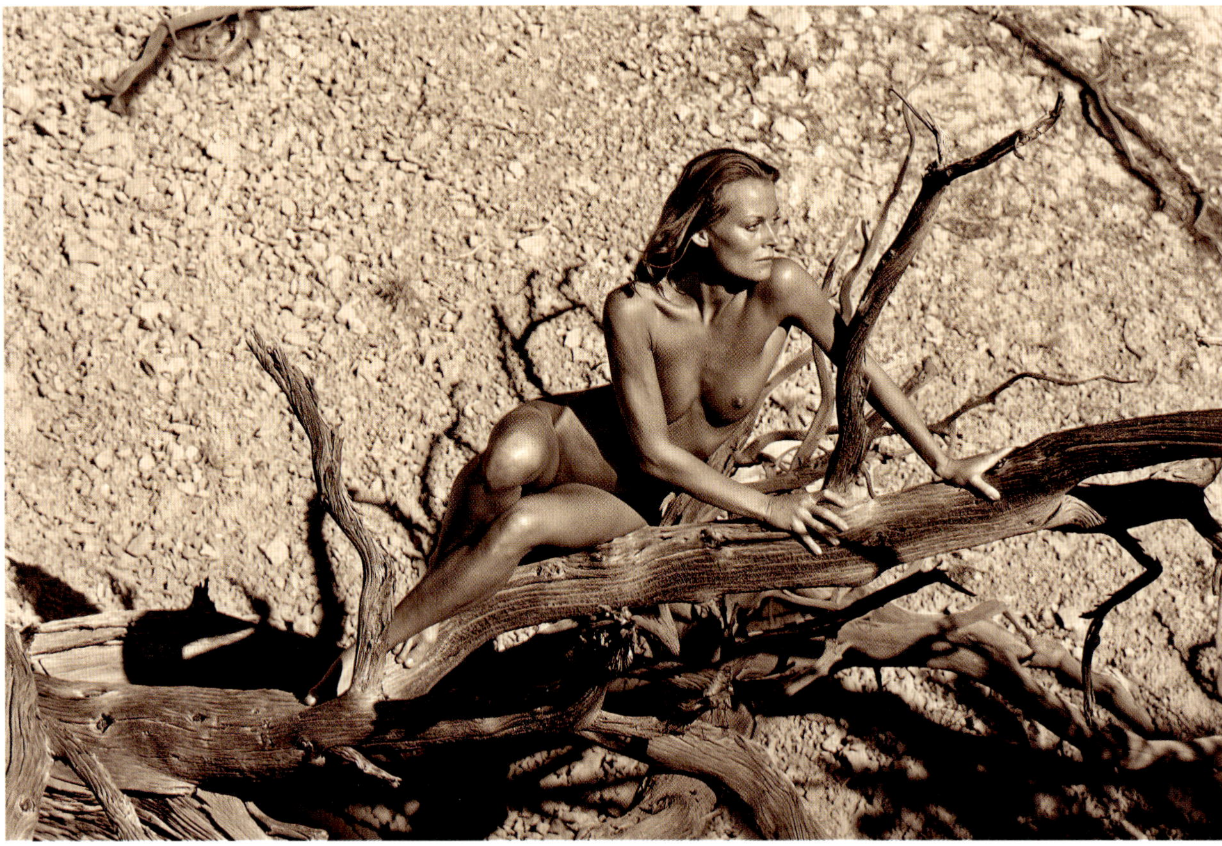

PL. 22 Pete Saloutos (American, born 1947), *Twinka and Juniper Tree*, 1974. Photo print on metal, 24 × 36 in. Collection of Pete Saloutos.

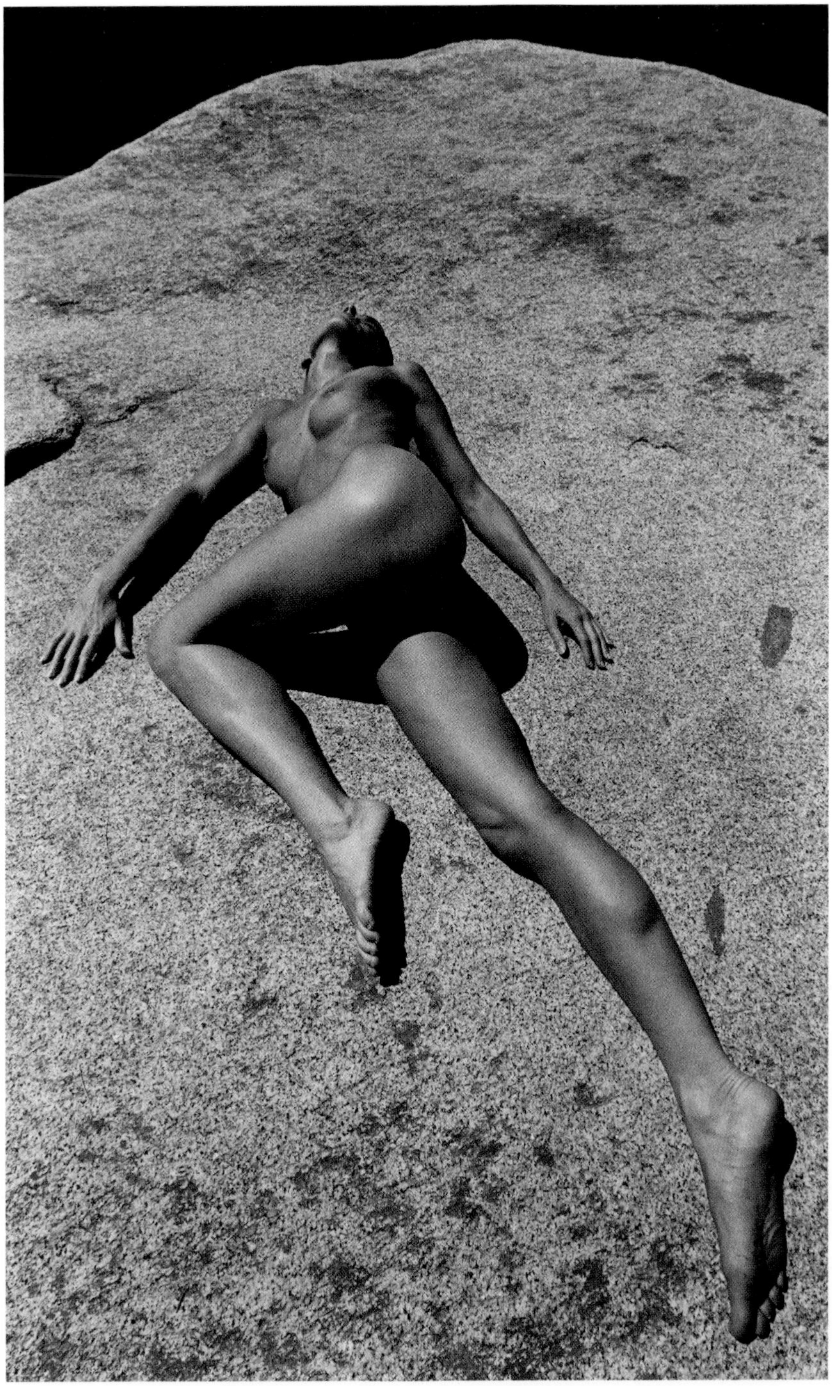

PL. 23 Larry Keenan Jr. (American, 1943–2012), *Untitled,* 1975. Gelatin silver print, 9 × 5 ½ in. Collection of Twinka Thiebaud.

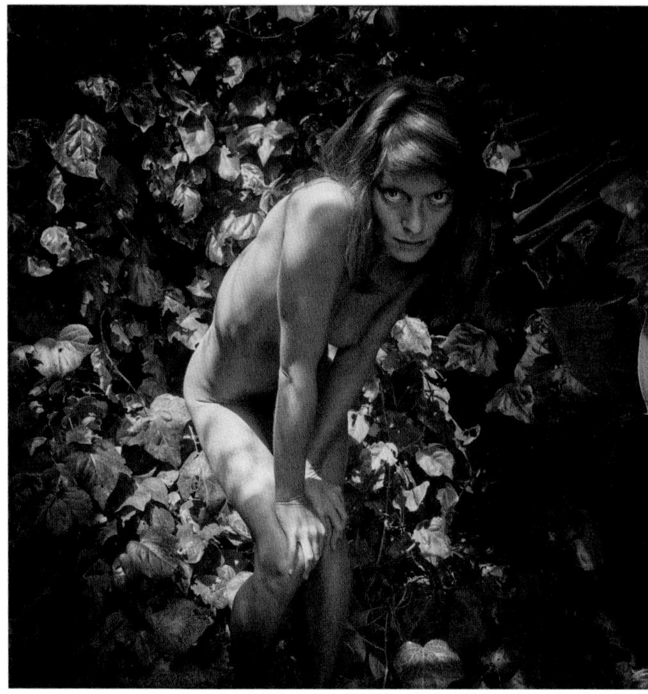

PL. 24 R. Michael Walker (American, born 1950), *Twinka in Henry's Garden, Pacific Palisades, CA*, 1975. Gelatin silver print, 14 ⅝ × 14 ¼ in. Collection of Twinka Thiebaud.

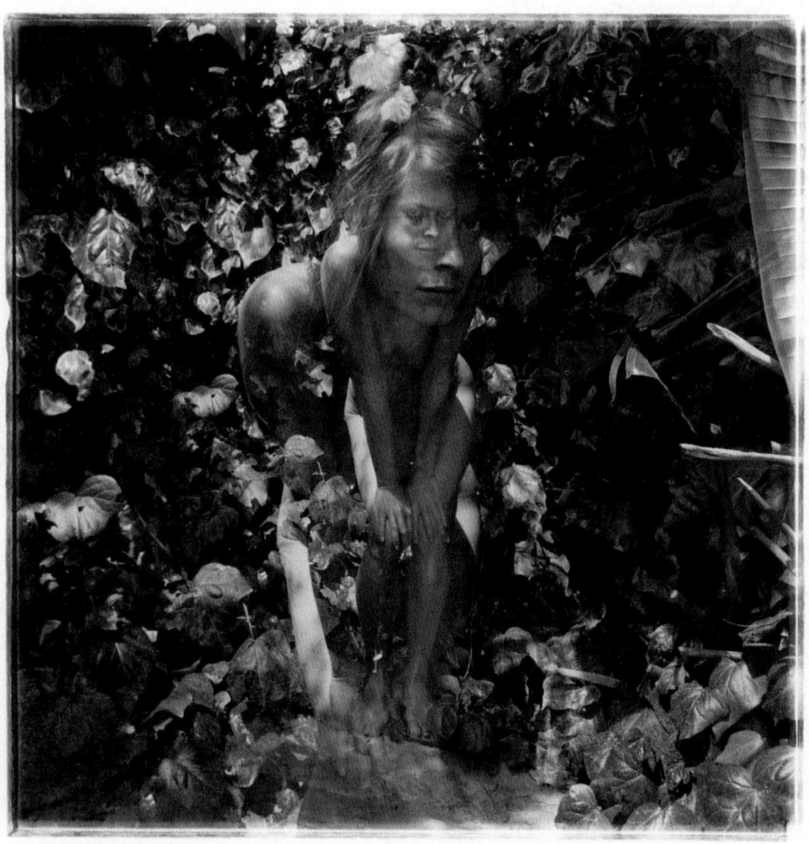

PL. 25 R. Michael Walker (American, born 1950), *Untitled*, 1975. Gelatin silver print, 7 × 7 ⅛ in. Collection of Twinka Thiebaud.

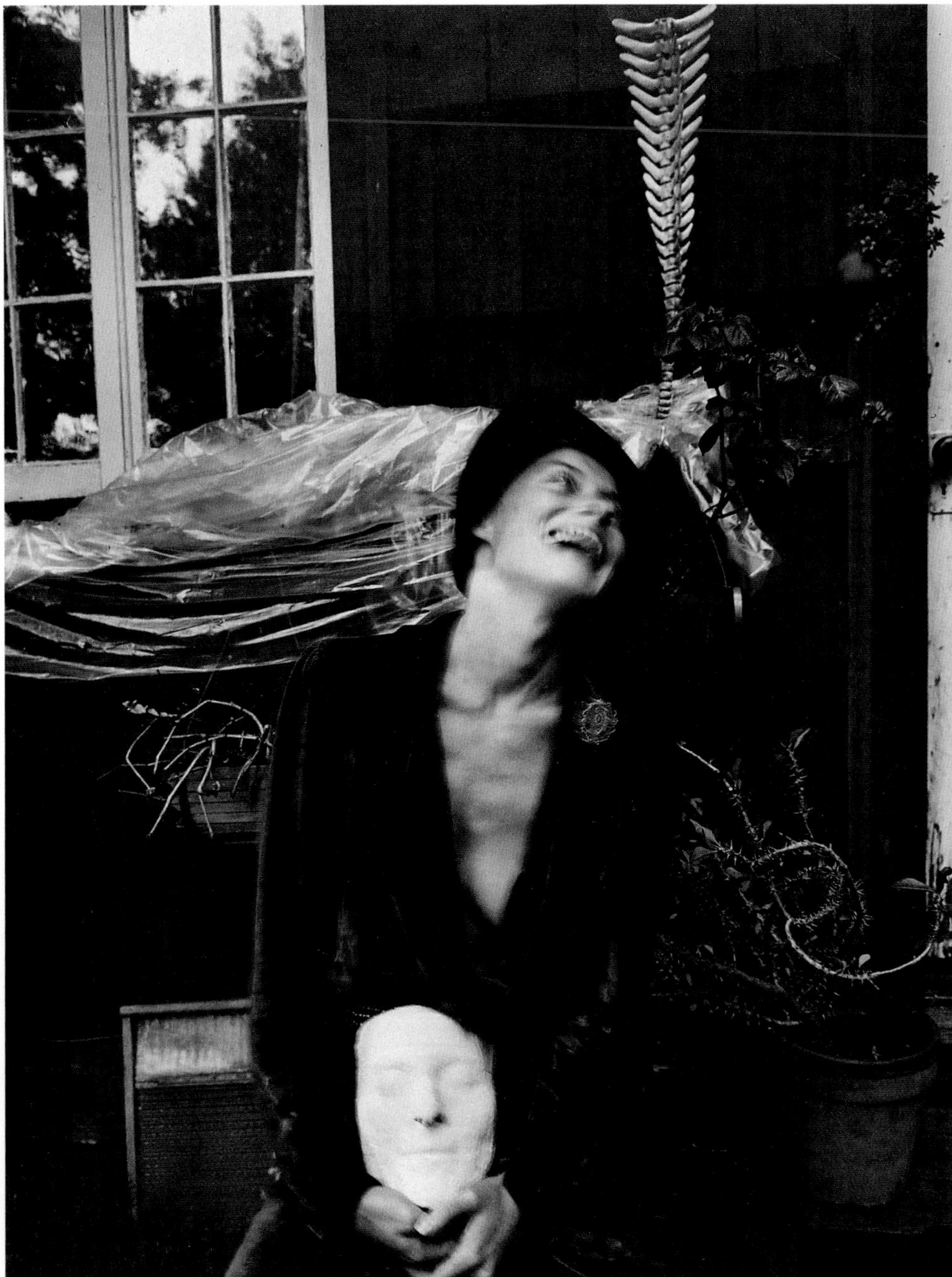

PL. 26 Judy Dater (American, born 1941), *Twinka with Lifemask*, 1975. Gelatin silver print, 11 ⅞ × 9 in. Collection of Twinka Thiebaud.

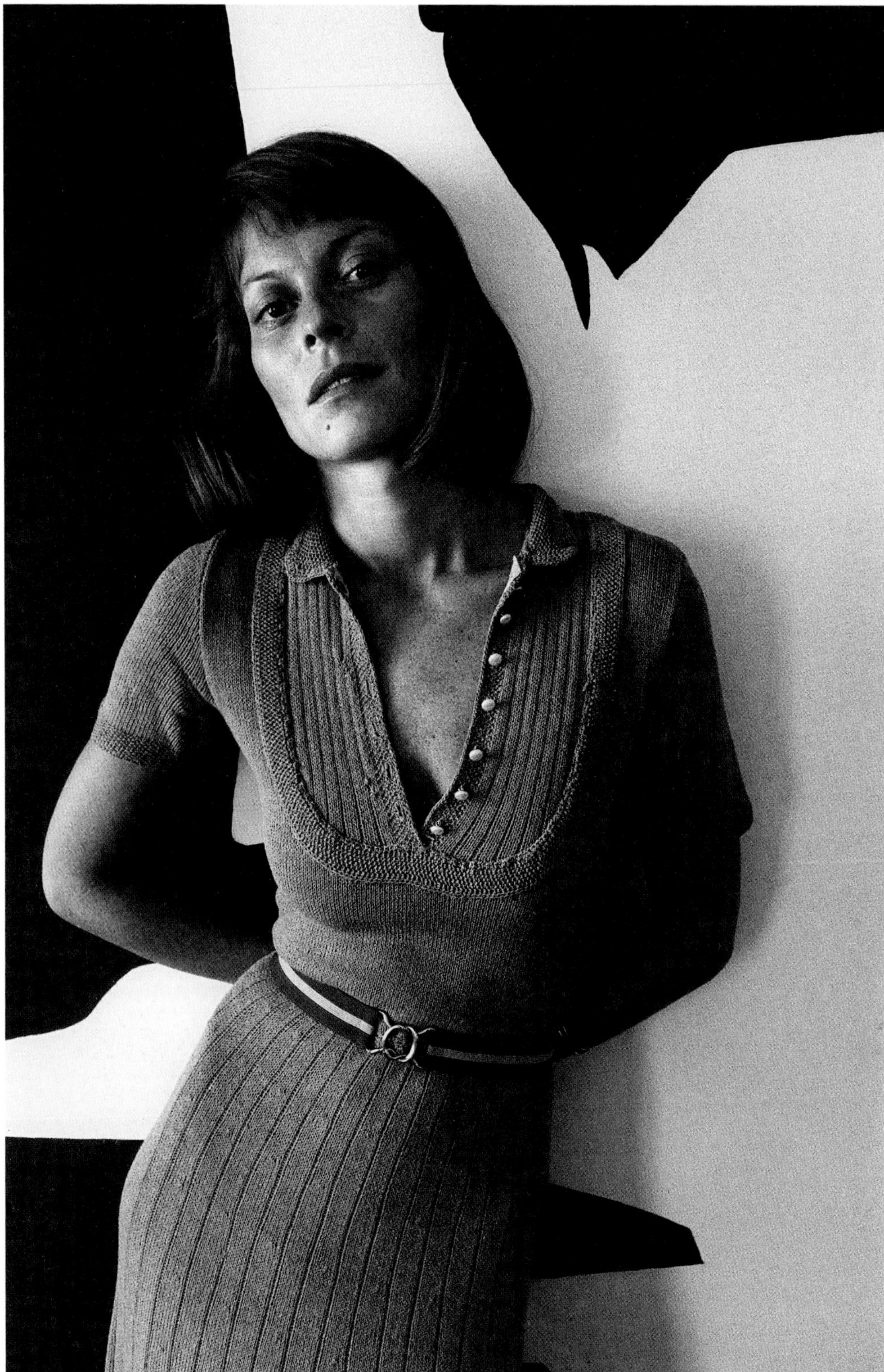

PL. 27 Arnold Newman (American, 1918–2006), *Untitled (Twinka Standing)*, 1975. Gelatin silver print, 9 ½ × 6 ½ in. Collection of Twinka Thiebaud.

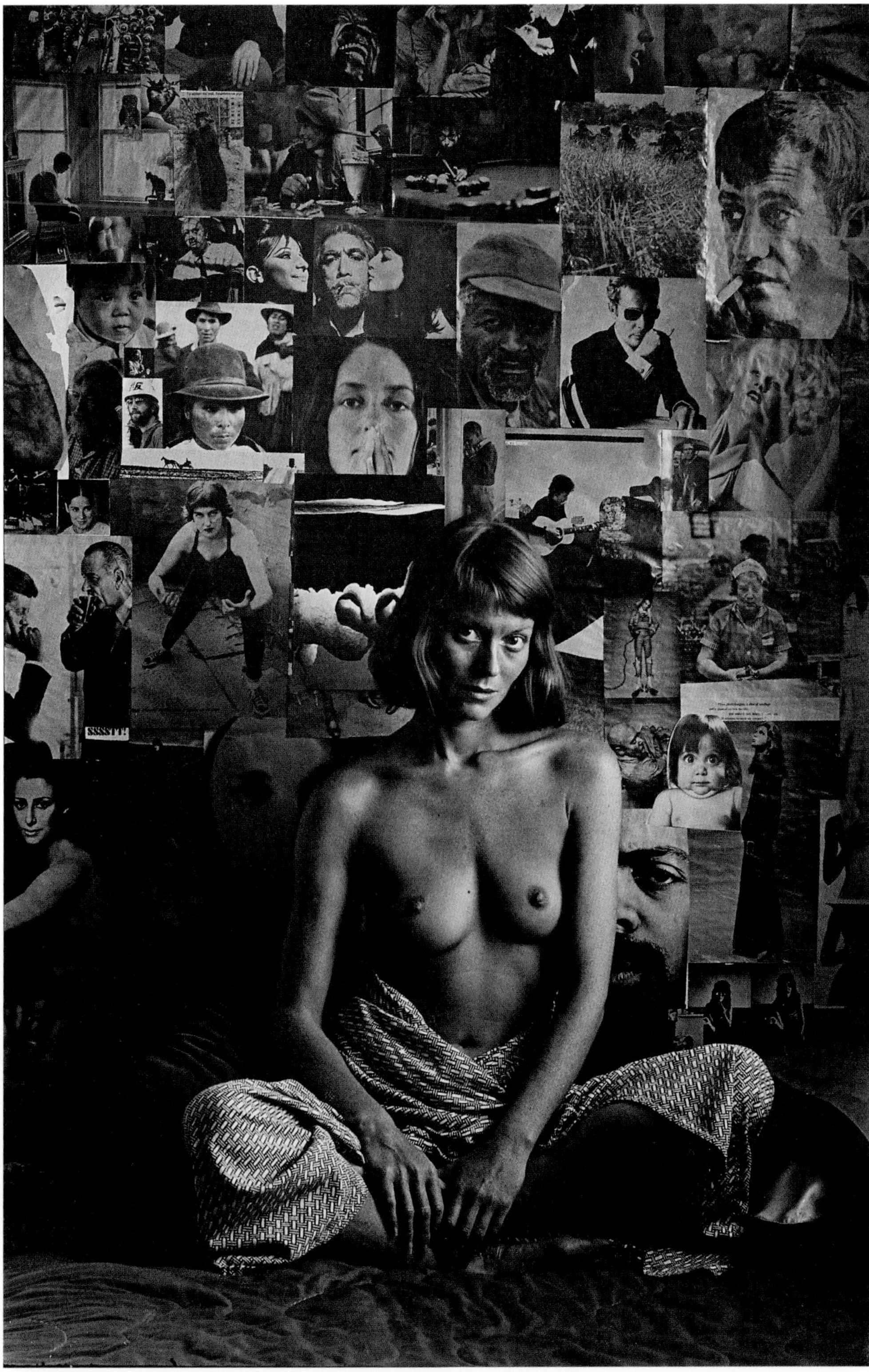

PL. 28 Arnold Newman (American, 1918–2006), *Untitled (Twinka Seated)*, 1975. Gelatin silver print, 9 5⁄8 × 6 3⁄8 in. Collection of Twinka Thiebaud.

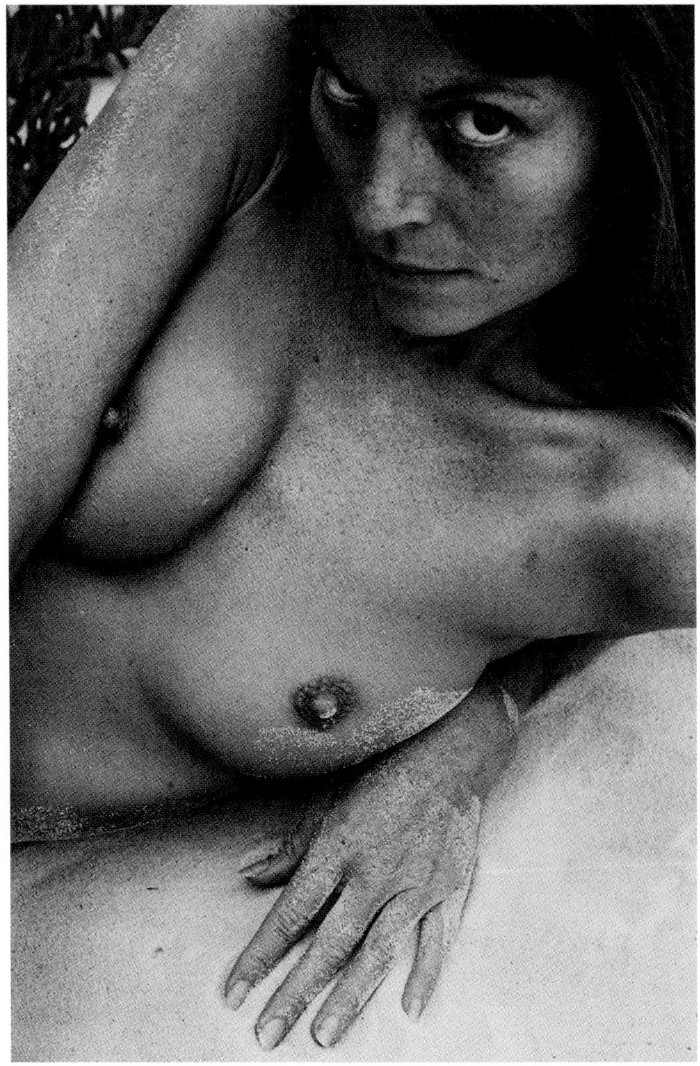

PL. 29 Lucien Clergue (French, 1934–2014), *Twinka at Pebble Beach, Monterey, CA (Looking Ahead),* 1975. Gelatin silver print, 14 ¼ × 9 ⅜ in. Collection of Twinka Thiebaud.

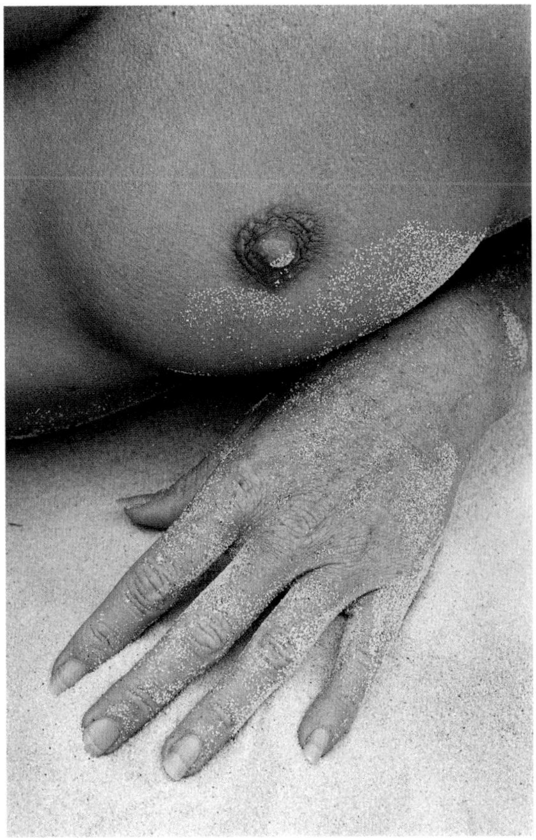

PL. 30 Lucien Clergue (French, 1934–2014), *Twinka at Pebble Beach, Monterey, CA (Hand and Breast)*, 1975. Gelatin silver print, 14 ¼ × 9 ⅜ in. Collection of Twinka Thiebaud.

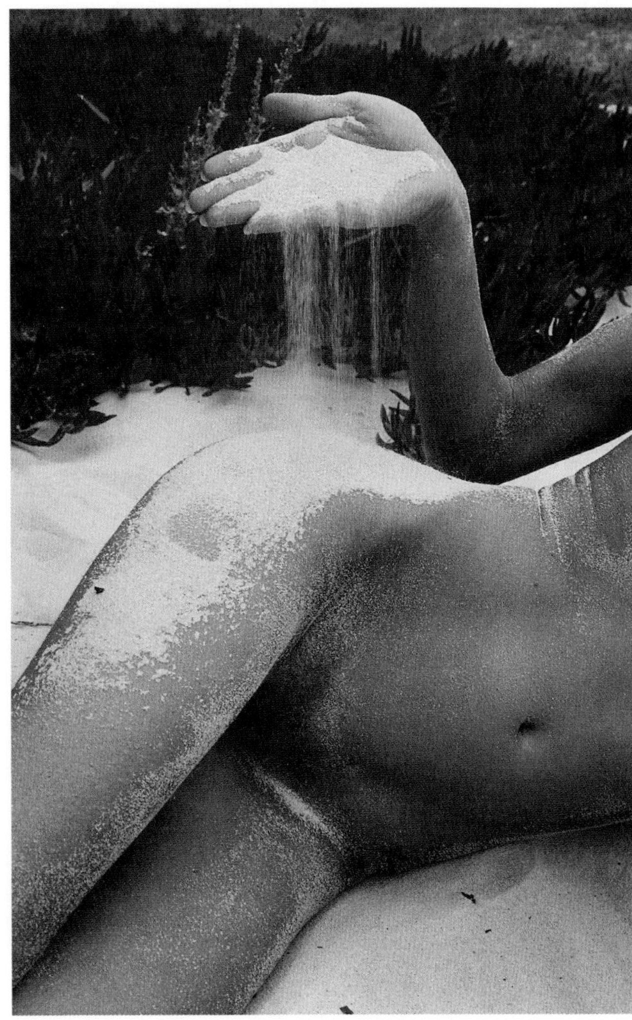

PL. 31 Lucien Clergue (French, 1934–2014), *Twinka at Pebble Beach, Monterey, CA (Falling Sand)*, 1975. Gelatin silver print, 14 ¼ × 9 ⅜ in. Collection of Twinka Thiebaud.

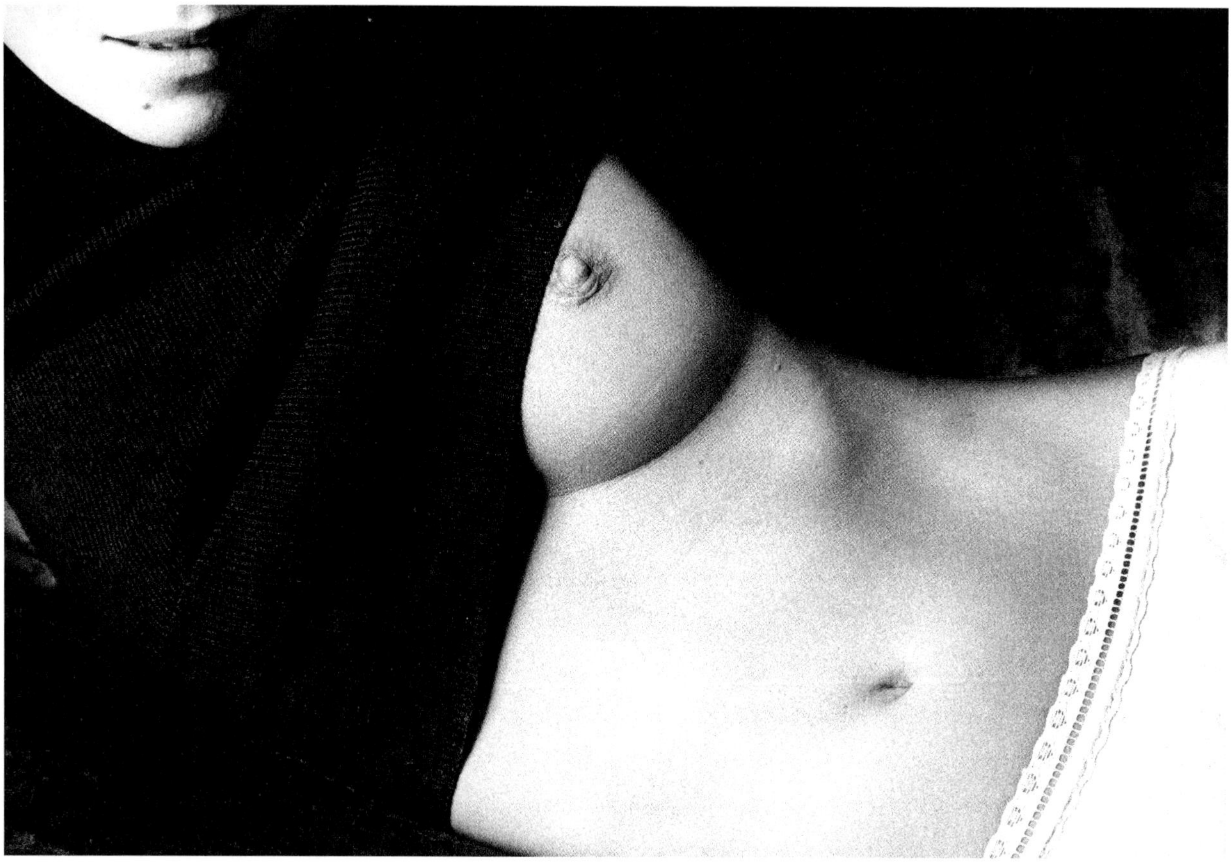

PL. 32 Ralph Gibson (American, born 1939), *Untitled*, 1976. Gelatin silver print, 8 × 12 3/8 in. Collection of Twinka Thiebaud.

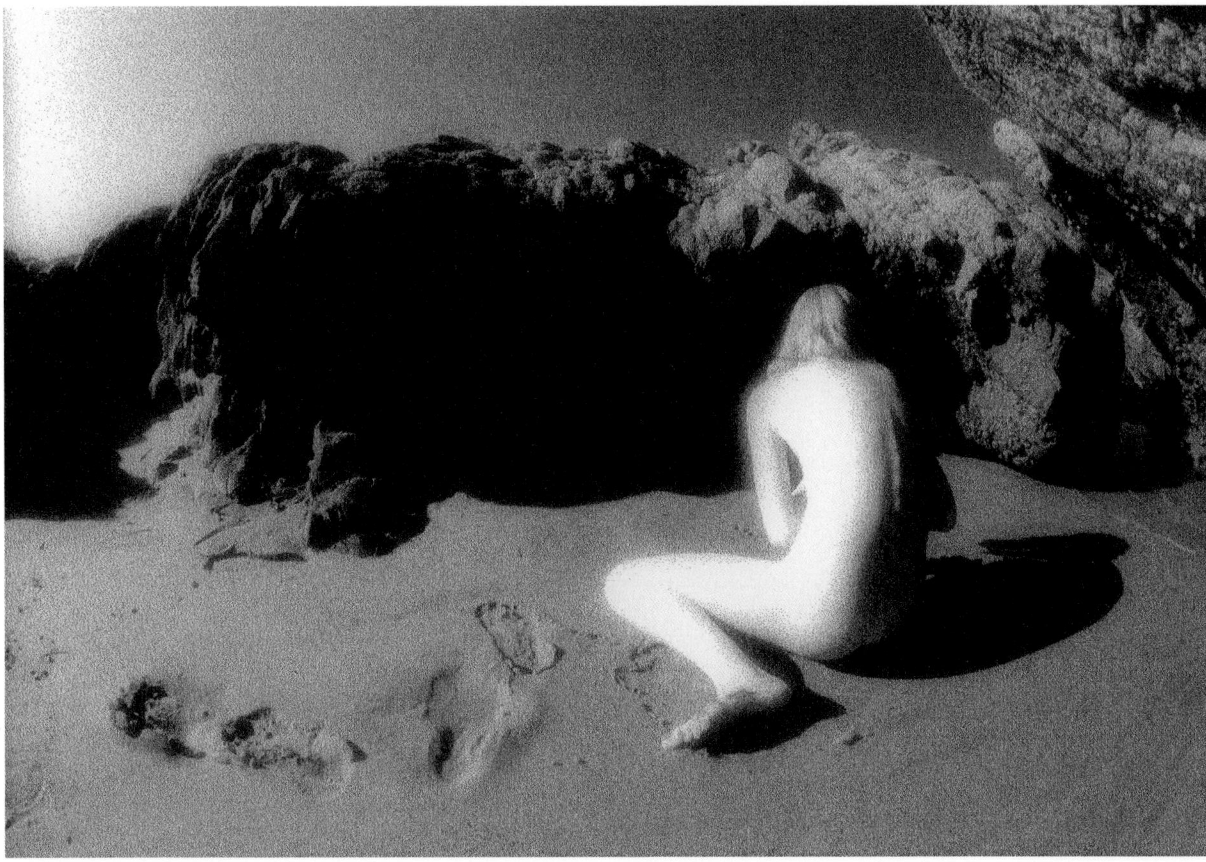

PL. 33 Pete Saloutos (American, born 1947), *Twinka at the Beach*, 1976. Infrared black-and-white film, 4 ¾ × 7 in. Collection of Twinka Thiebaud.

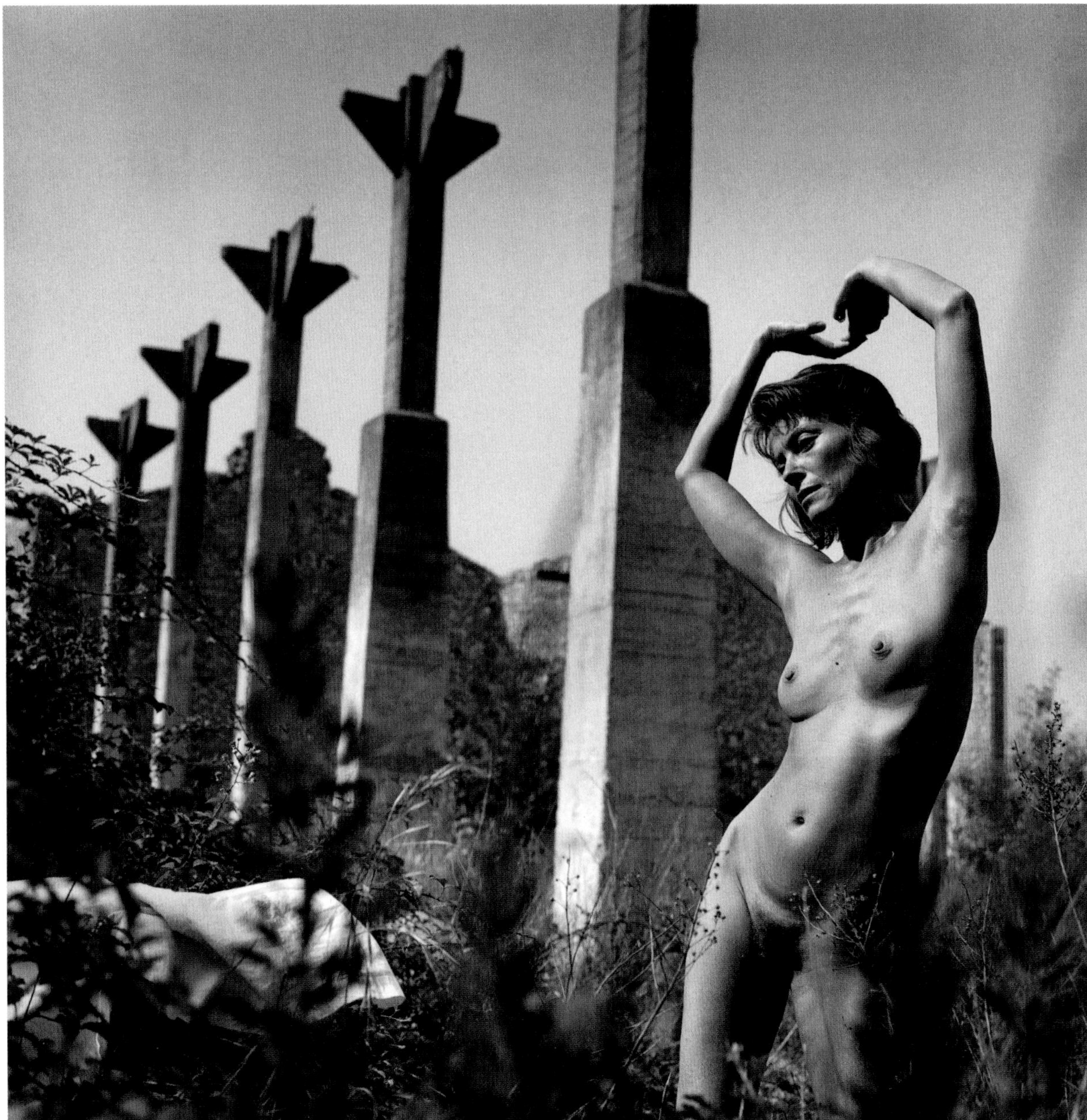

PL. 34 Arthur Tress (American, born 1940), *Twinka, Age 40, Bombed Paper Mill, Arles, France (Missile Columns),* 1985. Gelatin silver print, 7 ½ × 7 ½ in. Collection of Twinka Thiebaud.

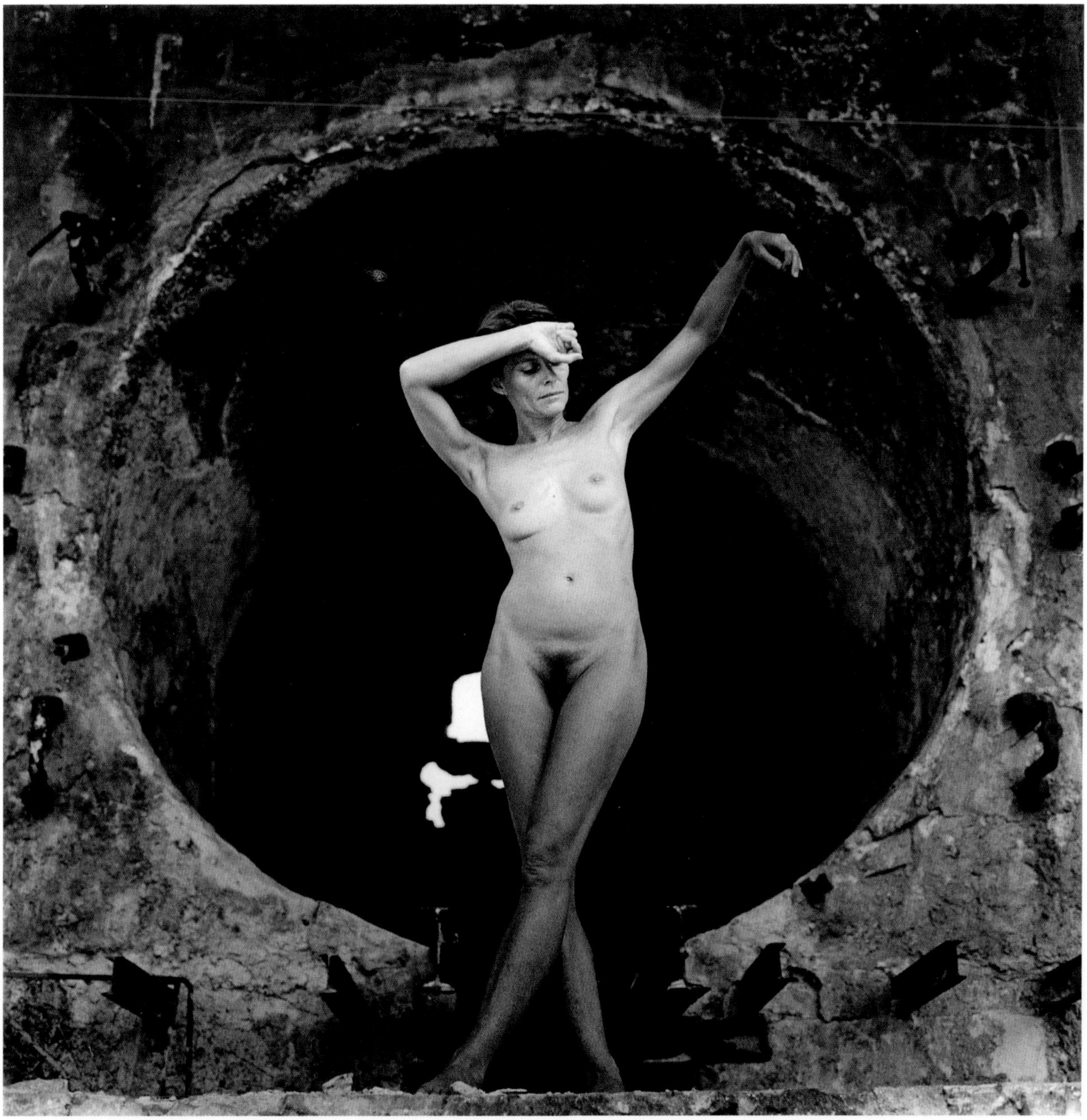

PL. 35 Arthur Tress (American, born 1940), *Twinka, Age 40, Bombed Paper Mill, Arles, France (Outside Tunnel),* 1985. Gelatin silver print, 7 ½ × 7 ½ in. Collection of Twinka Thiebaud.

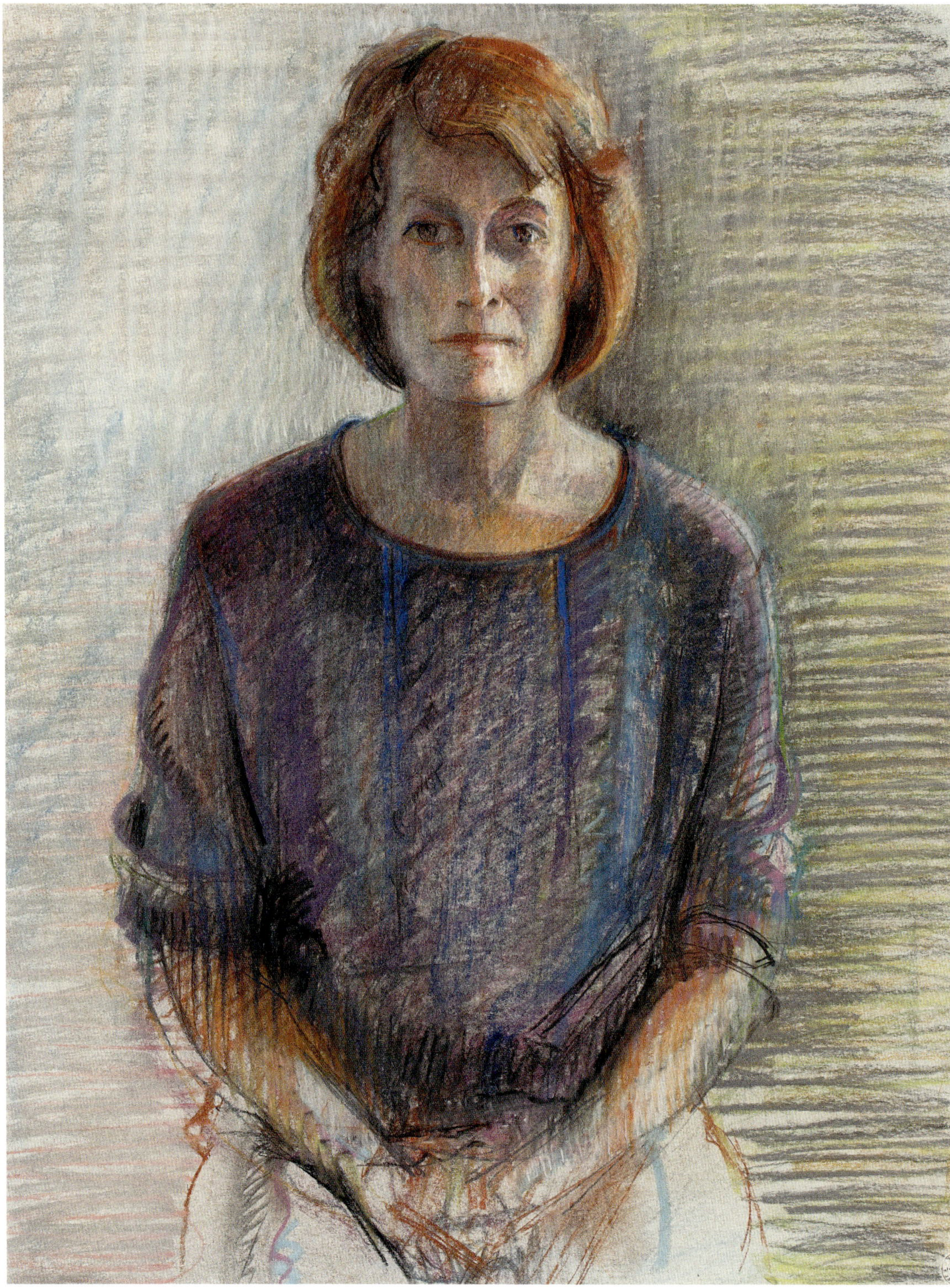

PL. 36 Wayne Thiebaud (American, 1920–2021), *Untitled*, circa 1985. Pastel on Schoeller's Parole paper, 27 ¾ × 21 ⅞ in. Collection of Twinka Thiebaud.

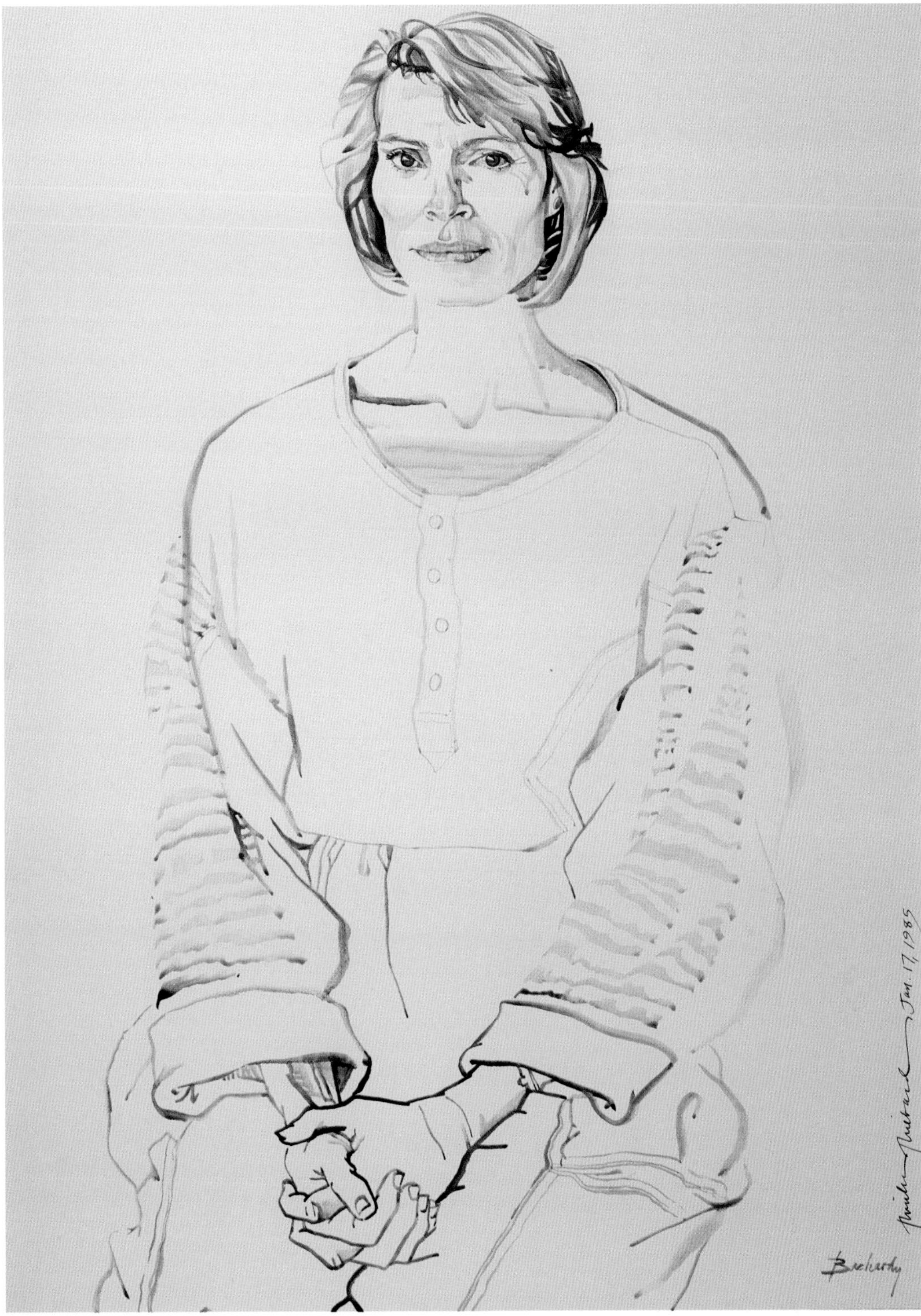

PL. 37 Don Bachardy (American, born 1934), *Twinka Thiebaud*, 1985. Ink on paper, 30 × 22 ¼ in. Crocker Art Museum, gift of the artist, 2021.37.4.

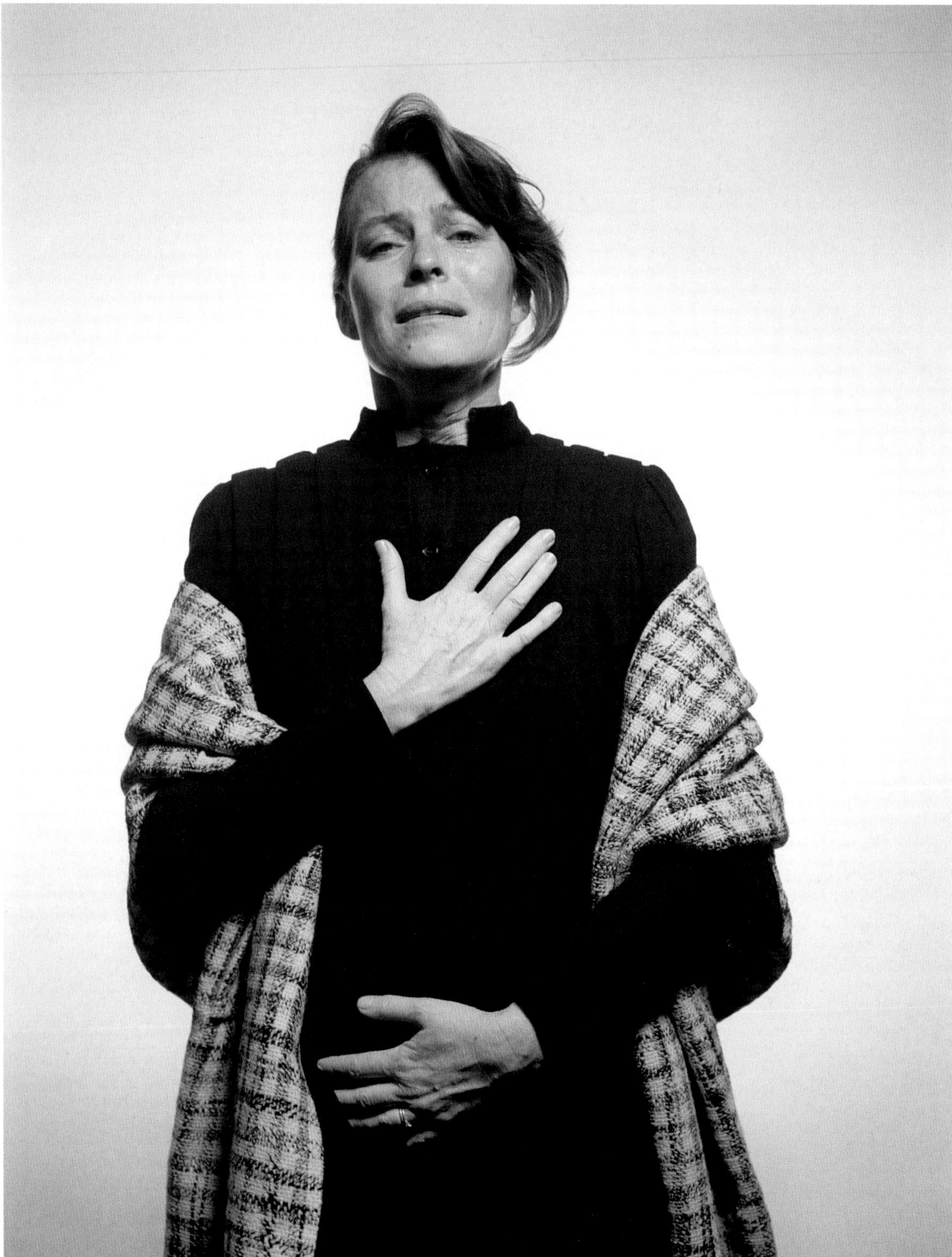

PL. 38 John Reiff Williams (American, born 1954), *Twinka Crying*, 1987. Gelatin silver print, 13 ⅝ × 9 ⅝ in. Collection of Twinka Thiebaud.

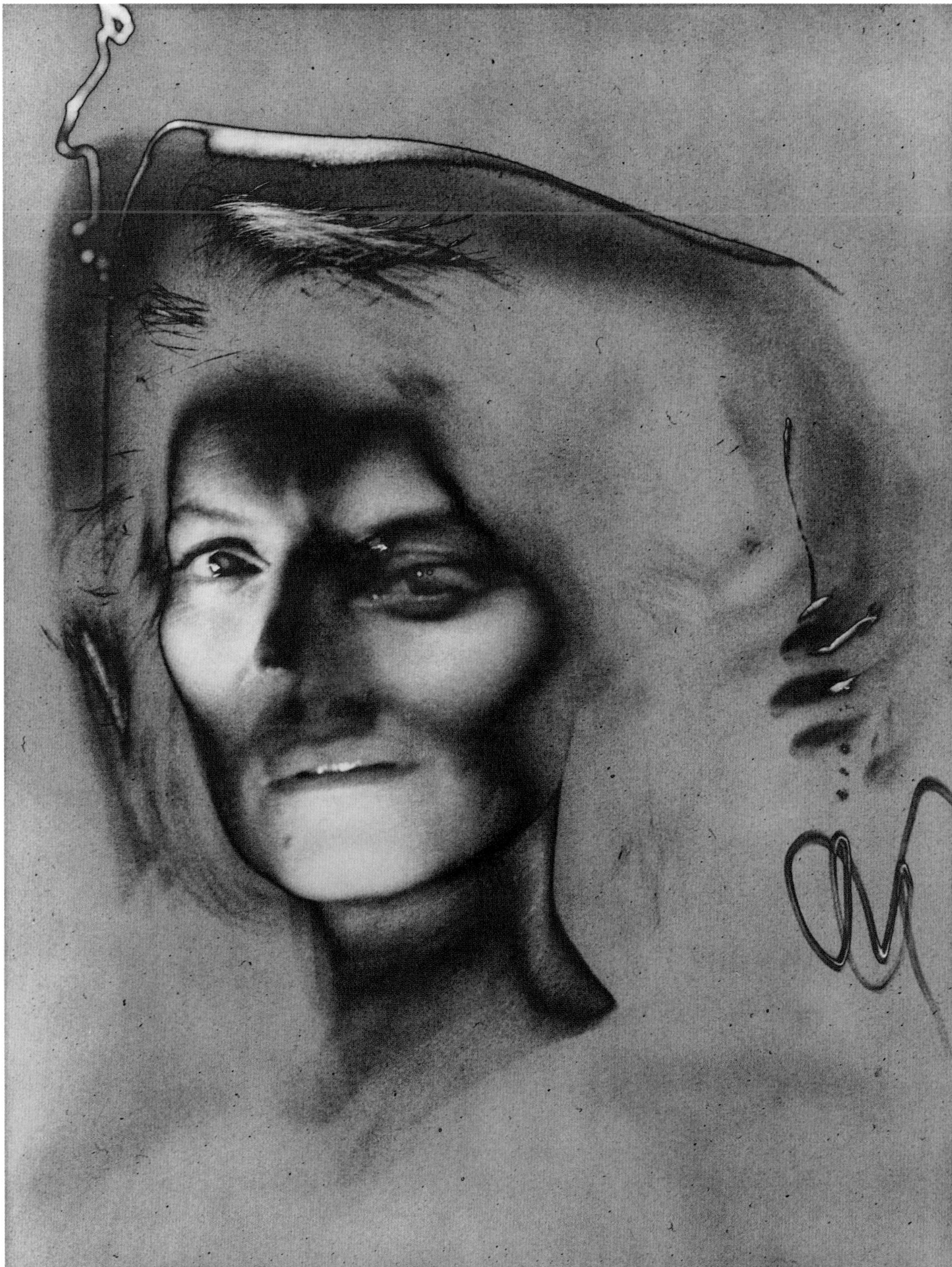

PL. 39 John Reiff Williams (American, born 1954), *Twinka Portrait,* 1987. Archival pigment print from solarized Polaroid process, 14 ⅝ × 11 in. Collection of John Reiff Williams.

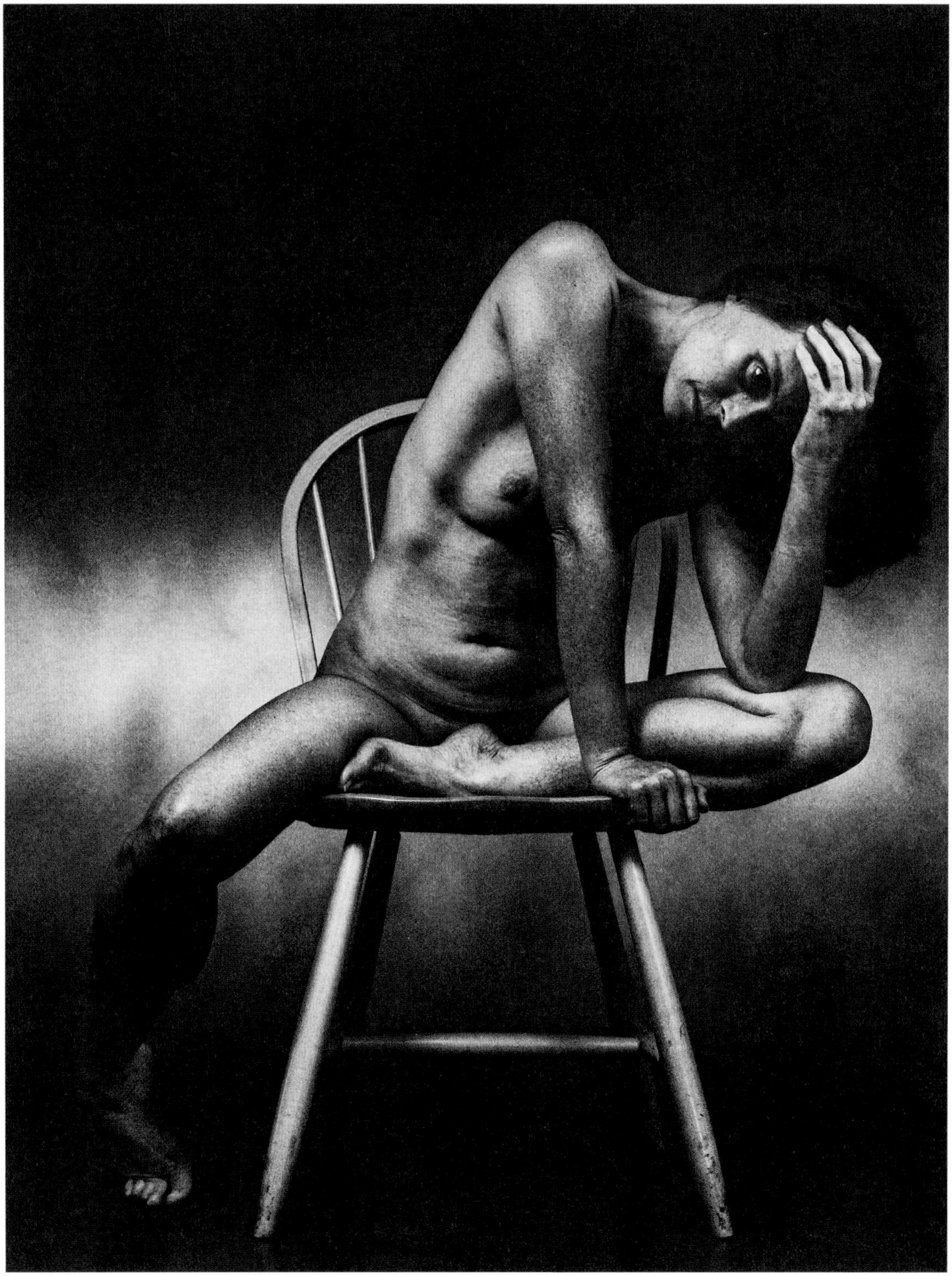

PL. 40 John Reiff Williams (American, born 1954), *Twinka: Nude in the Chair "C,"* 1987. Gelatin silver print, 14 ¼ × 11 in. Collection of Twinka Thiebaud.

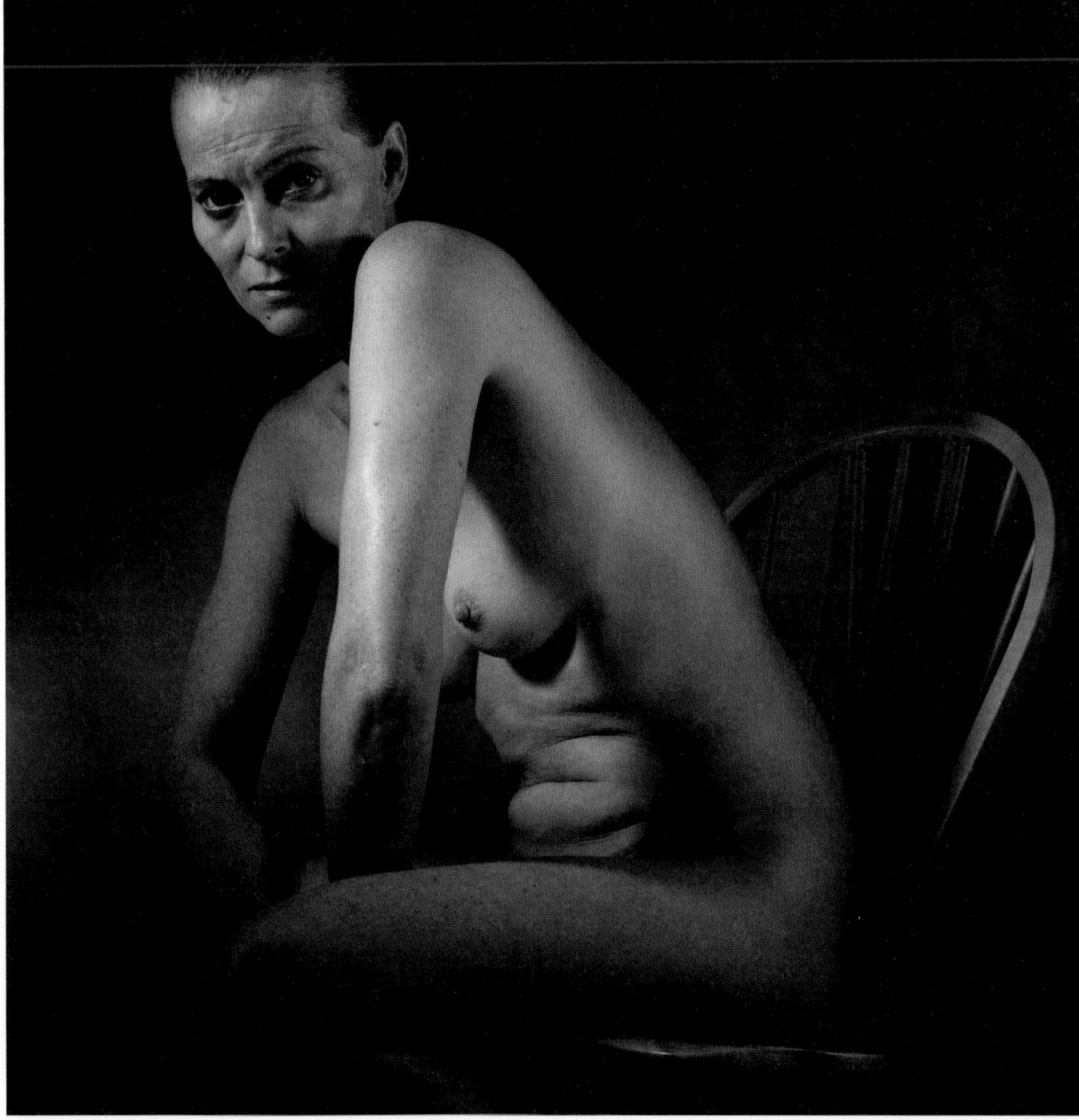

PL. 41 John Reiff Williams (American, born 1954), *Untitled (Twinka: Nude in Chair, Hands on Knees)*, 1987. Gelatin silver print, 6 ⅜ × 6 ¼ in. Collection of Twinka Thiebaud.

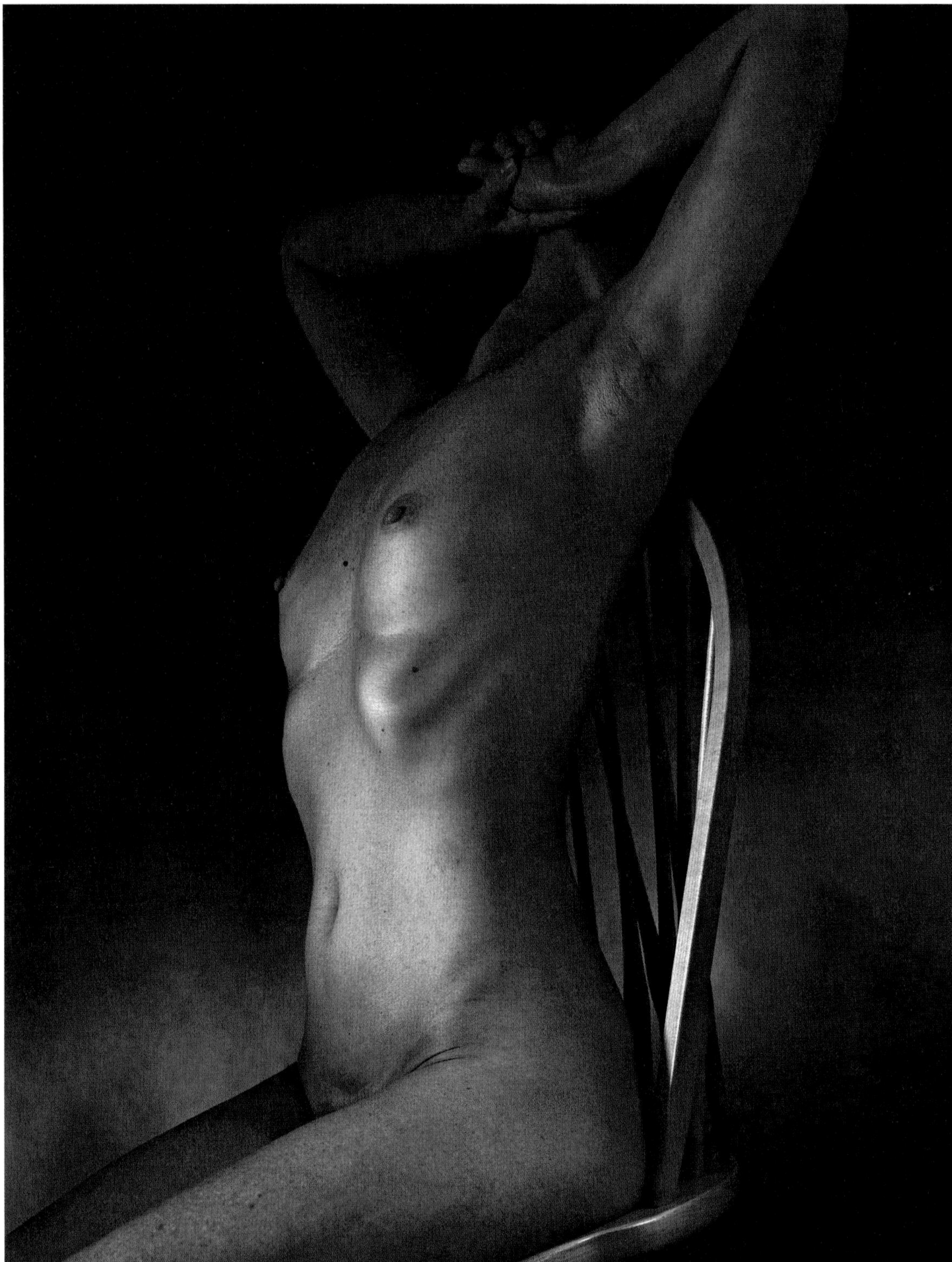

PL. 42 John Reiff Williams (American, born 1954), *Twinka: Nude in the Chair*, 1987. Gelatin silver print, 14 ⅛ × 11 in. Collection of Twinka Thiebaud.

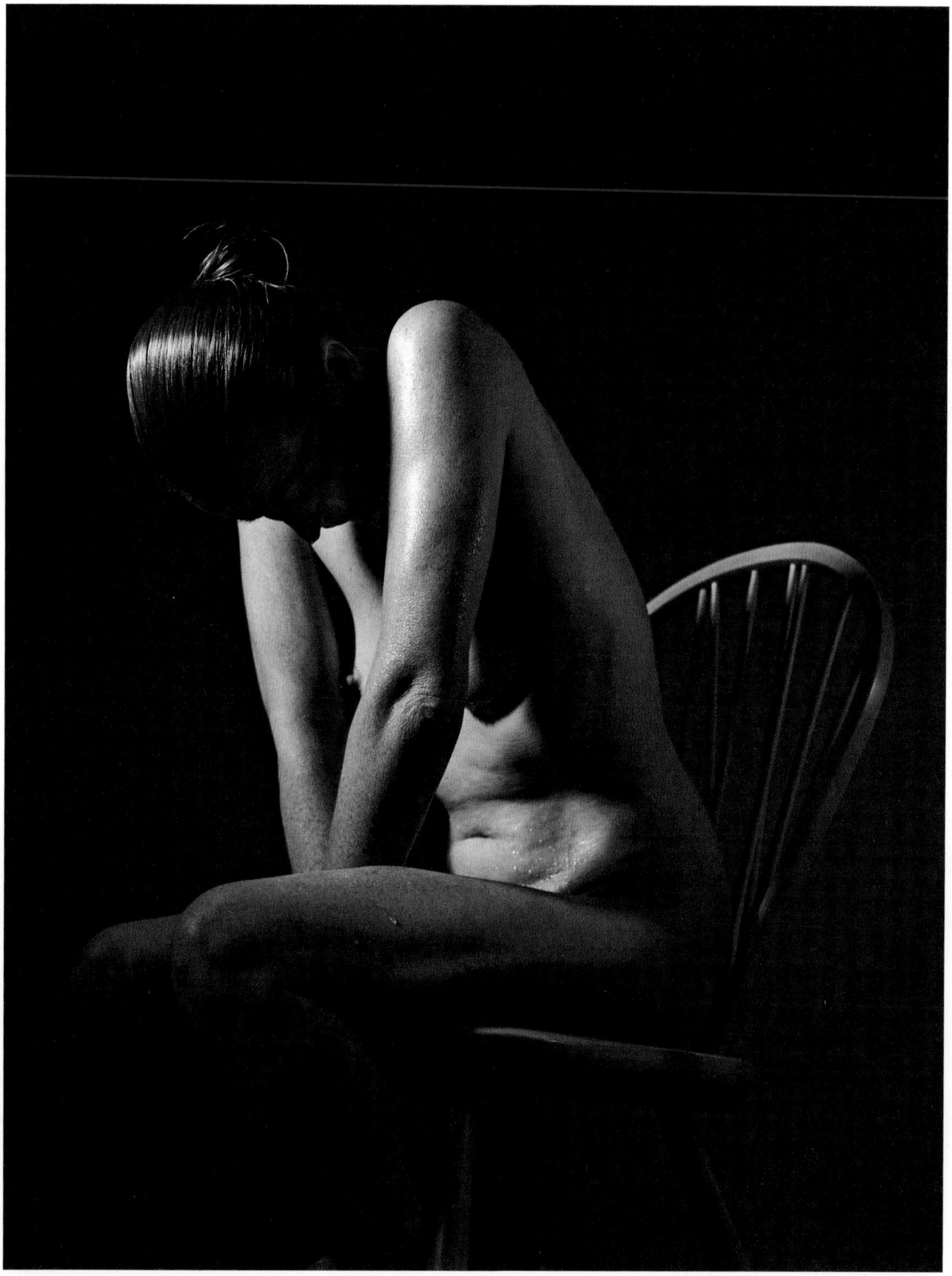

PL. 43 John Reiff Williams (American, born 1954), *Twinka: Nude in the Chair "F,"* 1987. Gelatin silver print, 14 ⅜ × 11 in. Collection of Twinka Thiebaud.

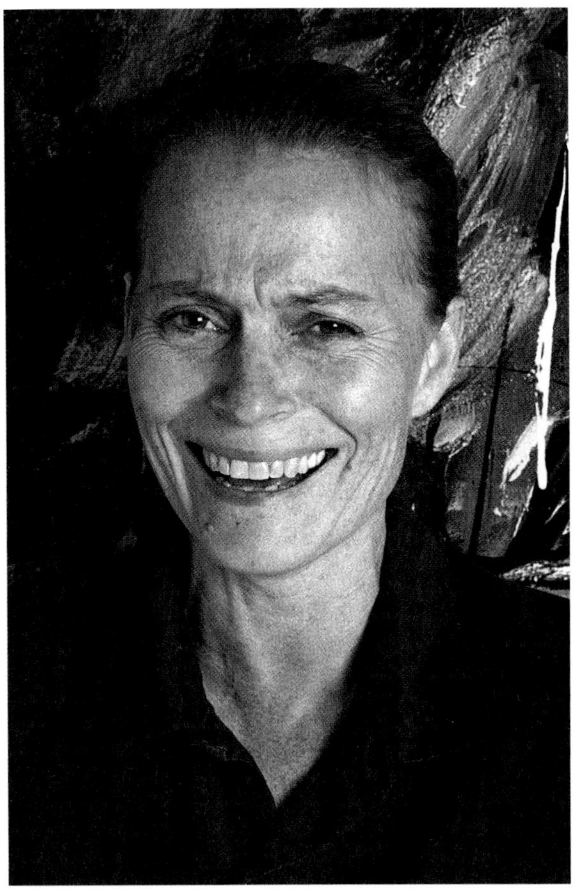

PL. 44 John Reiff Williams (American, born 1954), *Untitled (Twinka Laughing)*, from the *Funny Faces* series, 1987. Archival pigment print, 16 ½ × 11 in. Collection of John Reiff Williams.

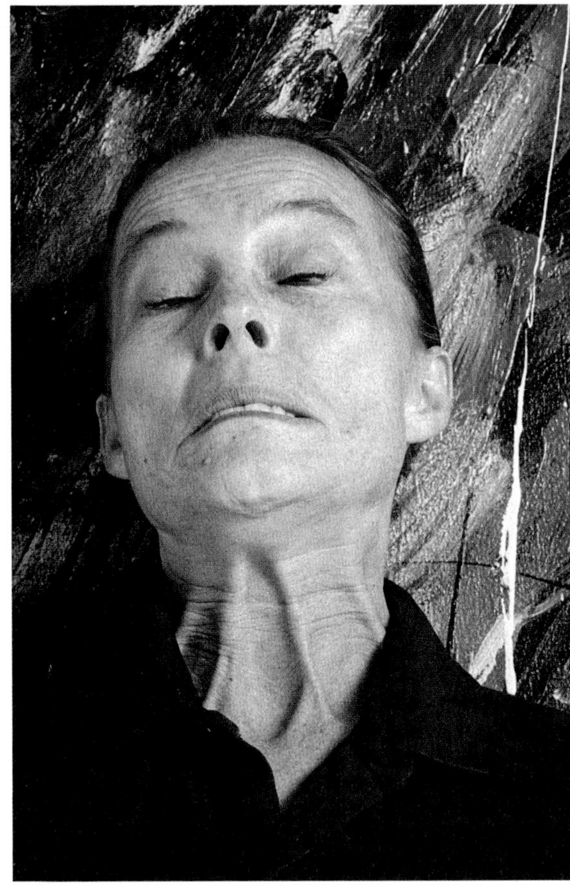

PL. 45 John Reiff Williams (American, born 1954), *Untitled (Twinka Straining Neck)*, from the *Funny Faces* series, 1987. Archival pigment print, 16 ½ × 11 in. Collection of John Reiff Williams.

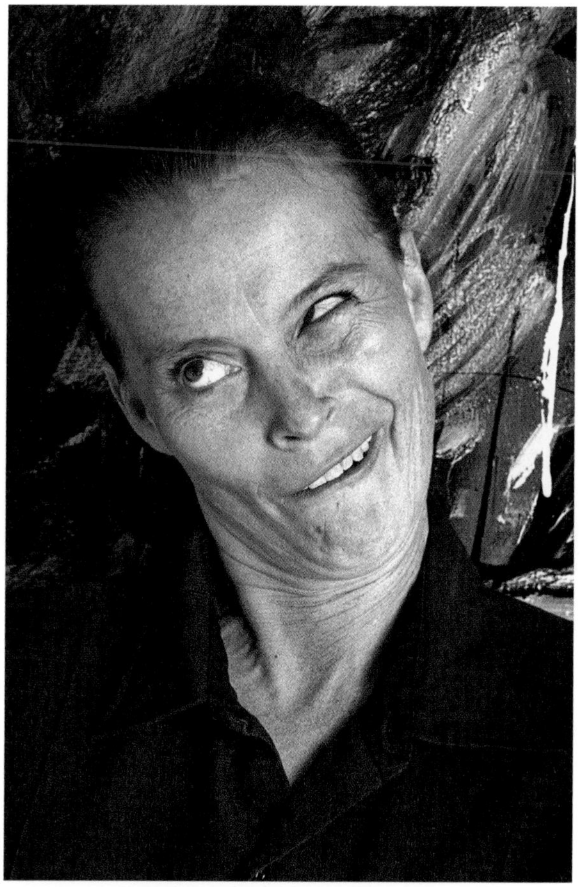

PL. 46 John Reiff Williams (American, born 1954), *Untitled (Twinka with One Eye Looking Up),* from the *Funny Faces* series, 1987. Archival pigment print, 16 ½ × 11 in. Collection of John Reiff Williams.

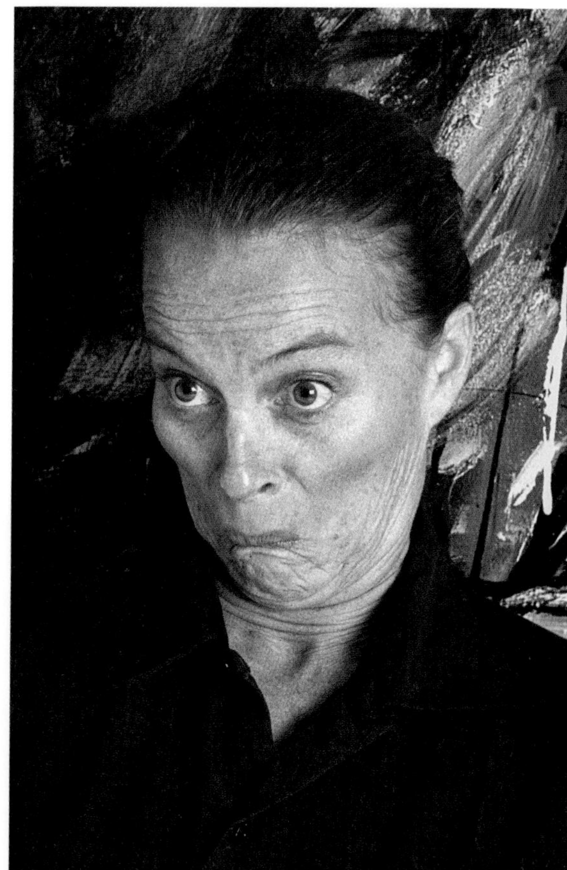

PL. 47 John Reiff Williams (American, born 1954), *Untitled (Twinka Holding Breath),* from the *Funny Faces* series, 1987. Archival pigment print, 16 ½ × 11 in. Collection of John Reiff Williams.

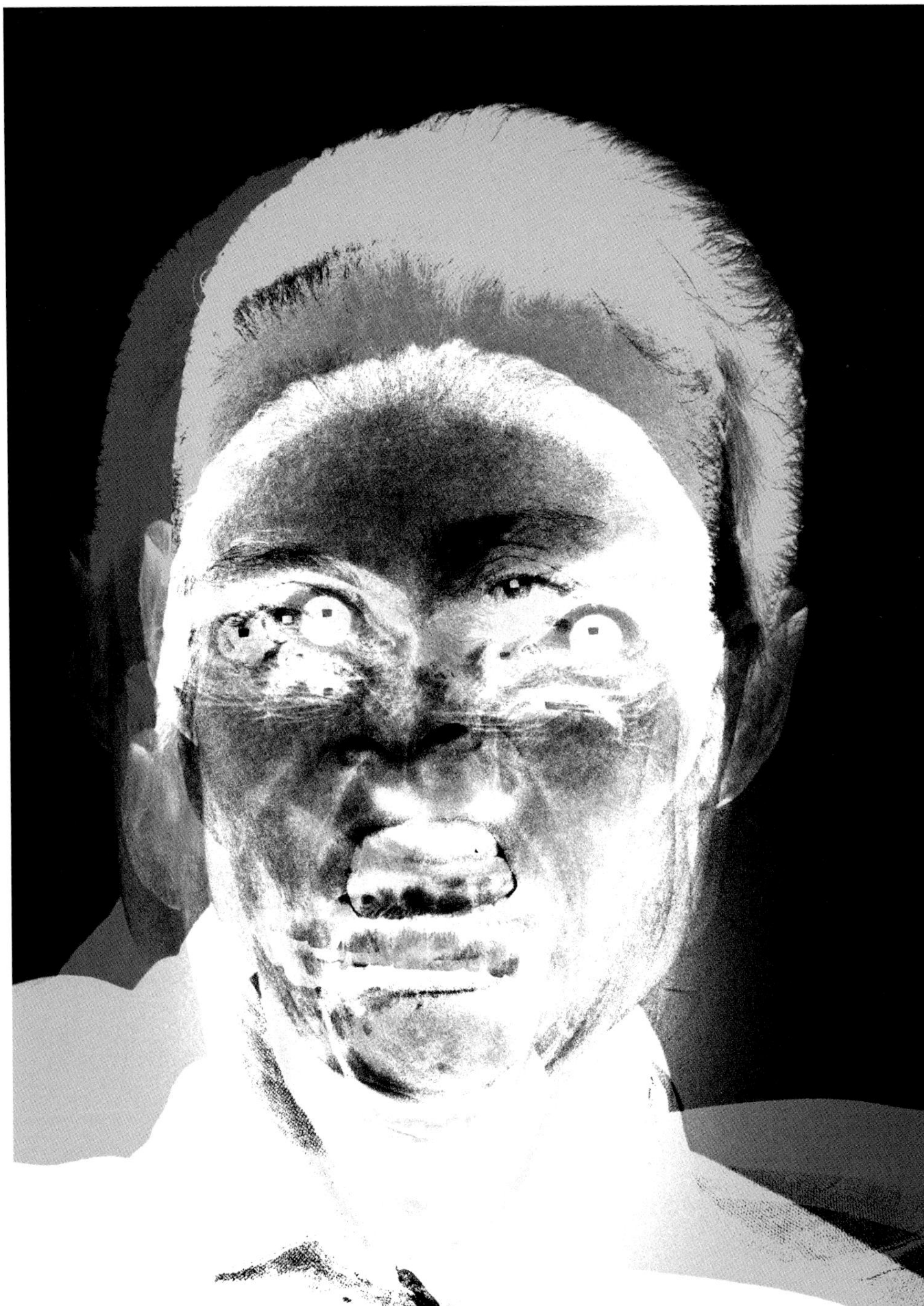

PL. 48 John Reiff Williams (American, born 1954), *Untitled (Monster Face 1)*, 1987. Archival pigment print, 15 ¼ × 11 in. Collection of John Reiff Williams.

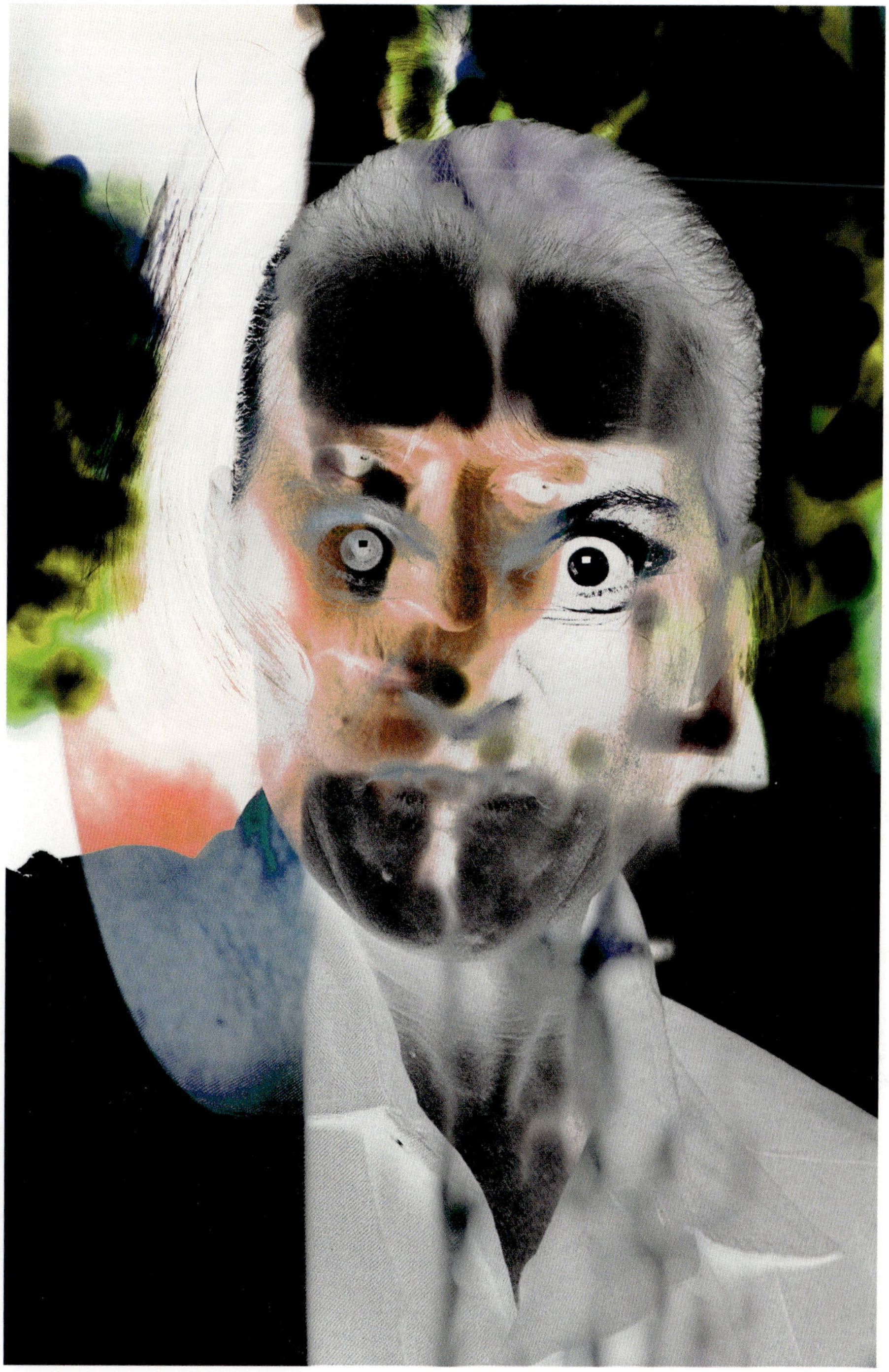

PL. 49 John Reiff Williams (American, born 1954), *Untitled (Monster Face 2),* 1987. Archival pigment print, 16 ½ × 11 in. Collection of John Reiff Williams.

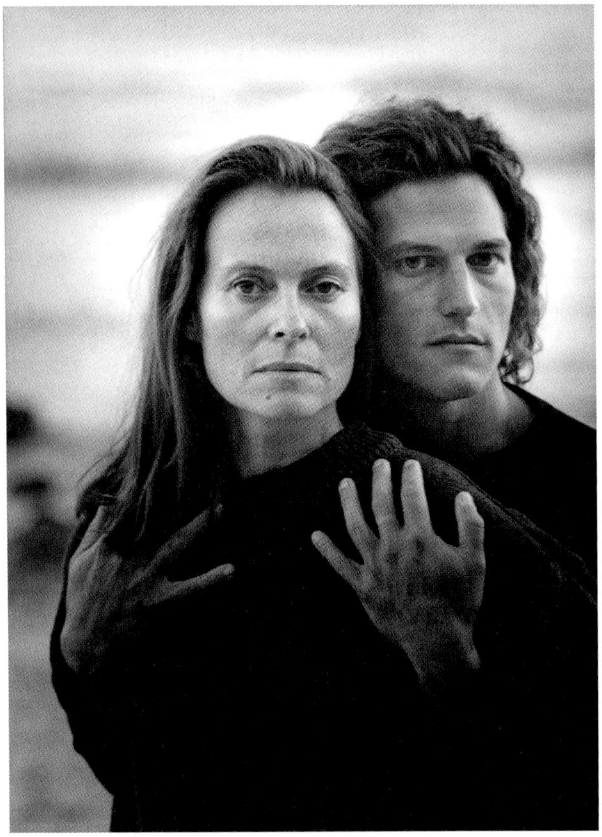

PL. 50 John Reiff Williams (American, born 1954), *Twinka Thiebaud (with Model 1),* 1991. Gelatin silver print, 7 ⅞ × 5 ⅞ in. Collection of Twinka Thiebaud.

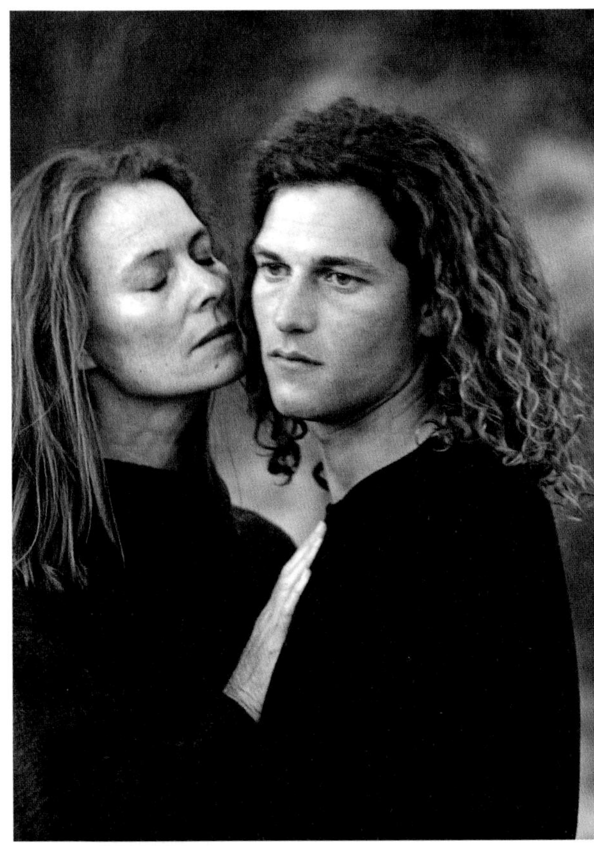

PL. 51 John Reiff Williams (American, born 1954), *Twinka Thiebaud (with Model 2),* 1991. Gelatin silver print, 7 ⅞ × 5 ⅞ in. Collection of Twinka Thiebaud.

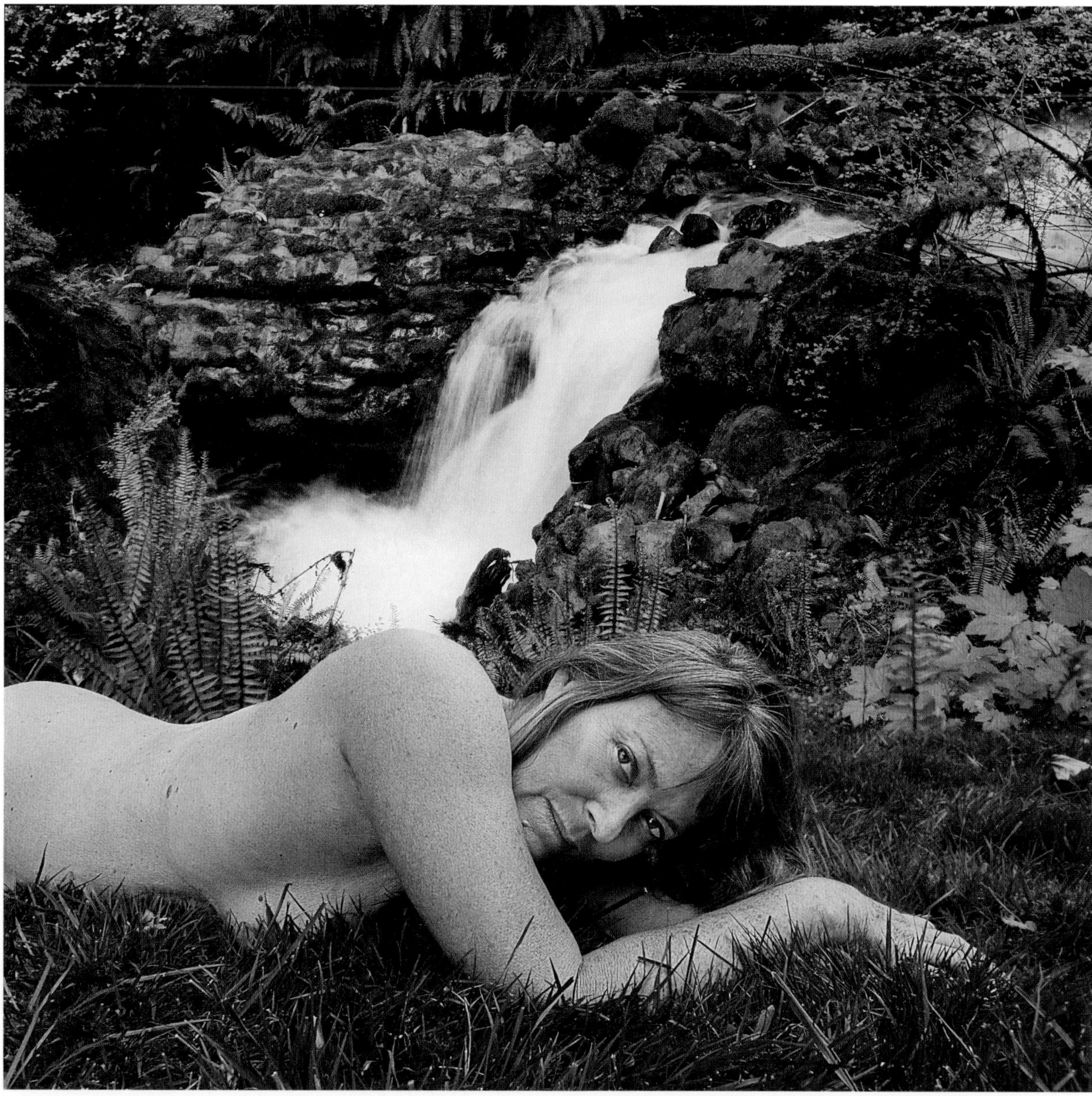

PL. 52 R. Michael Walker (American, born 1950), *Twinka, Portland, OR*, 2011. Archival inkjet print, 14 ⅜ × 14 ½ in. Collection of Twinka Thiebaud.

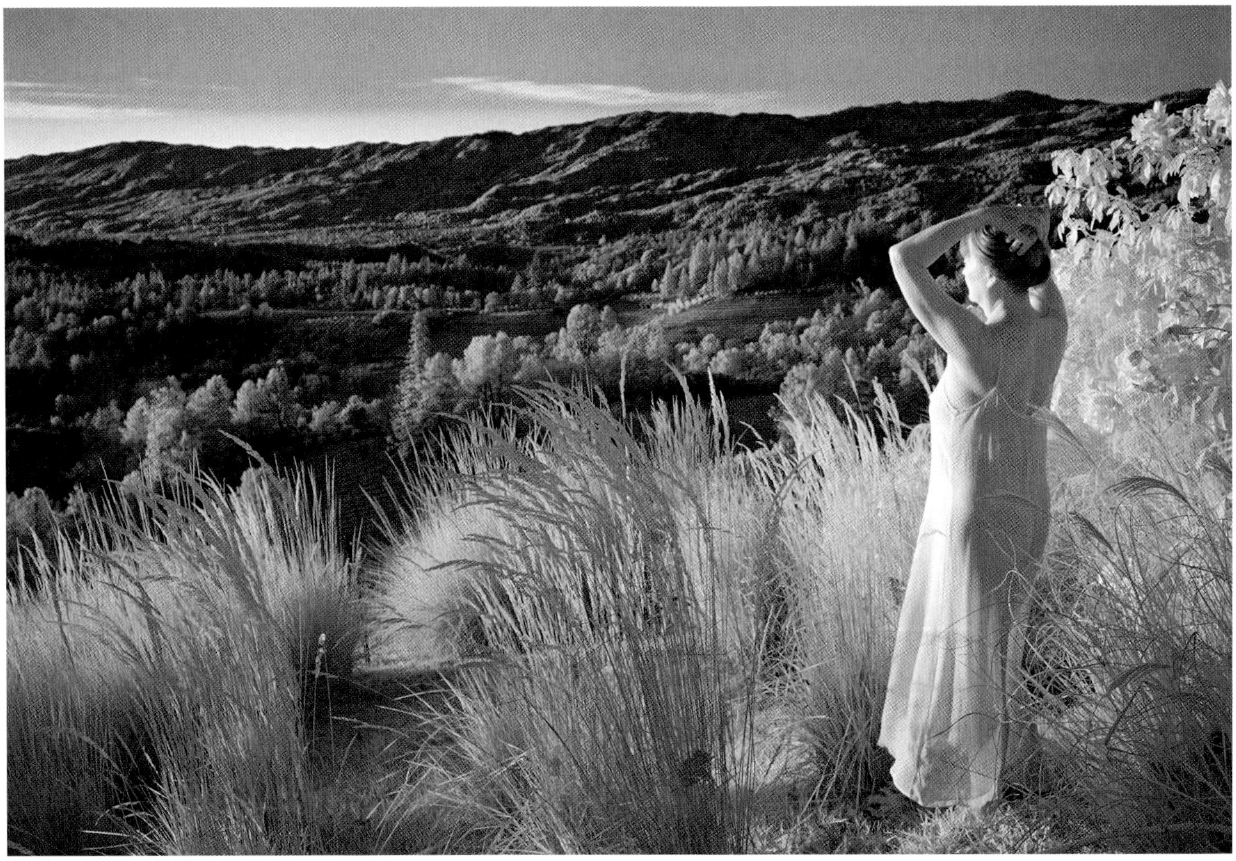

PL. 53 Elizabeth Opalenik (American, born 1947), *Twinka in Morning Light,* 2011. Archival pigment print, 9 × 13 ½ in. Collection of Elizabeth Opalenik.

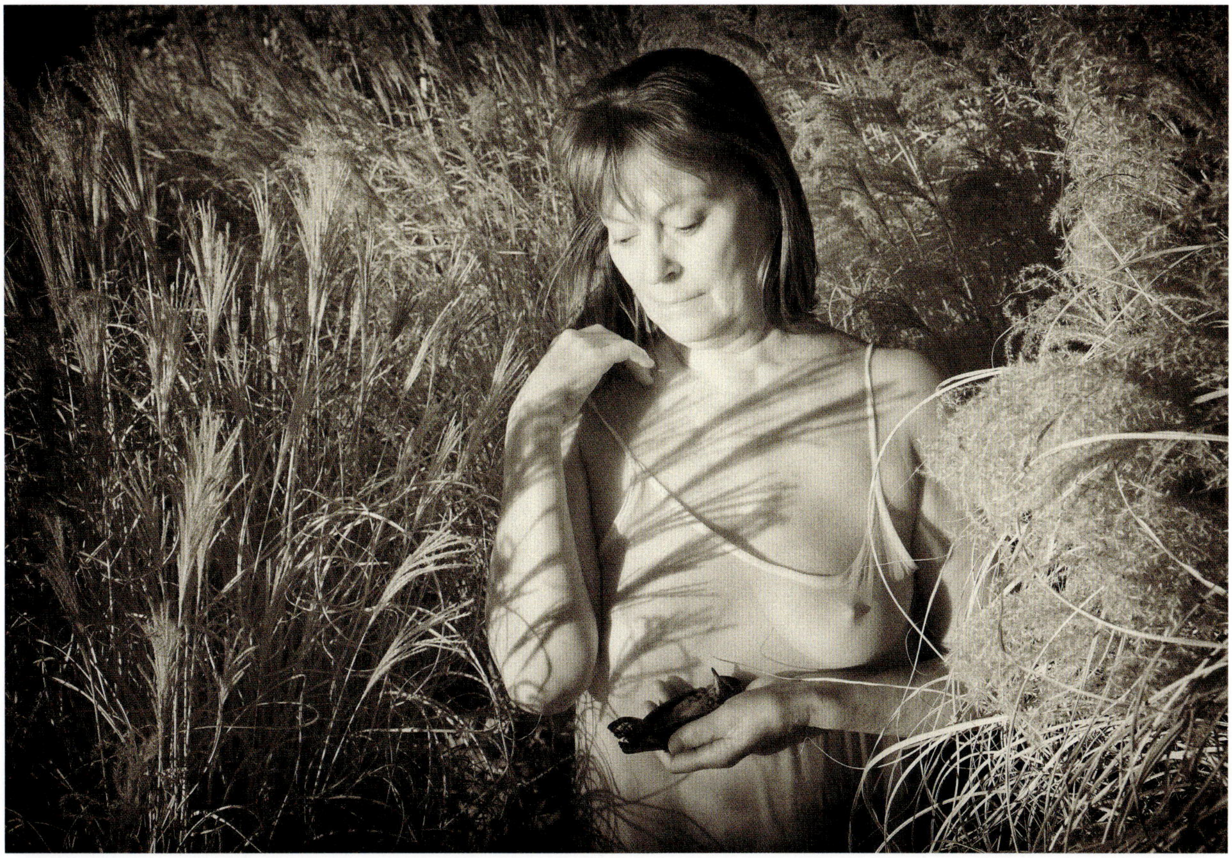

PL. 54 Elizabeth Opalenik (American, born 1947), *Bird in Hand*, 2011. Archival pigment print, 9 × 13 ½ in. Collection of Elizabeth Opalenik.

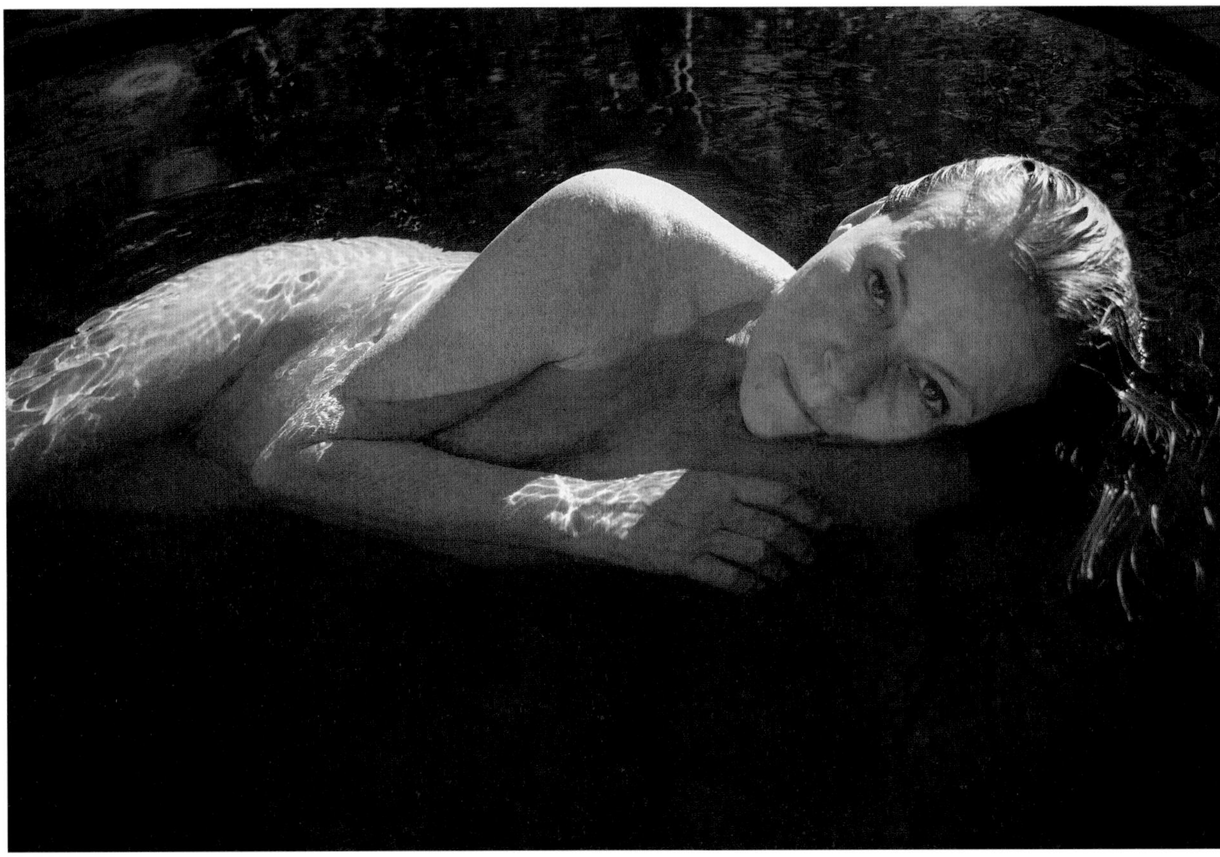

PL. 55 Elizabeth Opalenik (American, born 1947), *Twinka Reflective,* 2011. Archival pigment print, 9 × 13 ½ in. Collection of Elizabeth Opalenik.

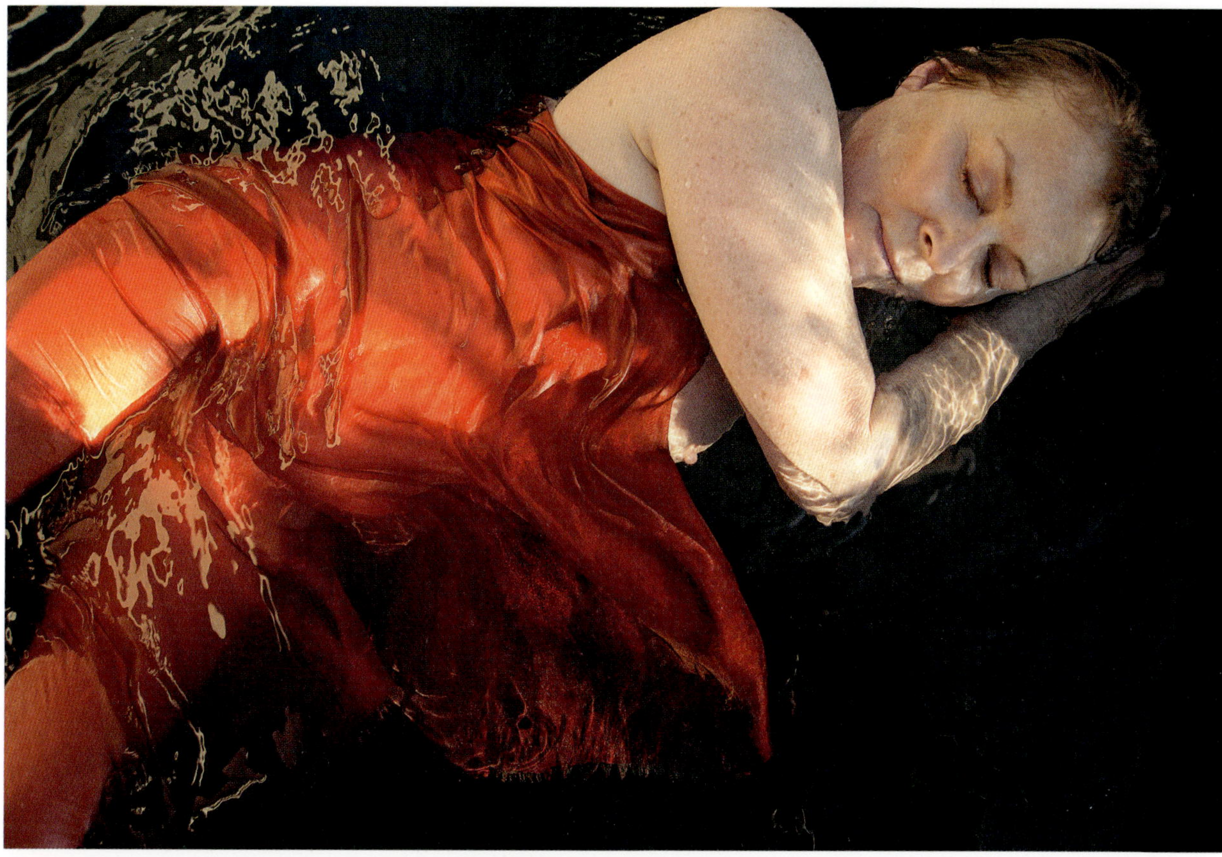

PL. 56 Elizabeth Opalenik (American, born 1947), *Twinka Floating in Red,* 2011. Archival pigment print, 14 ¾ × 22 in. Collection of Elizabeth Opalenik.

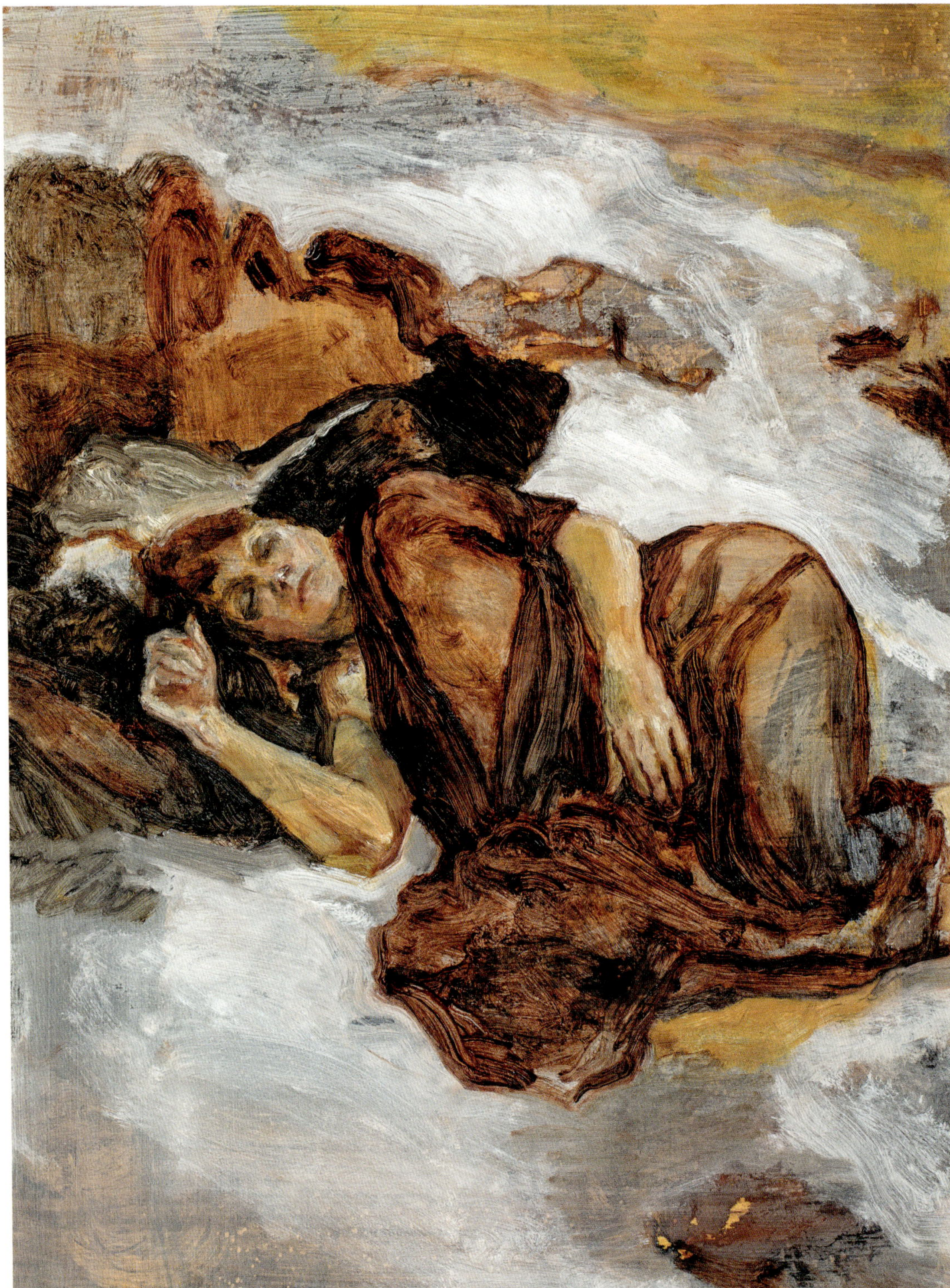

PL. 57 Kevin Kadar (American, born 1955), *Twinka's Dream*, 2011. Oil on museum board, 24 × 18 in. Collection of Twinka Thiebaud.

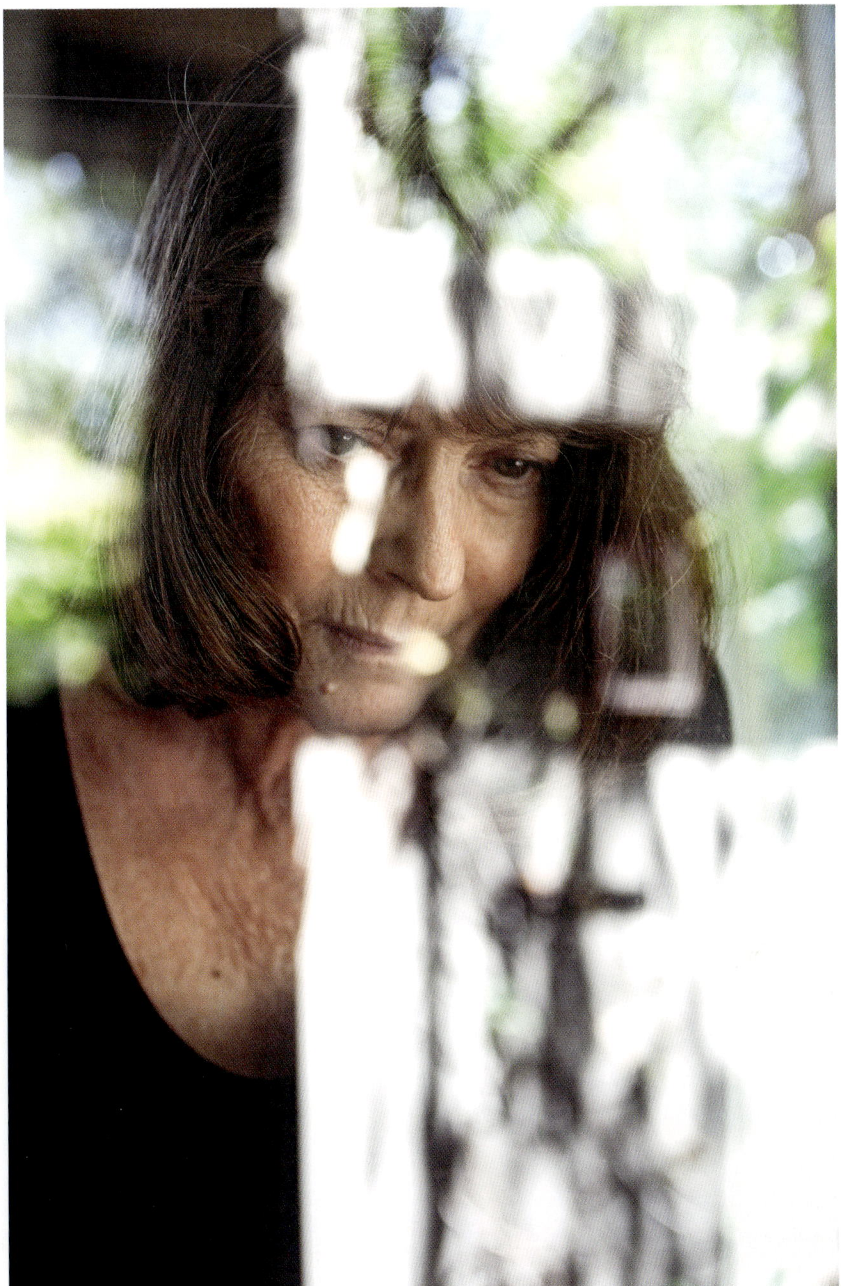

PL. 58 John Reiff Williams (American, born 1954), *Untitled (Twinka Reflection)*, 2011. Archival pigment print, 16 ½ × 11 in. Collection of John Reiff Williams.

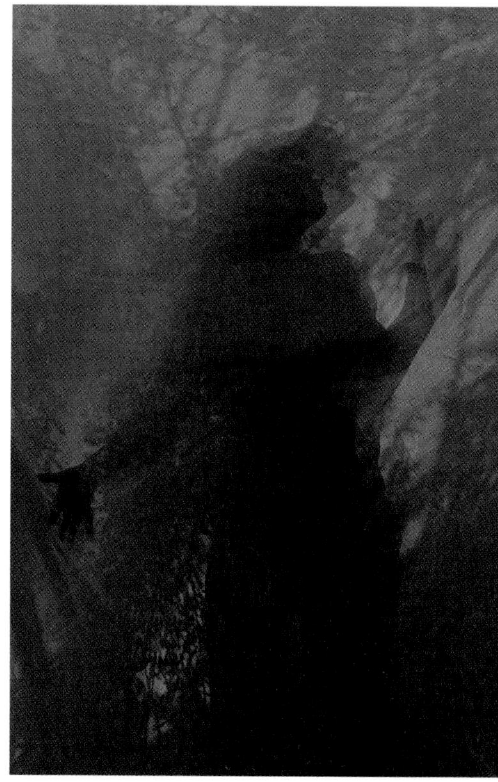

PL. 60 John Reiff Williams (American, born 1954), *Untitled (Twinka with Sheet 2),* 2011. Archival pigment print, 16 ½ × 11 in. Collection of John Reiff Williams.

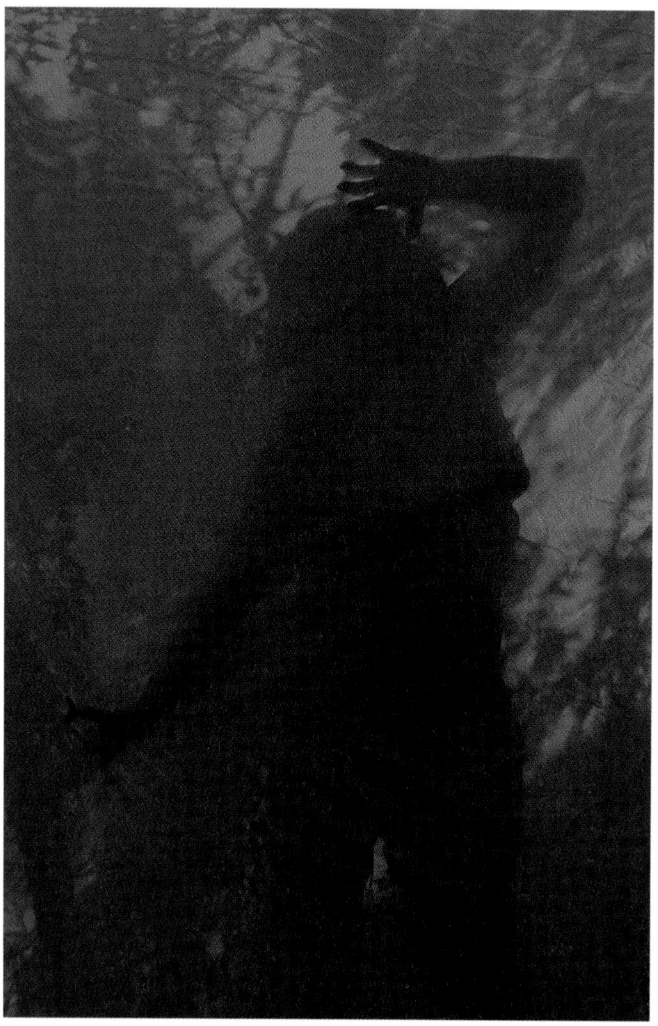

PL. 59 John Reiff Williams (American, born 1954), *Untitled (Twinka with Sheet 4),* 2011. Archival pigment print, 16 ½ × 11 in. Collection of John Reiff Williams.

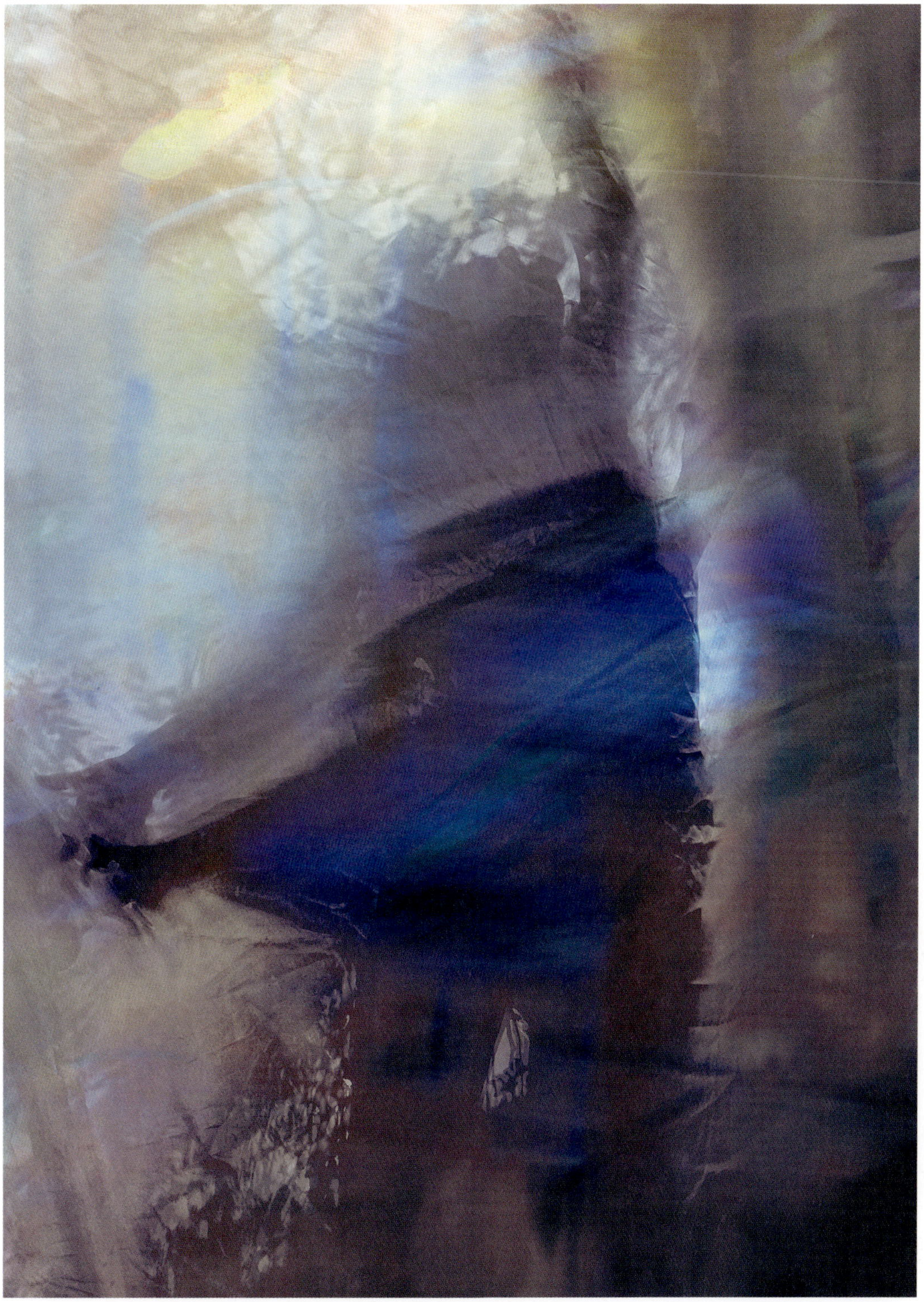

PL. 61 John Reiff Williams (American, born 1954), *Untitled (Twinka with Sheet 1),* 2011. Archival pigment print, 14 ⅝ × 11 in. Collection of John Reiff Williams.

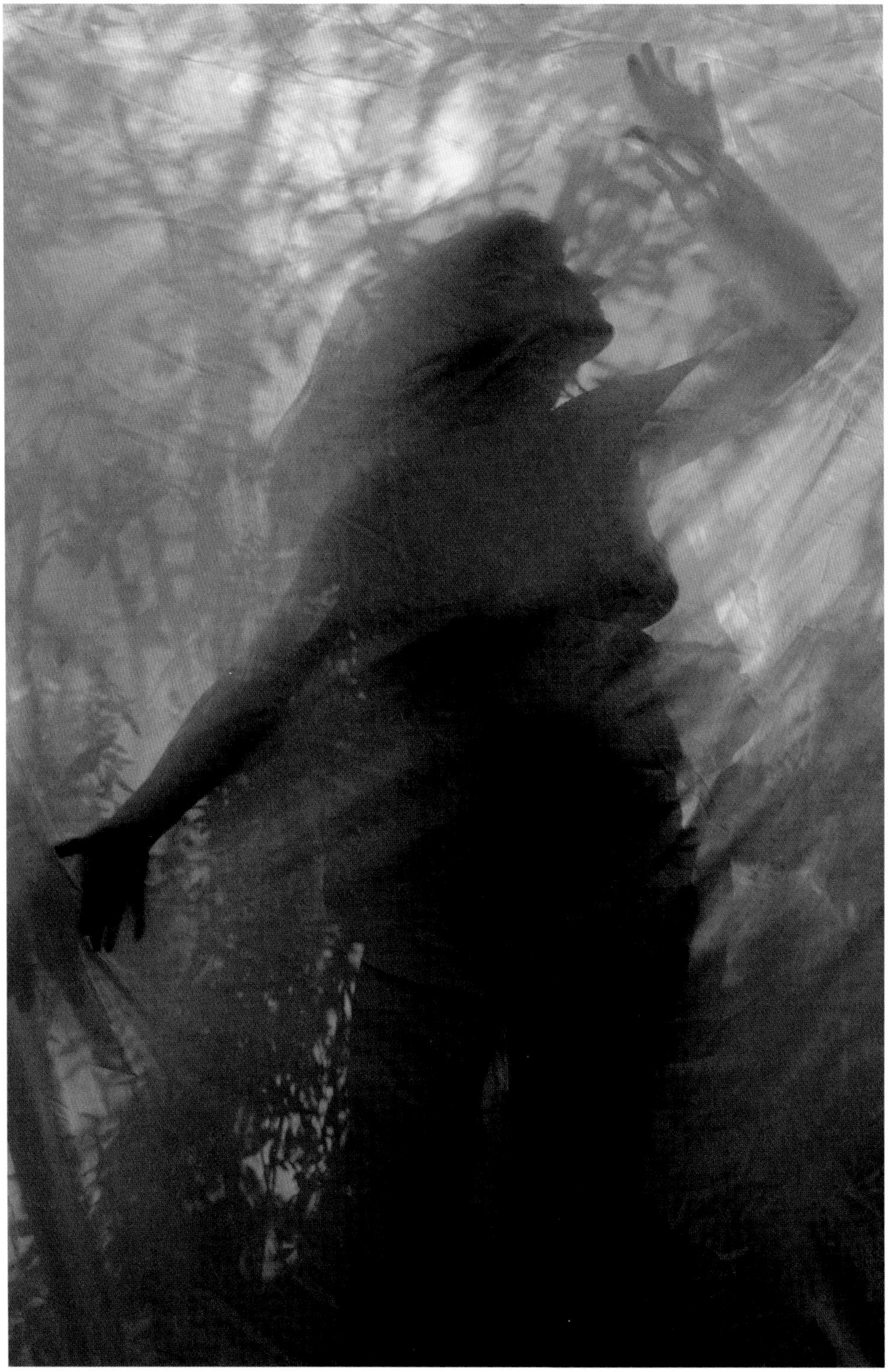

PL. 62 John Reiff Williams (American, born 1954), *Untitled (Twinka with Sheet 3),* 2011. Archival pigment print, 16 ½ x 11 in. Collection of John Reiff Williams.

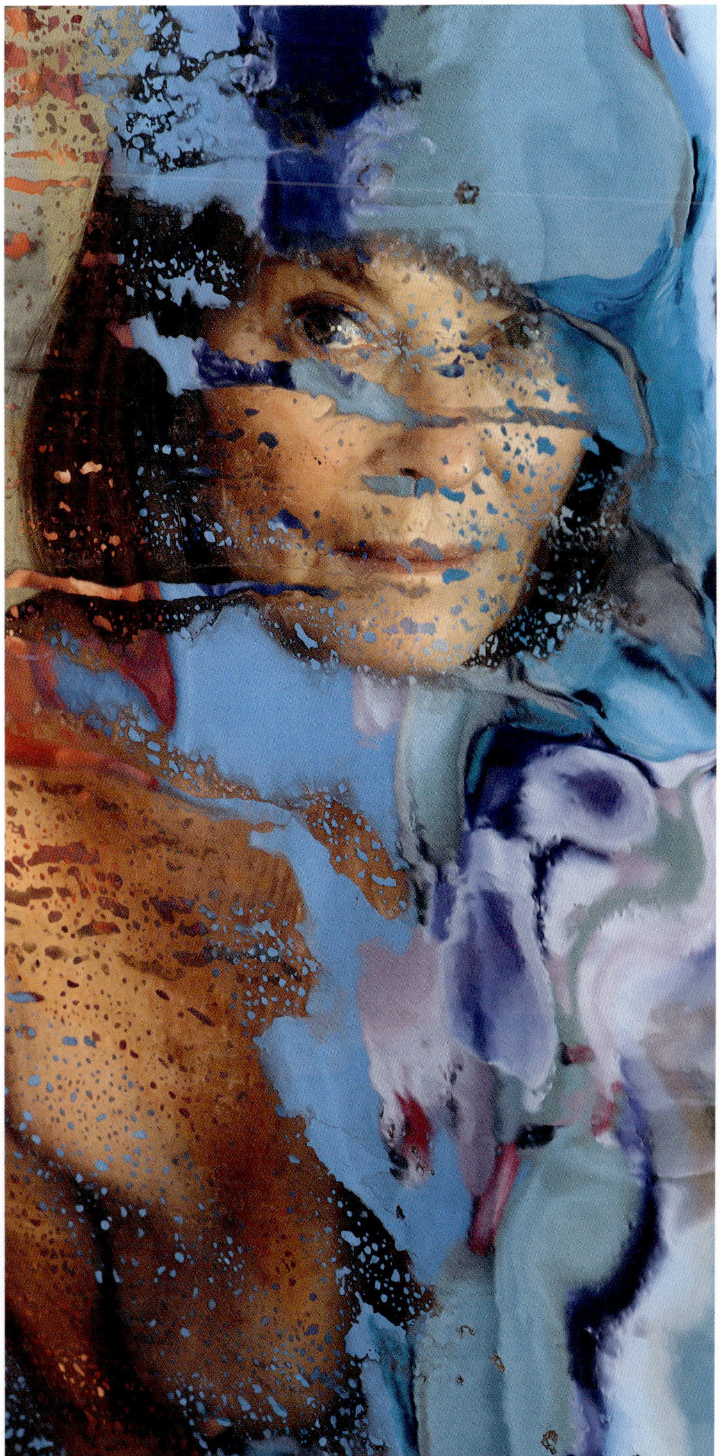

PL. 63 Elizabeth Opalenik (American, born 1947), *Twinka, the French Look,* 2013. Archival pigment print, 33 × 16 ½ in. Collection of Elizabeth Opalenik.

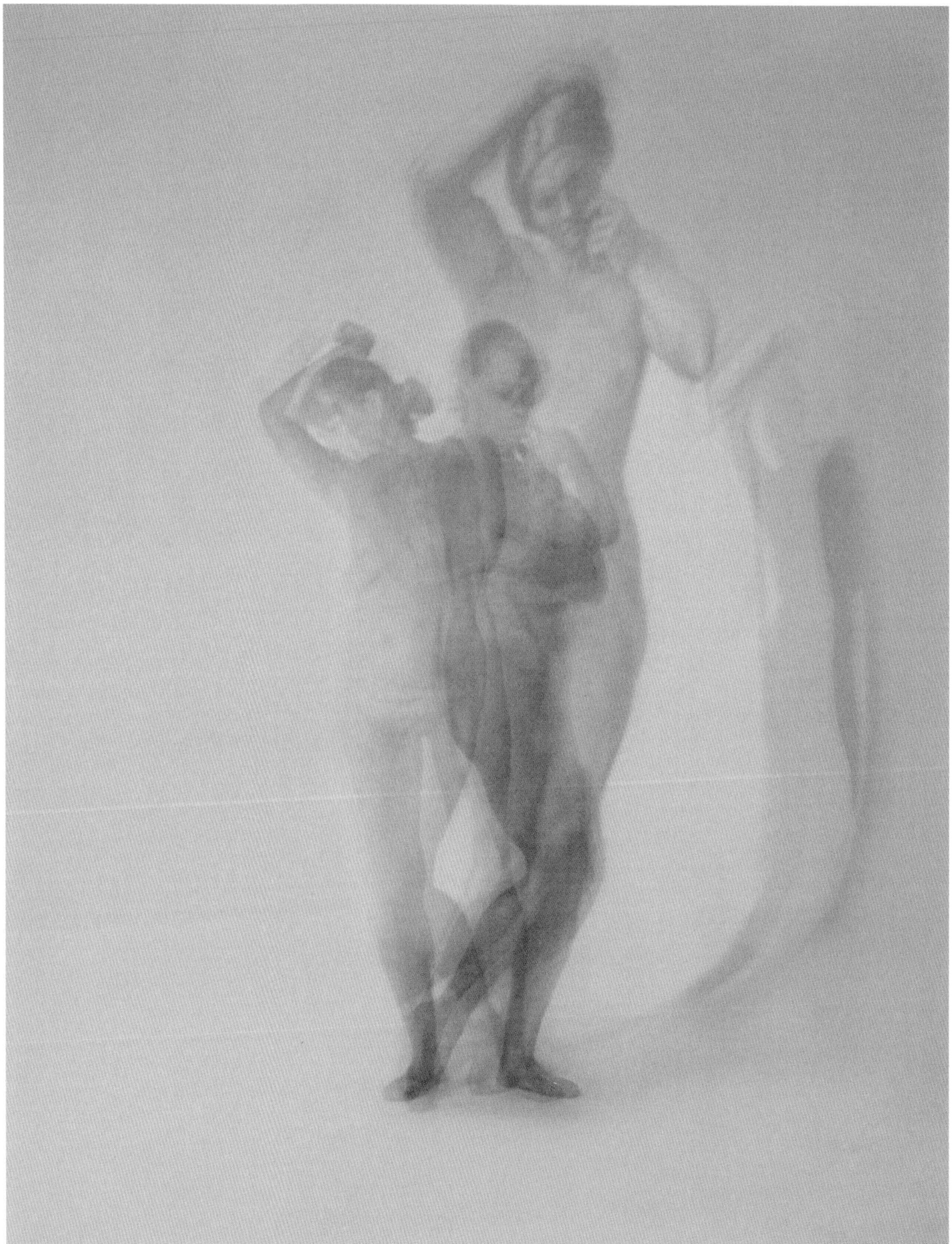

PL. 64 Michele Mattei (French), *Duality*, from the *Emerging Essence* series, 2014. C-print, 19 ¾ × 15 ⅜ in. Collection of Twinka Thiebaud.

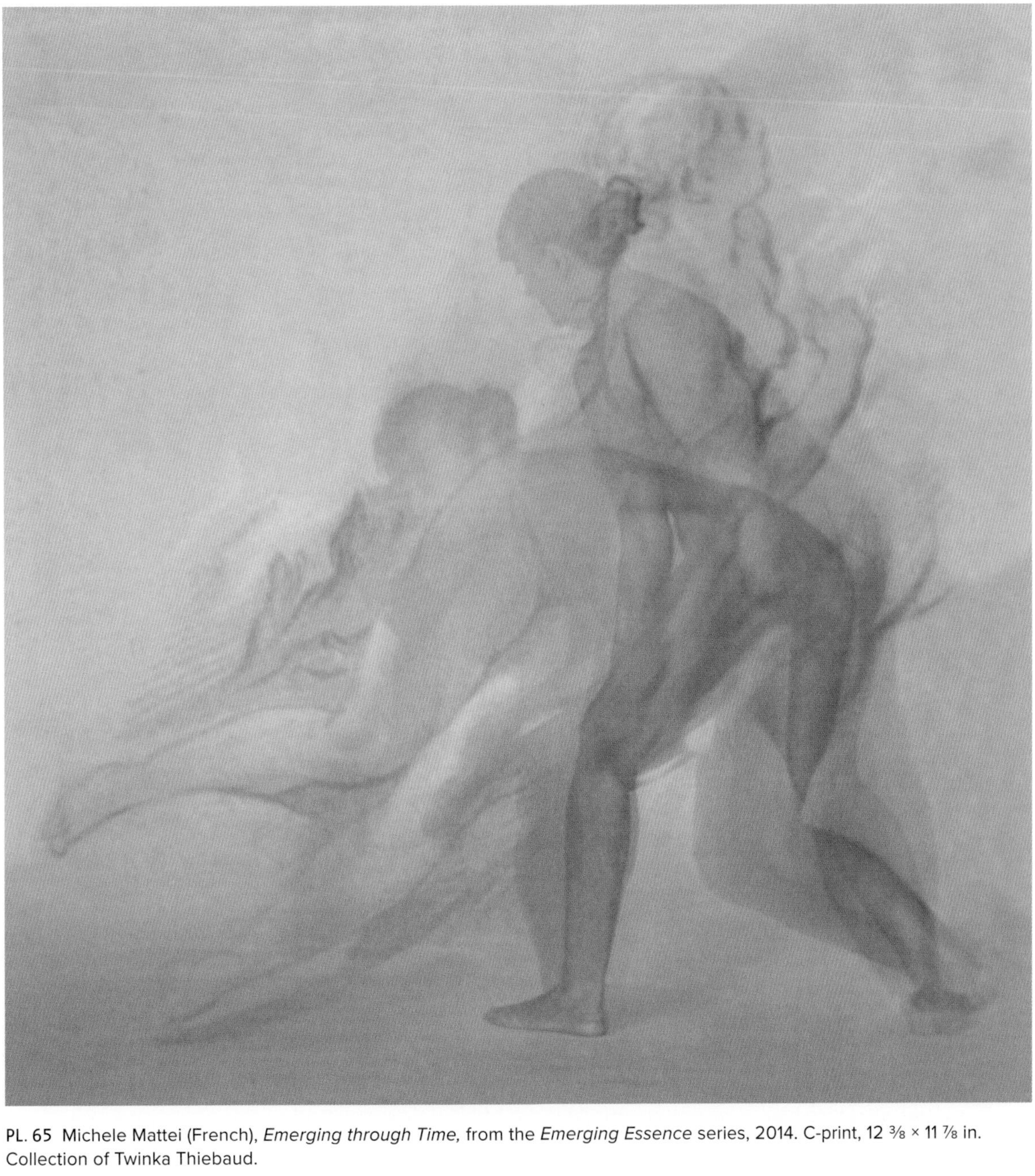

PL. 65 Michele Mattei (French), *Emerging through Time,* from the *Emerging Essence* series, 2014. C-print, 12 ⅜ × 11 ⅞ in. Collection of Twinka Thiebaud.

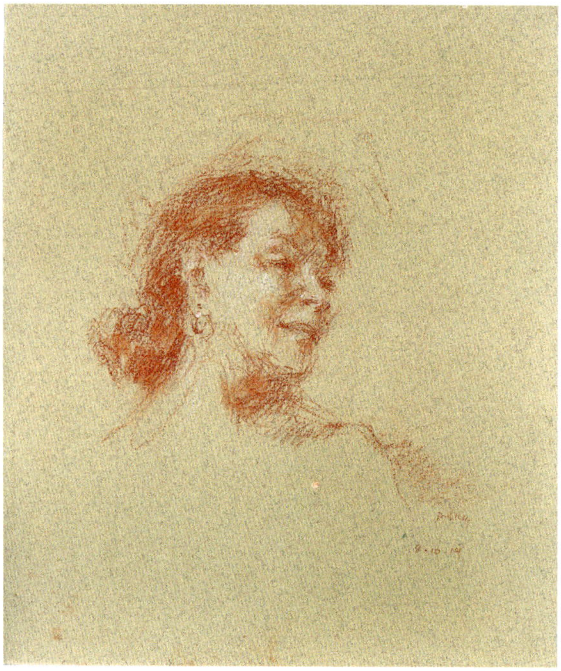

PL. 66 Fred Dalkey (American, born 1943), *Untitled (Twinka Portrait),* 2014. Pastel on paper, 9 ⅛ × 8 in. Collection of Twinka Thiebaud.

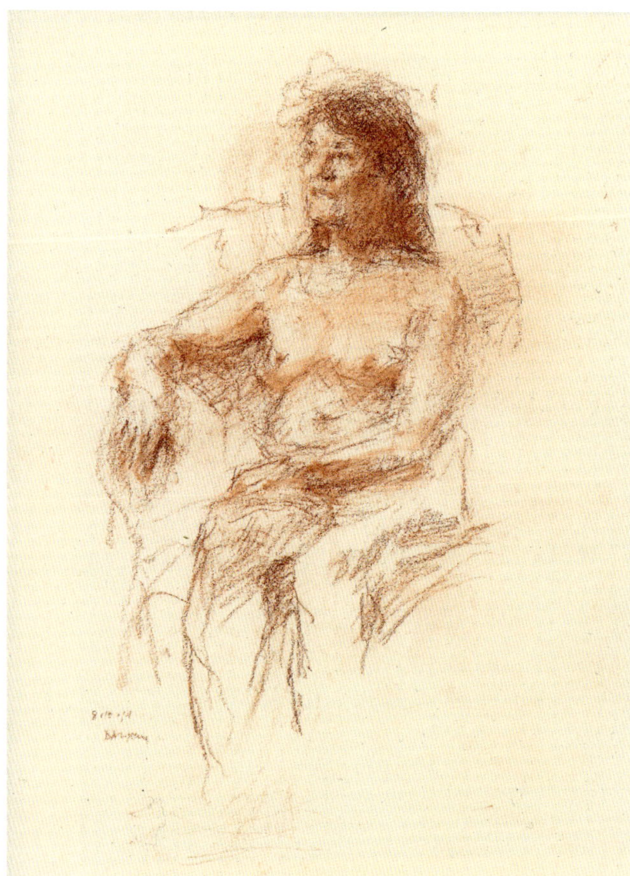

PL. 67 Fred Dalkey (American, born 1943), *Untitled (Twinka Seated),* 2014. Pastel on paper, 10 ⅛ × 7 ½ in. Collection of Twinka Thiebaud.

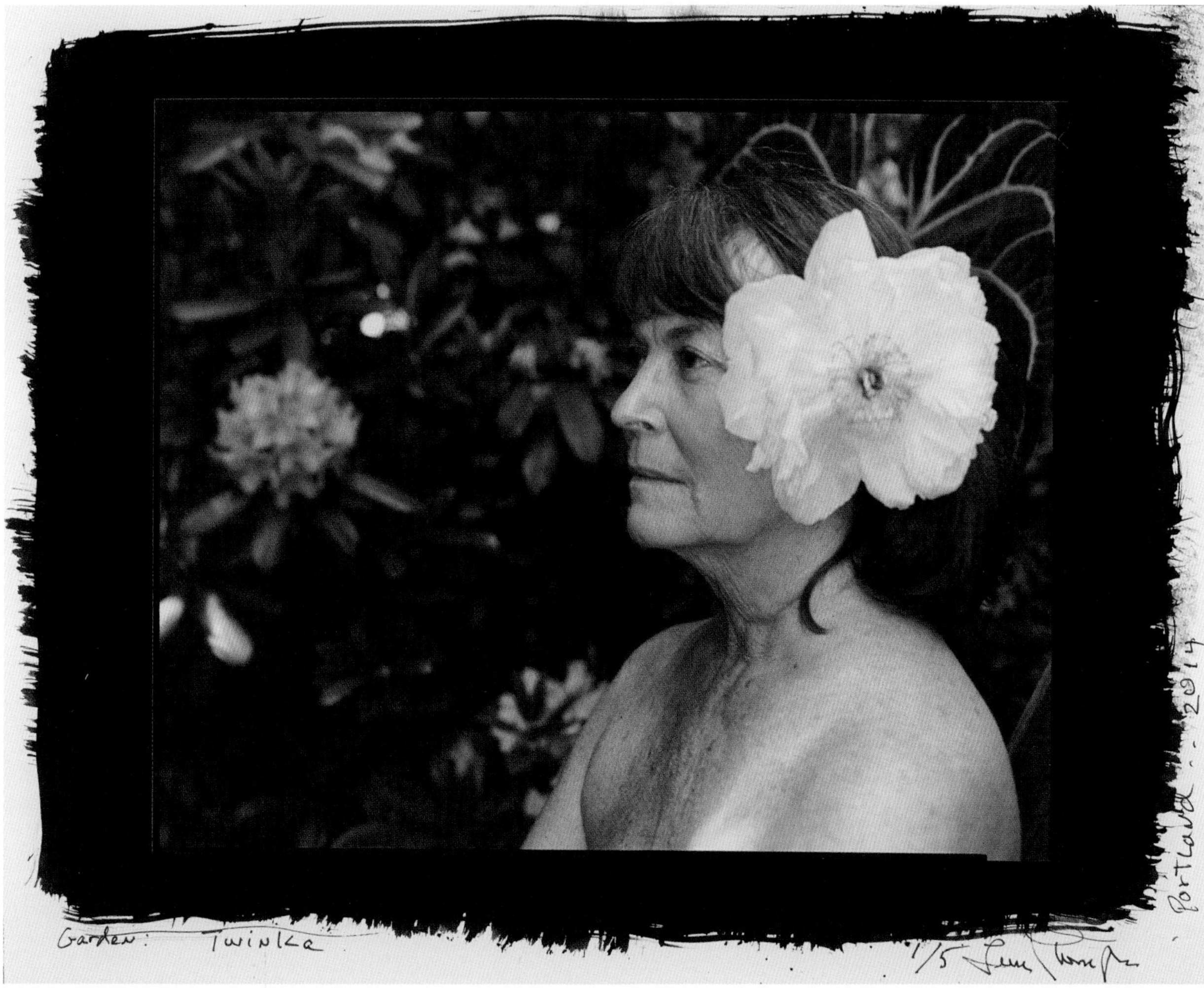

PL. 68 T. K. Thompson (American, born 1947), *Twinka*, from the *Garden* series, 2014. Platinum/gold print, 10 ¼ × 13 in. Collection of Twinka Thiebaud.

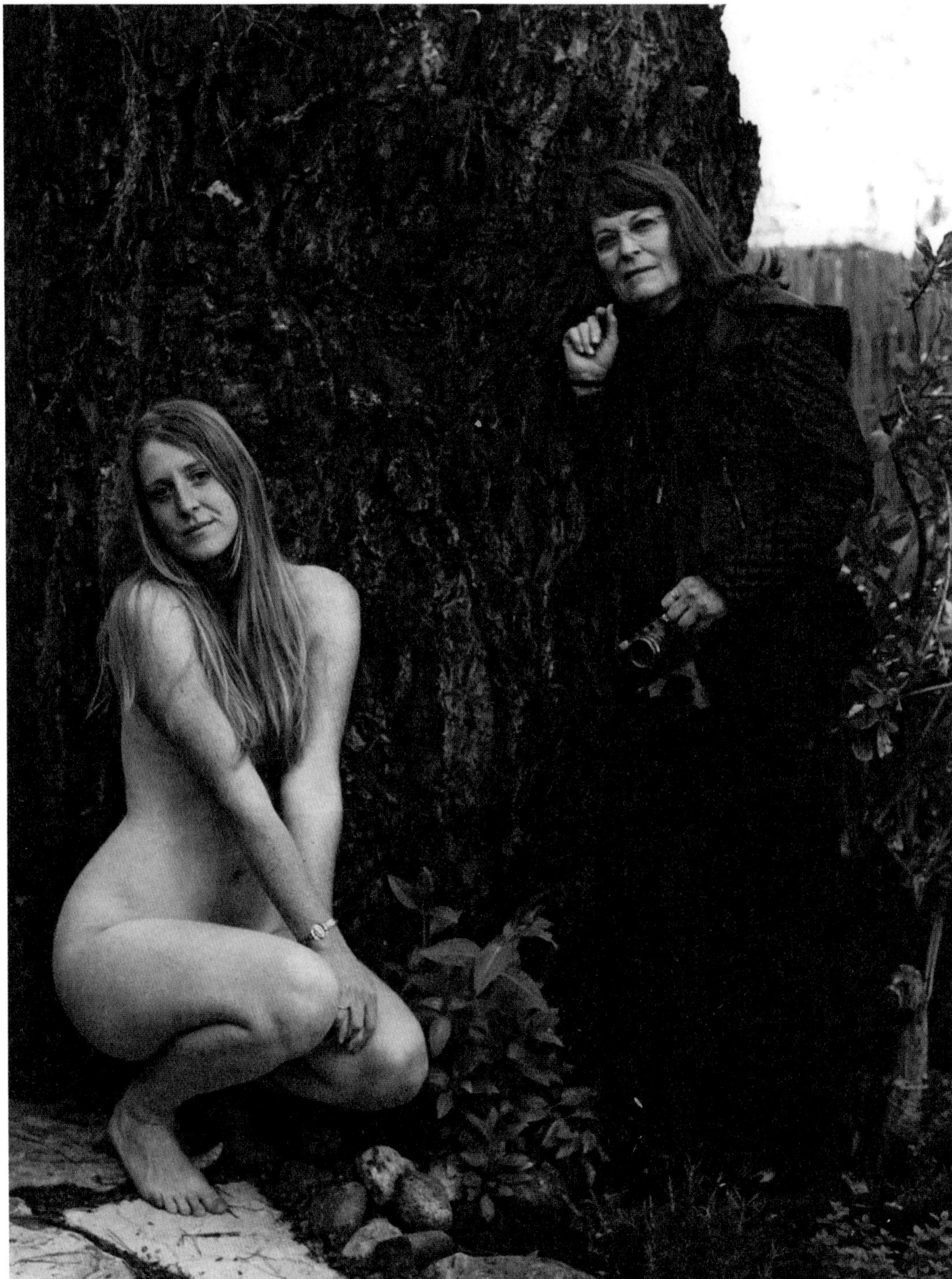

PL. 69 Michelle Magdalena (American, born 1985), *For Imogen*, 2014. Gelatin silver print, 6 ⅜ × 4 ⅞ in. Collection of Twinka Thiebaud.

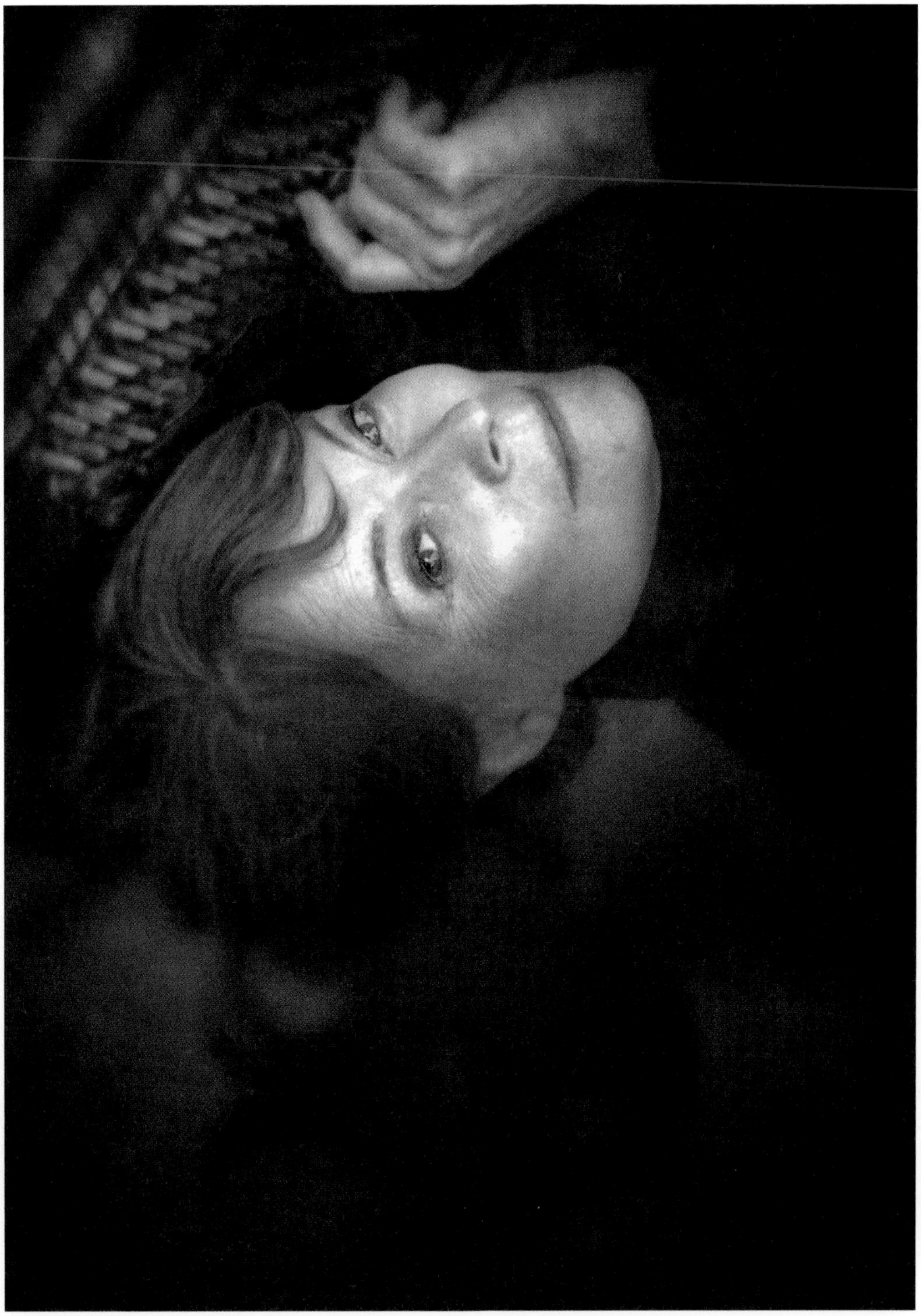

PL. 70 Ellis Christopher (American, born 1970), *Untitled*, 2015. Gelatin silver print, 12 × 8 ⅜ in. Collection of Twinka Thiebaud.

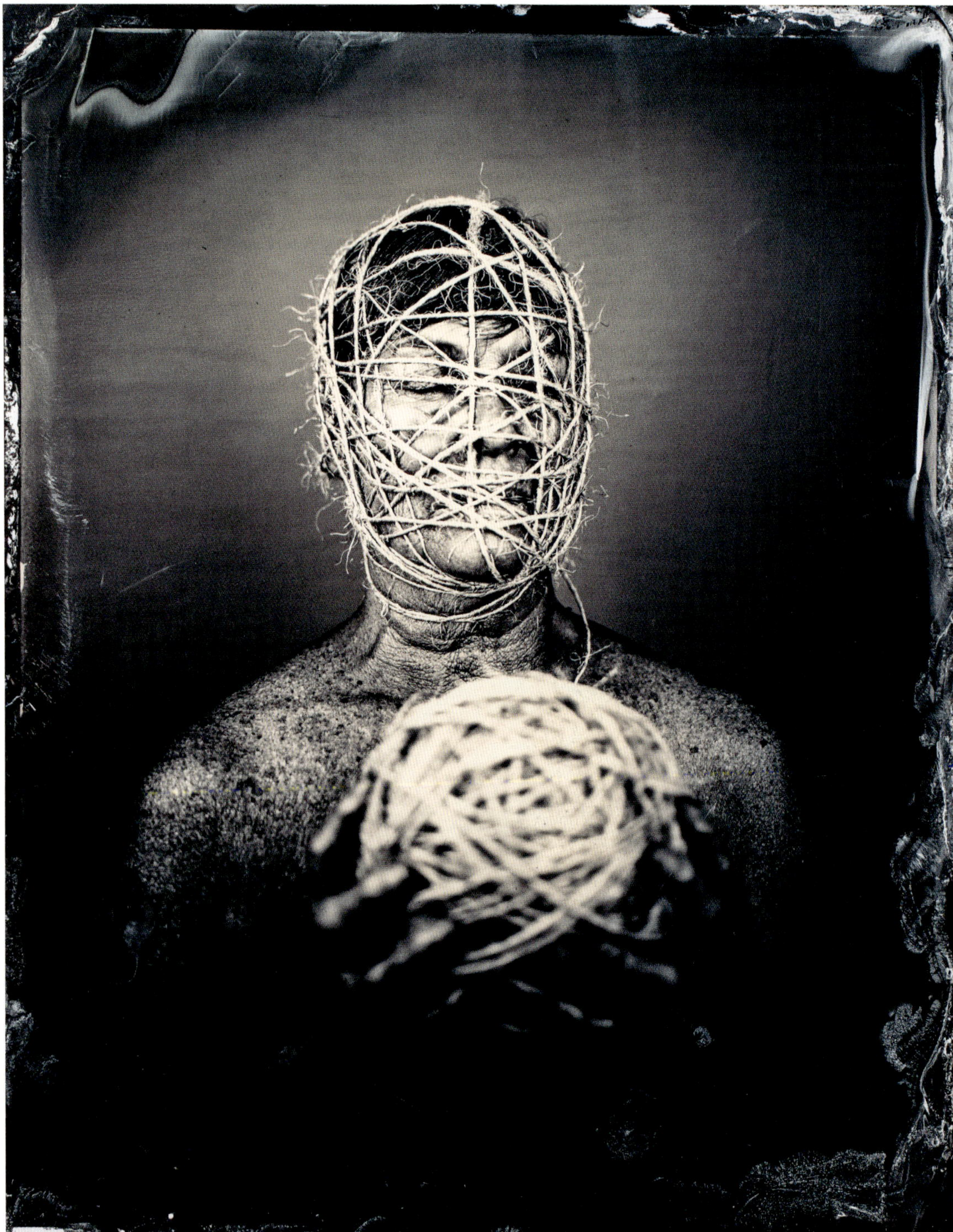

PL. 71 Susan Seubert (American, born 1970), *Entwined*, 2014. Digital pigment print from wet plate collodion negative, 18 × 14 ½ in. Collection of Twinka Thiebaud.

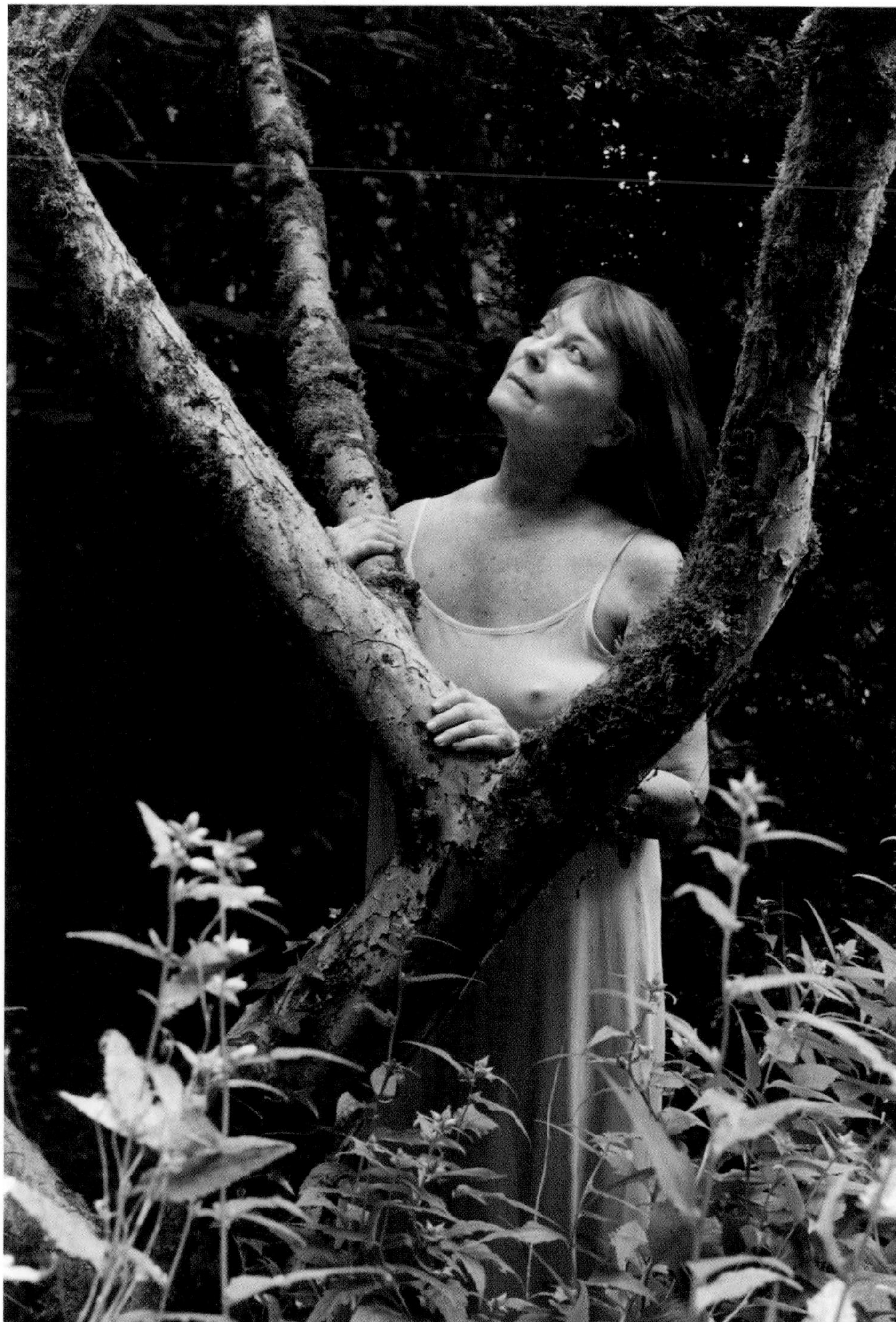

PL. 72 Kathleen Malan-Thompson (American, born 1953), *Twinka at 65*, 2014. Gelatin silver print, 10 × 8 in. Collection of Twinka Thiebaud.

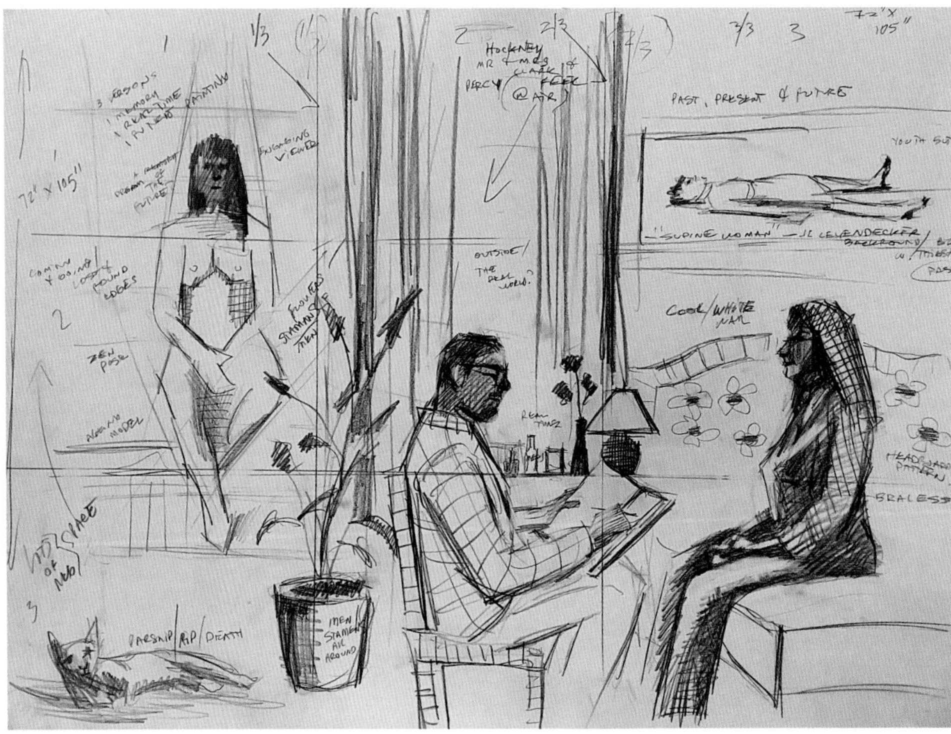

PL. 73 Bradford J. Salamon (American, born 1963), *Triple Twinka Study*, 2015. Pencil on Bristol vellum paper, 22 × 29 ½ in. Private collection.

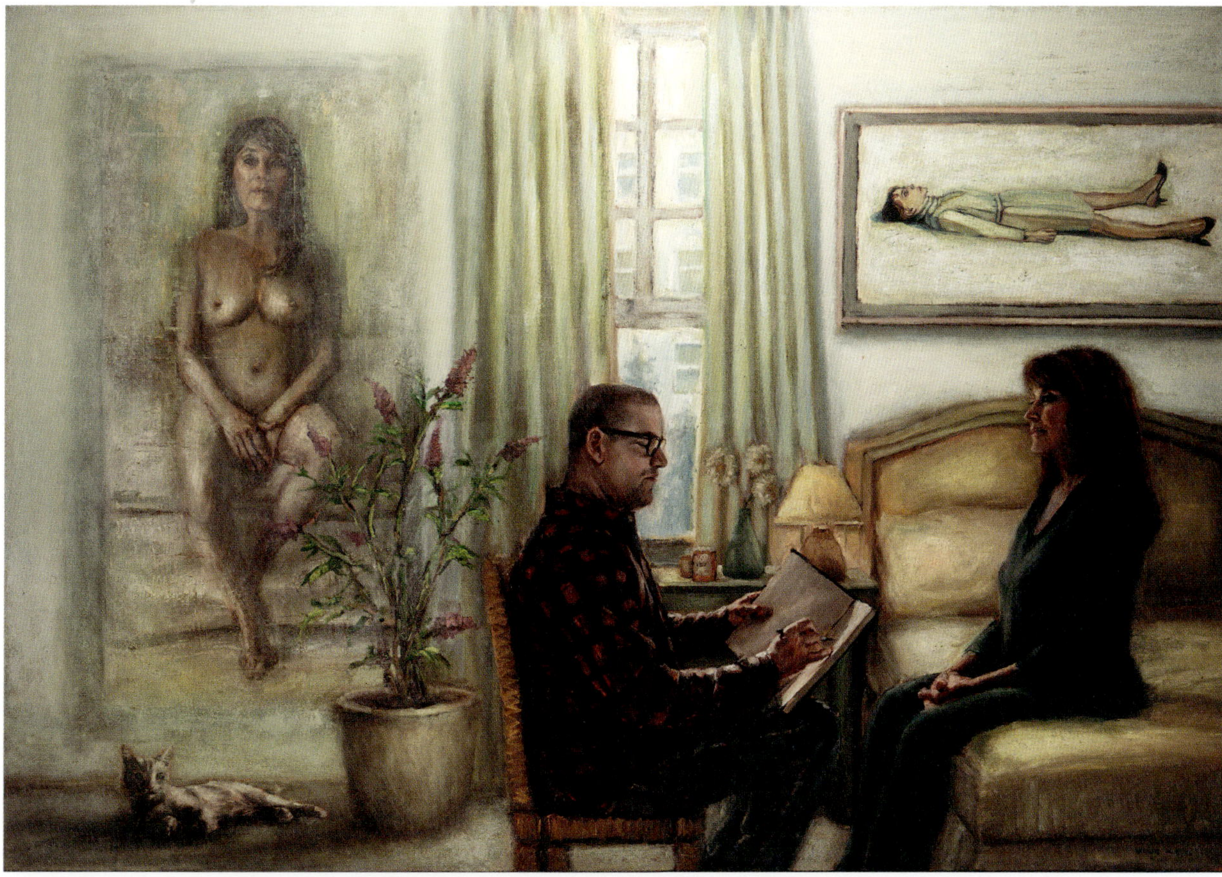

PL. 74 Bradford J. Salamon (American, born 1963), *Triple Twinka*, 2015. Oil on canvas, 72 × 105 in. Private collection.

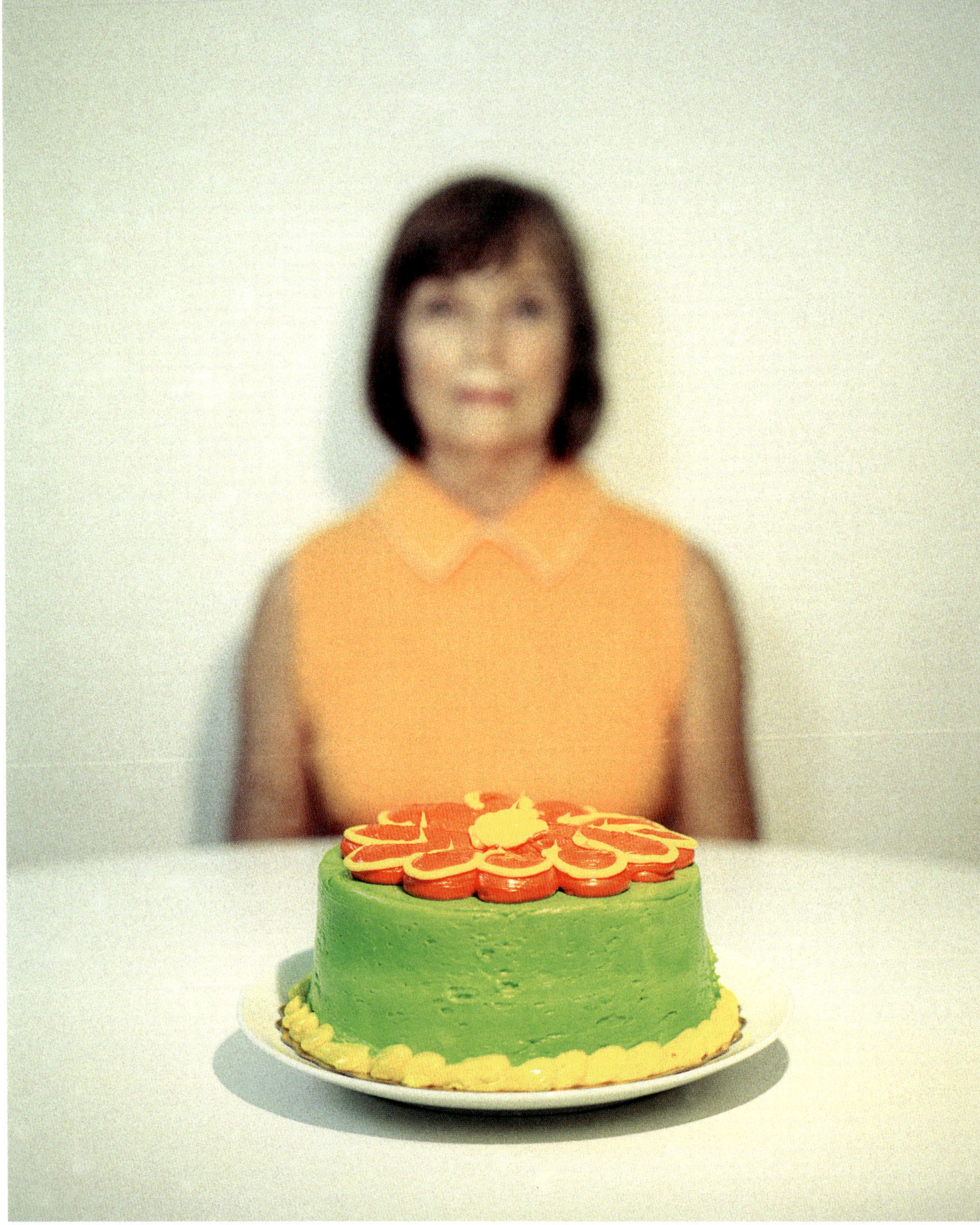

PL. 75 Aline Smithson (American, born 1953), *Twinka with a Cake*, 2017. Archival pigment print, 20 × 14 in. Collection of Aline Smithson, artist.

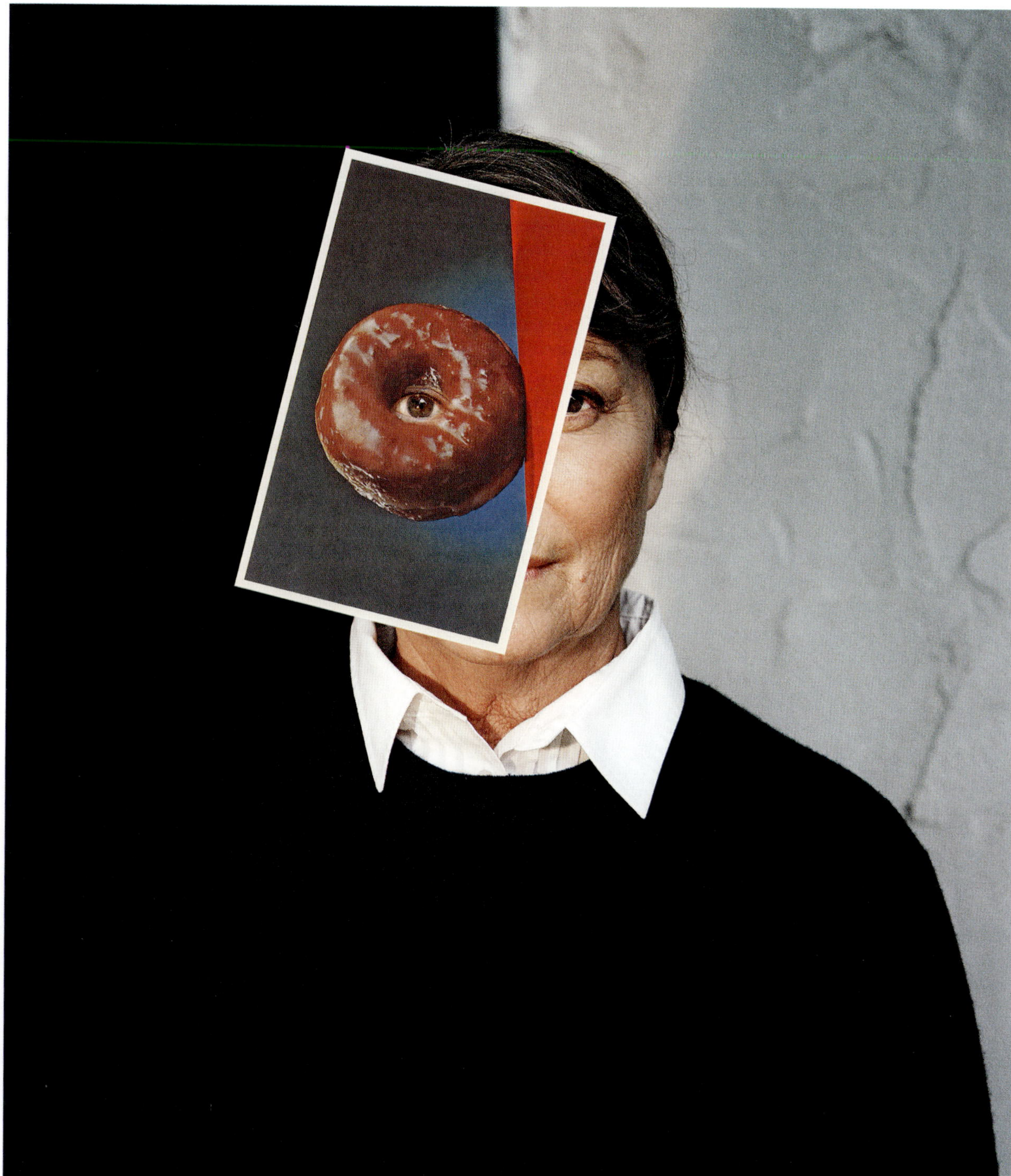

PL. 76 Aline Smithson (American, born 1953), *Twinka with a Donut*, 2017. Archival pigment print, 29 × 26 in. Collection of Aline Smithson, artist.

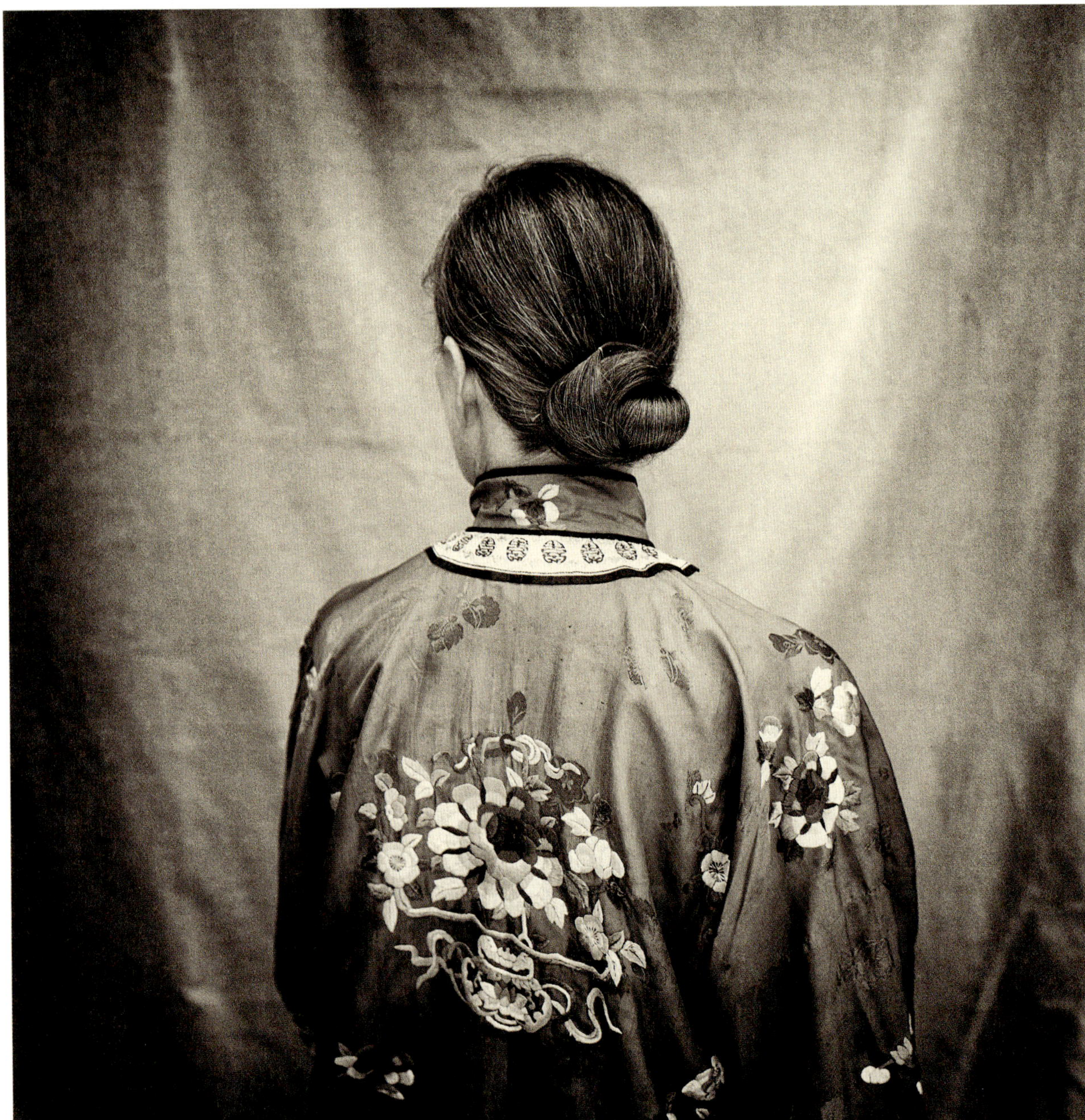

PL. 77 Aline Smithson (American, born 1953), *Twinka Turned*, 2017. Archival pigment print, 30 × 30 in. Collection of Aline Smithson, artist.

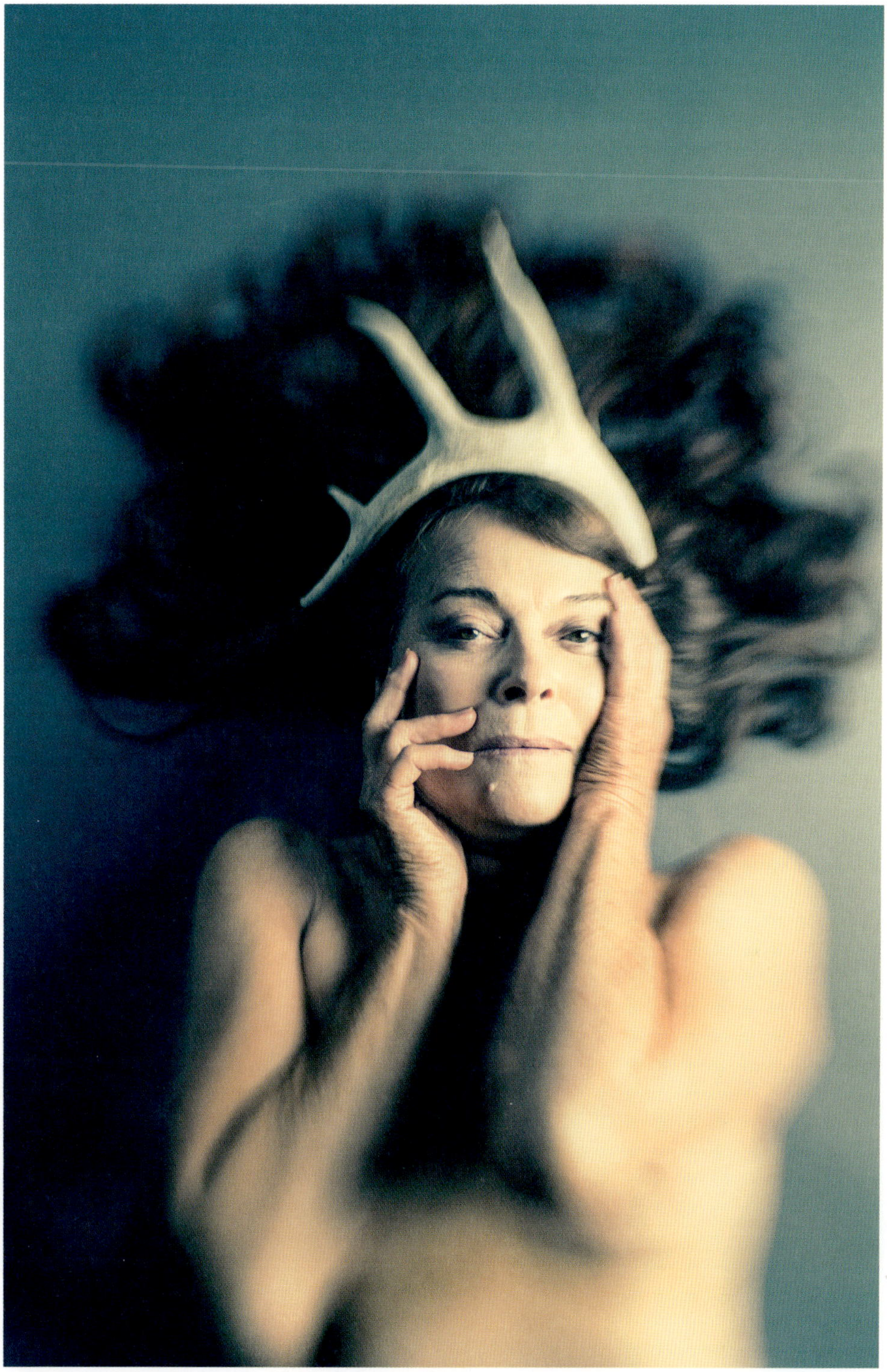

PL. 78 Kim Campbell (American, born 1970), *Beguiling,* from the *Deep in Between* series, 2017. Archival pigment print on fiber paper, 15 × 10 in. Collection of Kim Campbell.

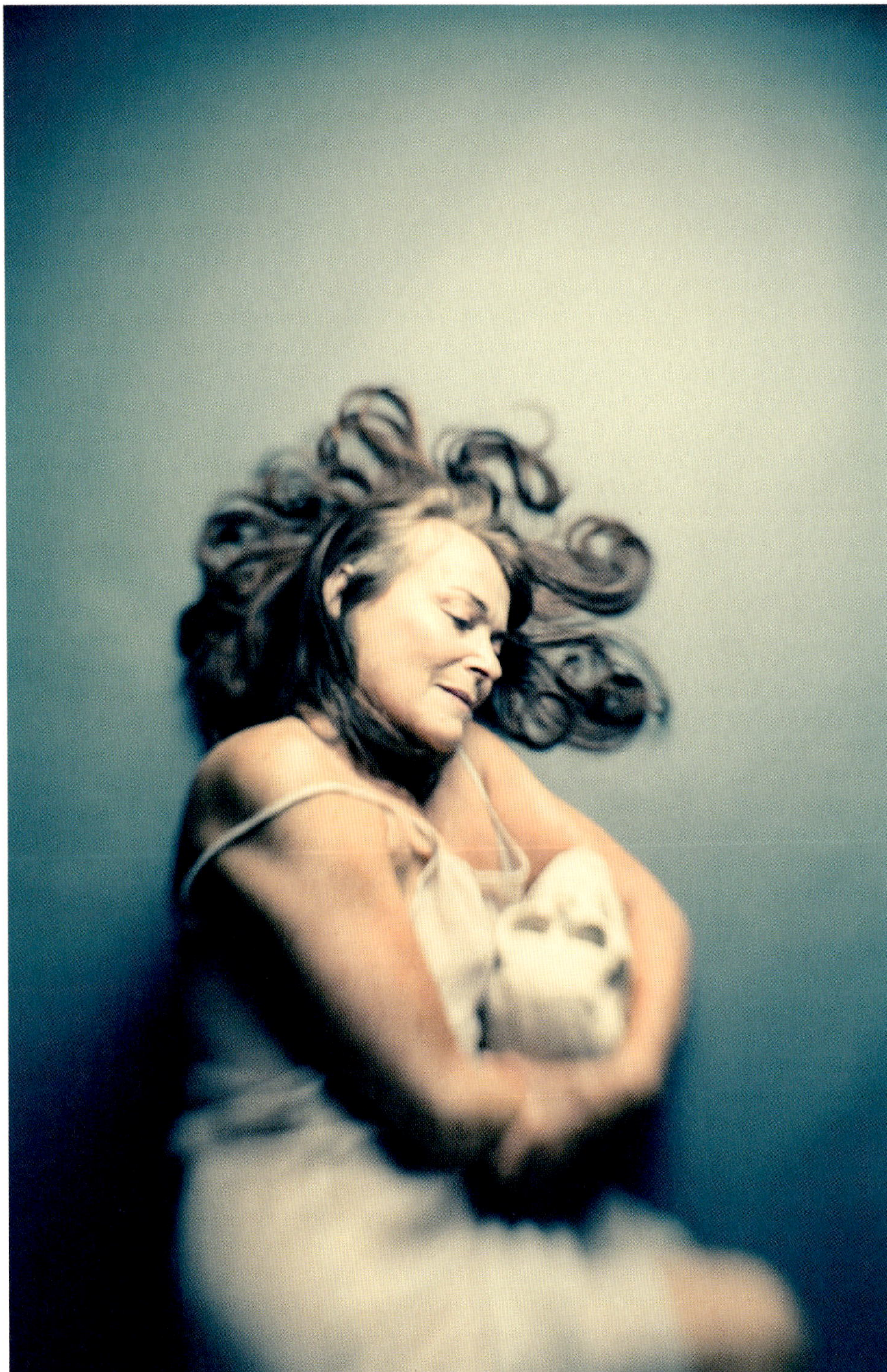

PL. 79 Kim Campbell (American, born 1970), *Biding*, from the *Deep in Between* series, 2017. Archival pigment print on fiber paper, 15 × 10 in. Collection of Kim Campbell.

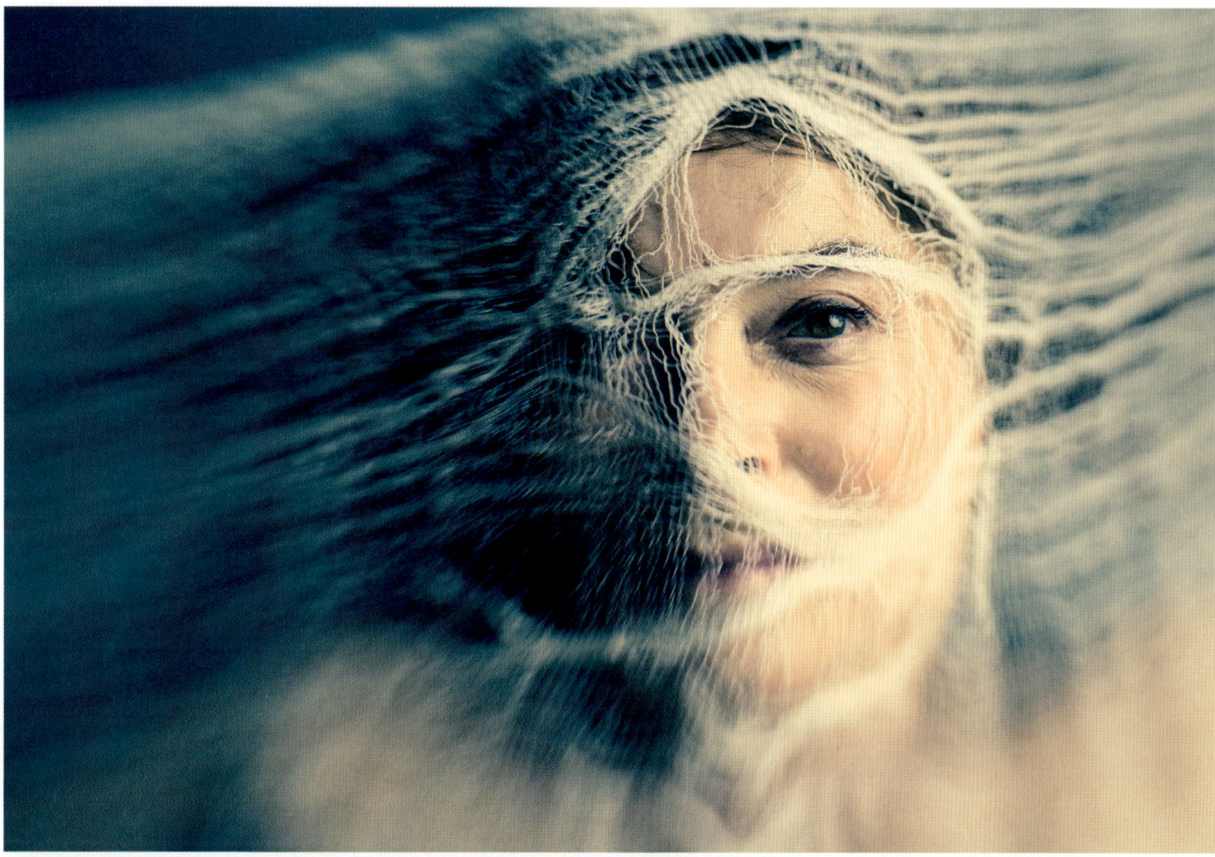

PL. 80 Kim Campbell (American, born 1970), *Perceiving*, from the *Deep in Between* series, 2017. Archival pigment print on fiber paper, 10 × 15 in. Collection of Kim Campbell.

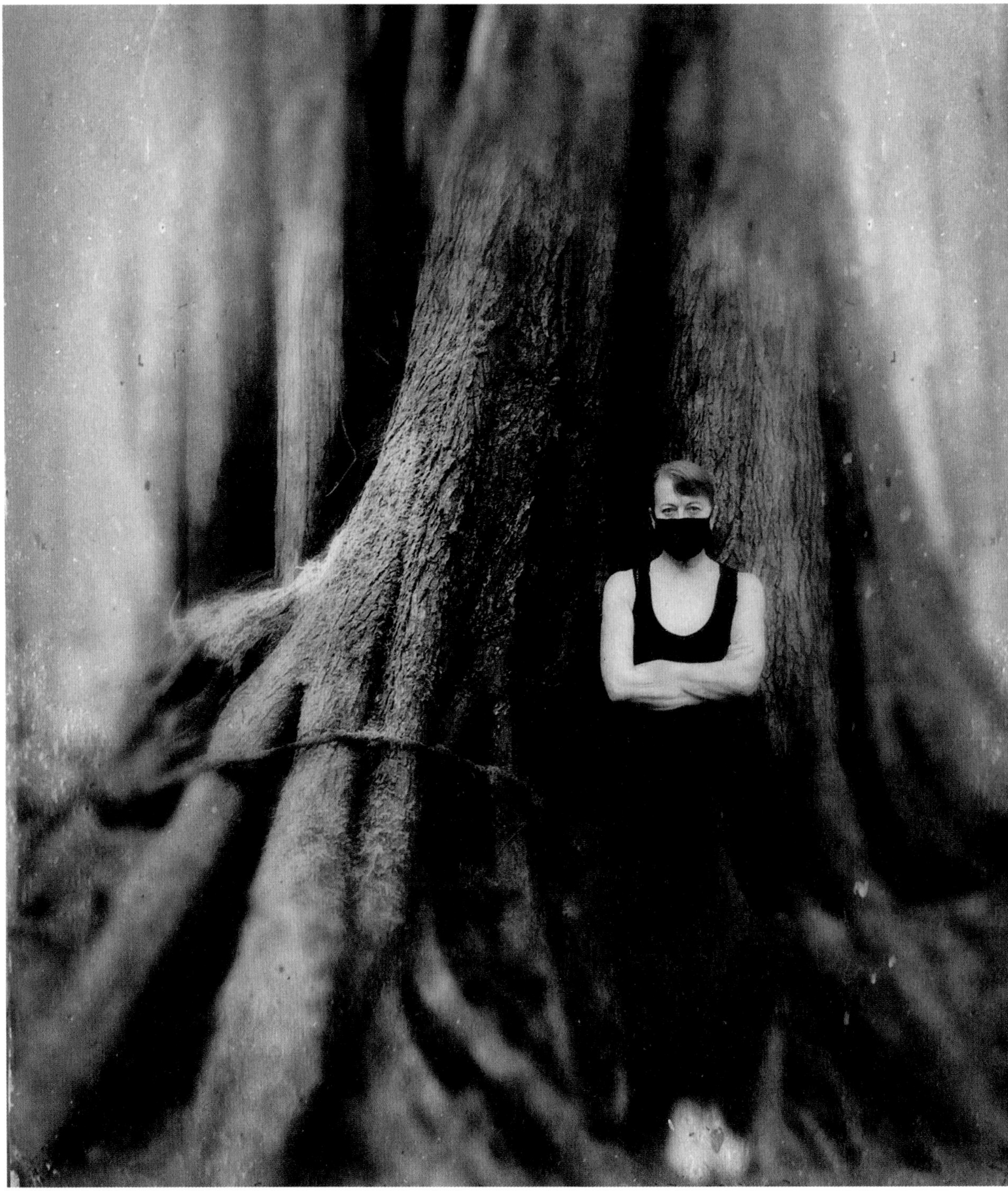

PL. 81 Lorijo Daniels (American, born 1965), *You Name It*, 2020. Tintype, 5 ⅜ × 5 in. Collection of Twinka Thiebaud.

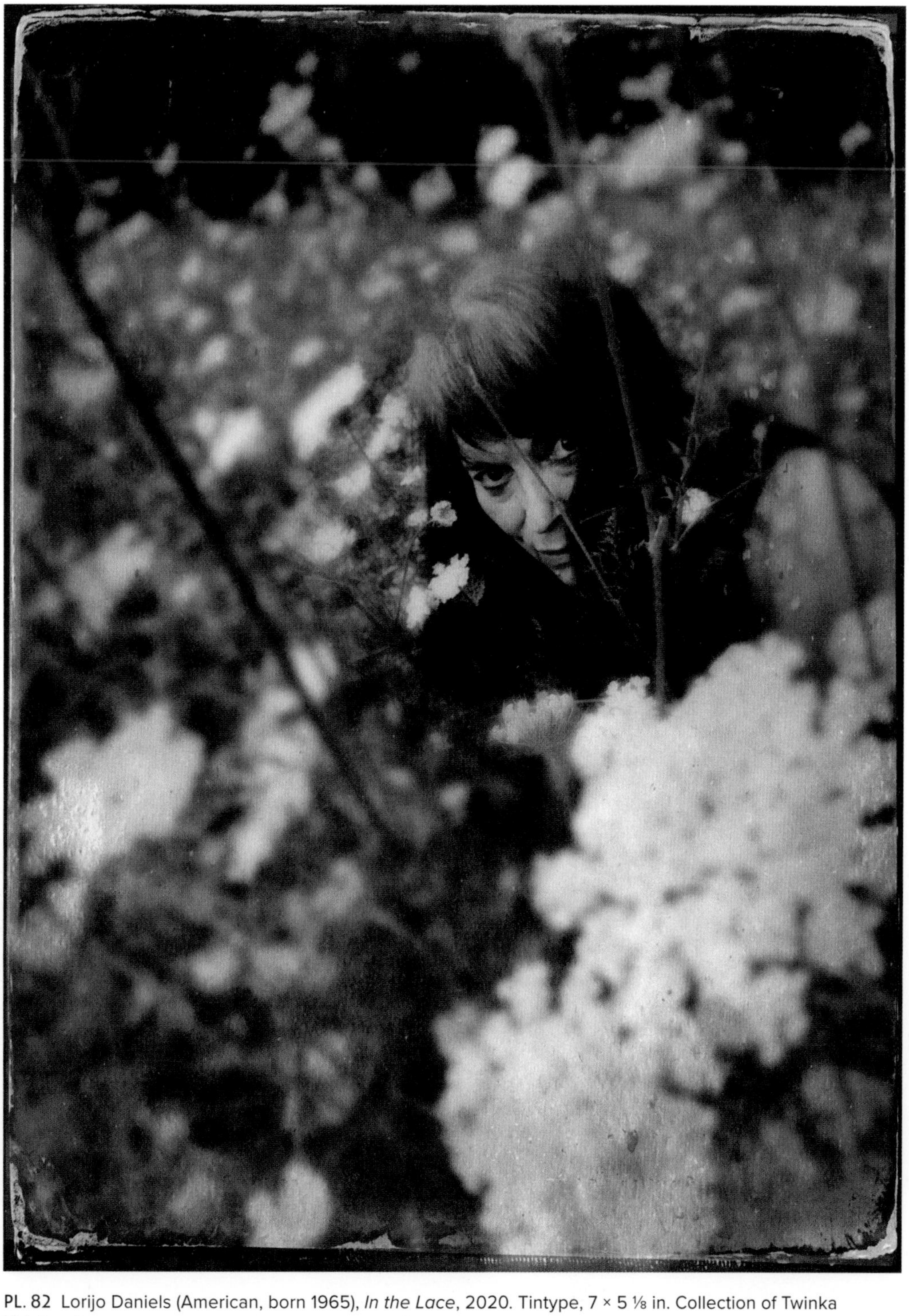

PL. 82 Lorijo Daniels (American, born 1965), *In the Lace*, 2020. Tintype, 7 × 5 ⅛ in. Collection of Twinka Thiebaud.

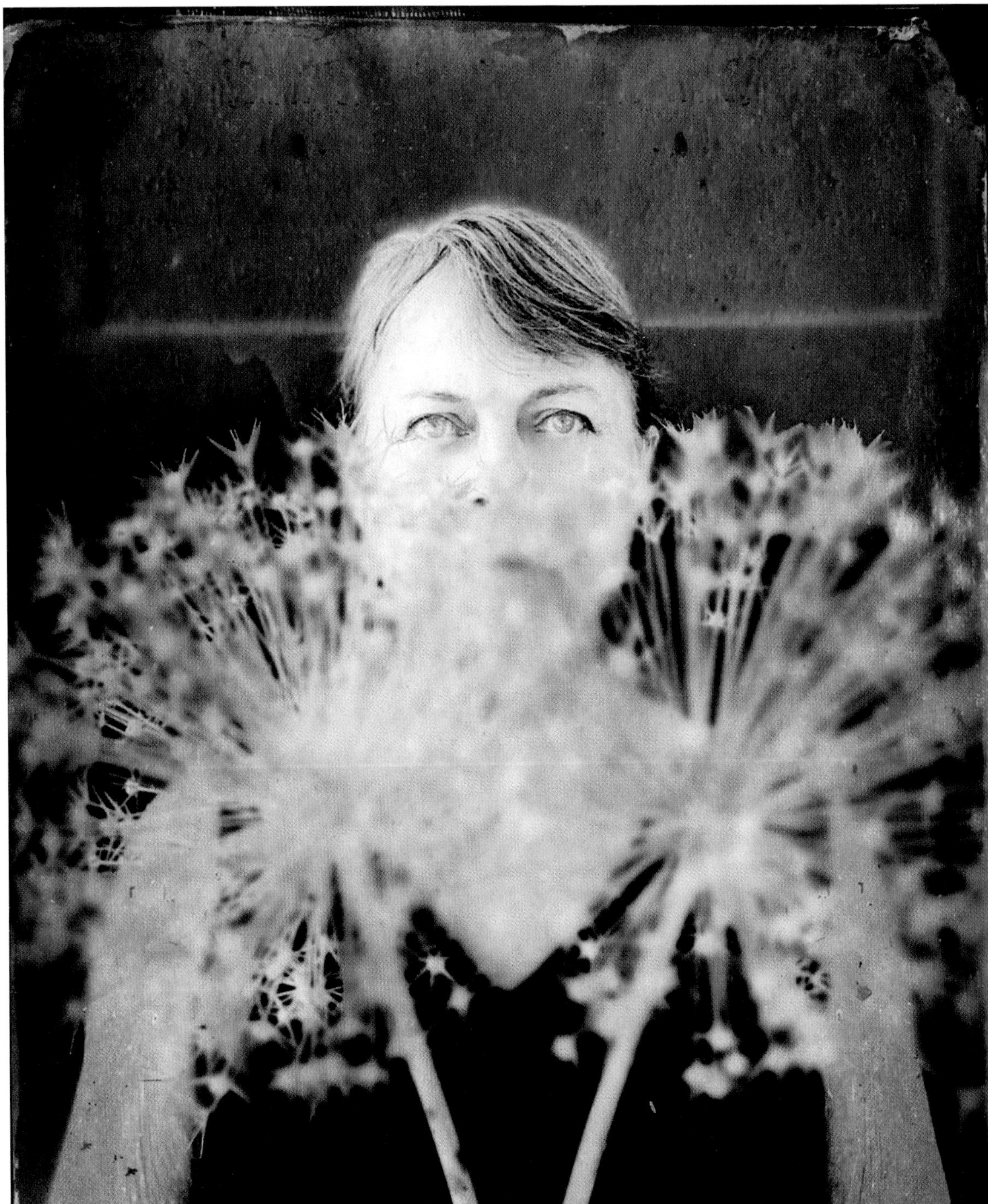

PL. 83 Lorijo Daniels (American, born 1965), *Double Allium*, 2021. Tintype, 5 ⅞ × 5 in. Collection of Twinka Thiebaud.

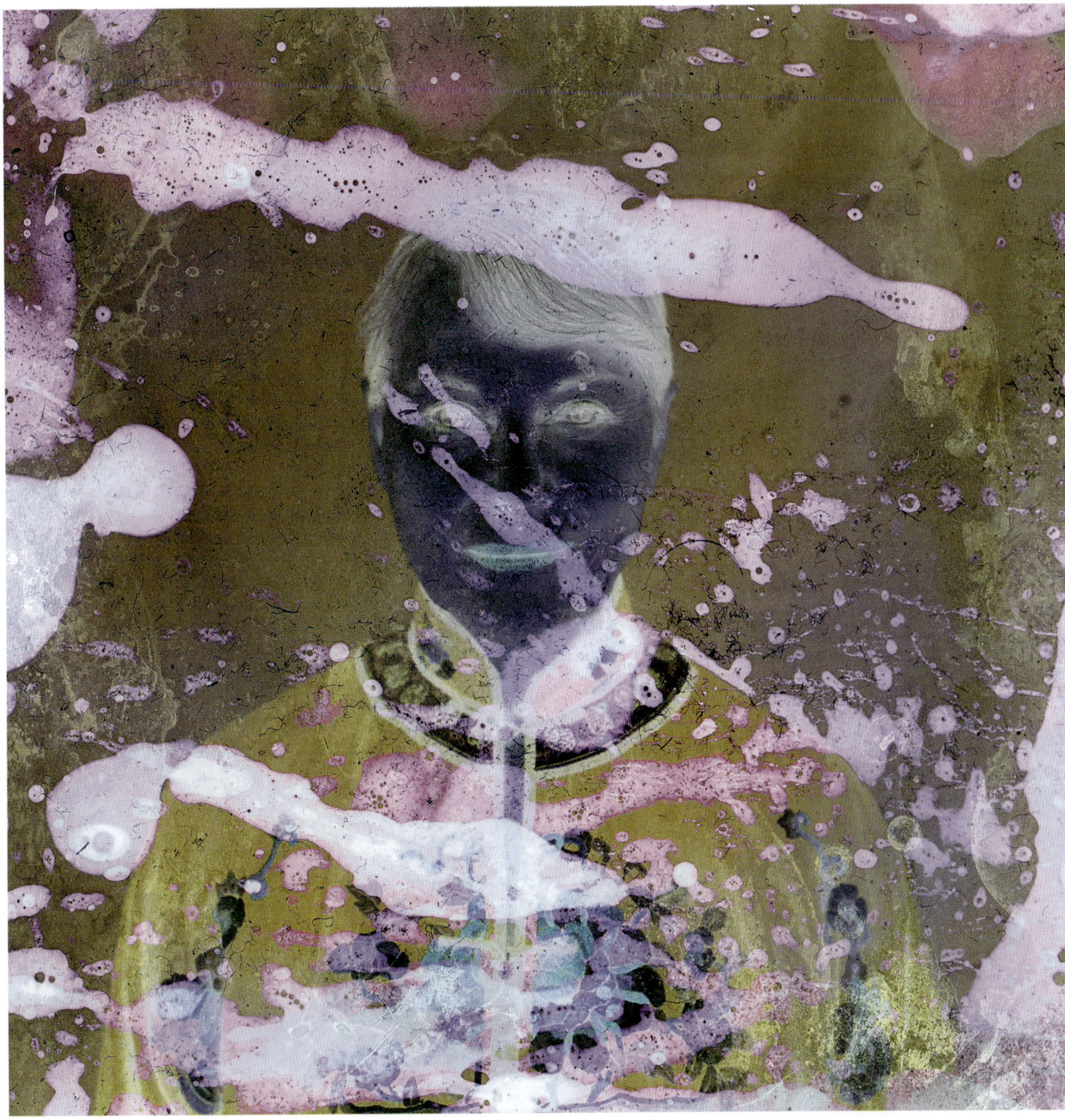

PL. 84 Aline Smithson (American, born 1953), *Twinka*, from *Fugue State*, 2021. Archival pigment print, 24 × 24 in. Collection of Aline Smithson, artist.

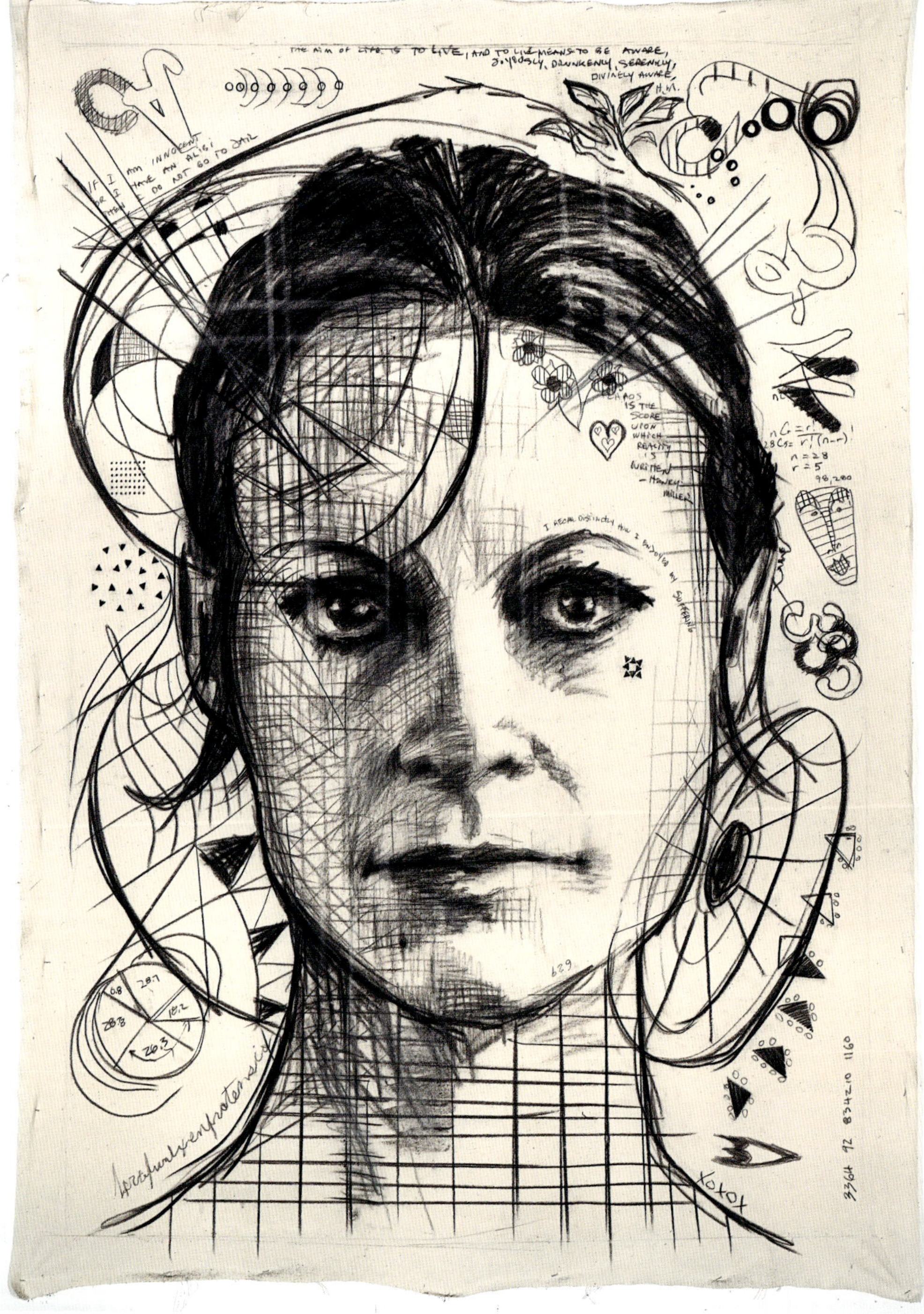

PL. 85 Bradford J. Salamon (American, born 1963), *V-V #15 Twinka Thiebaud*, 2021. Charcoal on canvas, 84 × 60 in. Private collection.

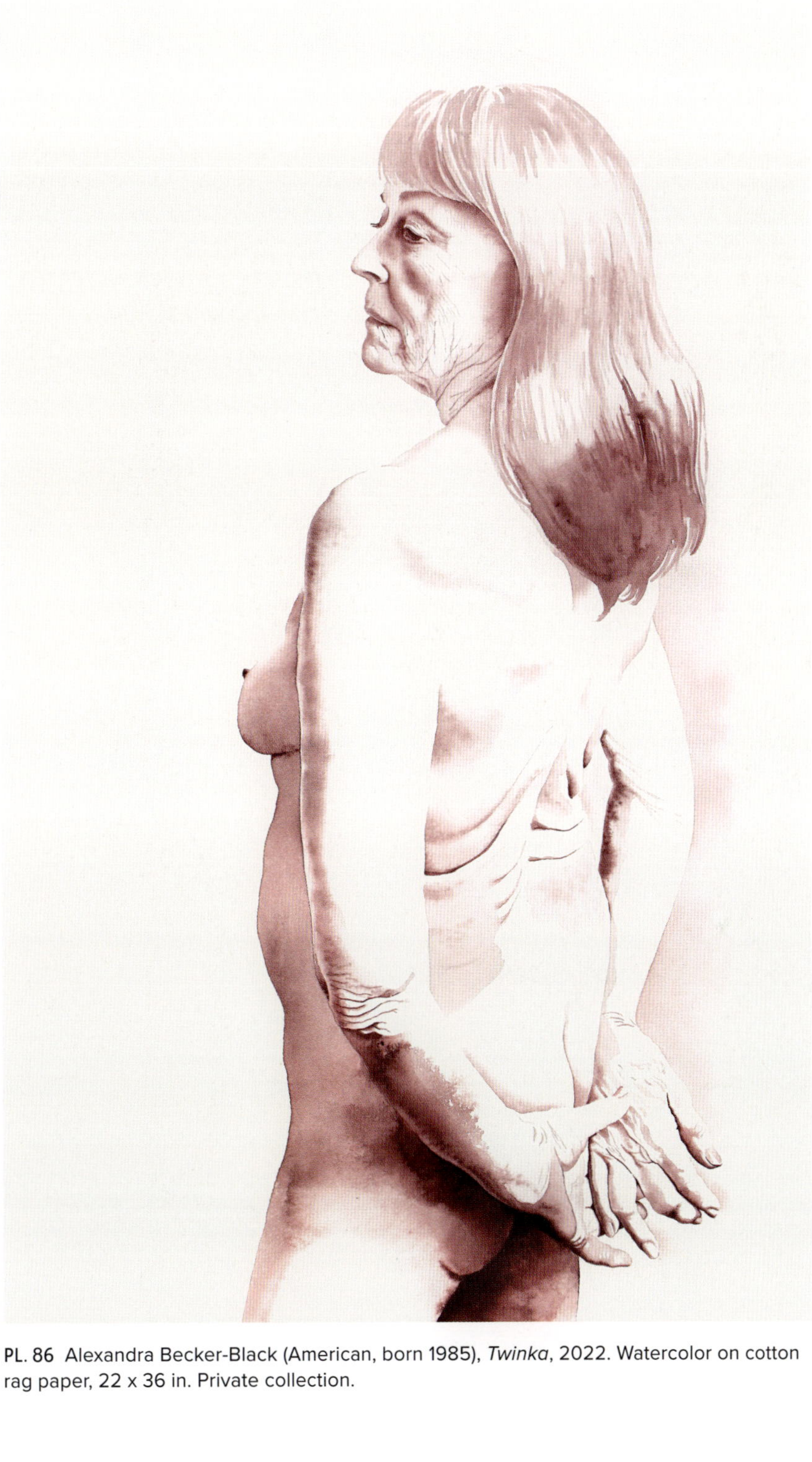

PL. 86 Alexandra Becker-Black (American, born 1985), *Twinka*, 2022. Watercolor on cotton rag paper, 22 x 36 in. Private collection.

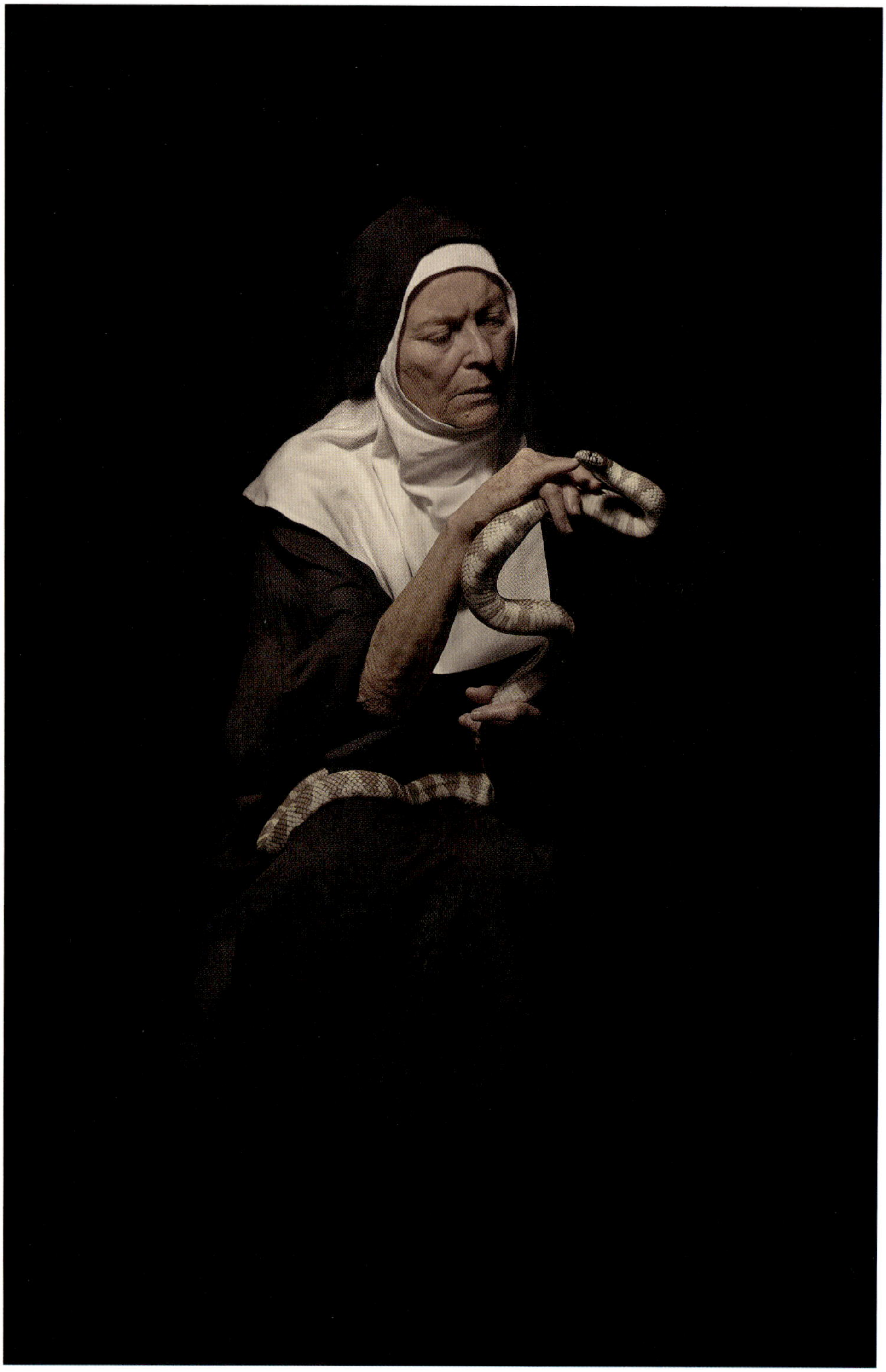

PL. 87 Tami Bahat (American, born Israel, 1979), *The Encounter*, 2022. Archival pigment print, 20 x 16 in. Collection of the artist.

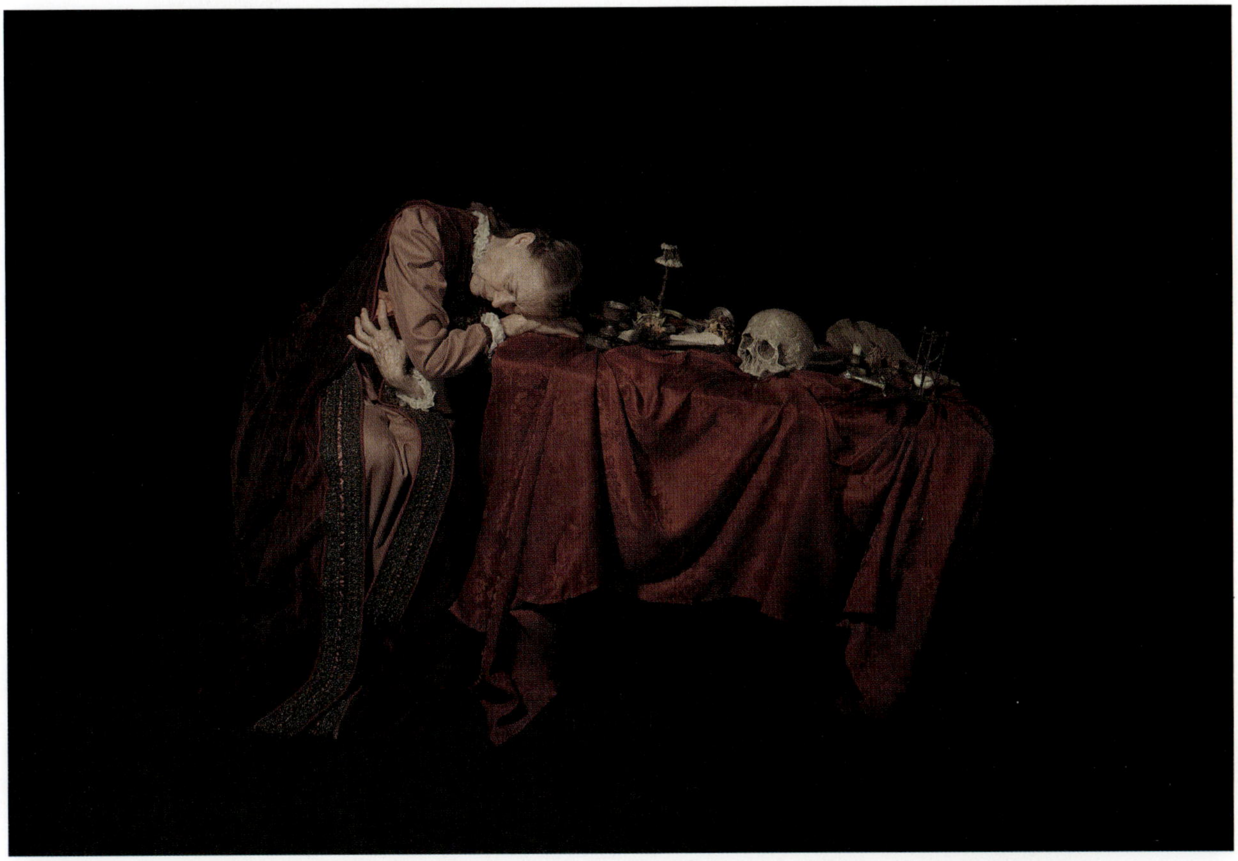

PL. 88 Tami Bahat (American, born Israel, 1979), *The Elegy*, 2022. Archival pigment print, 16 x 20 in. Collection of the artist.

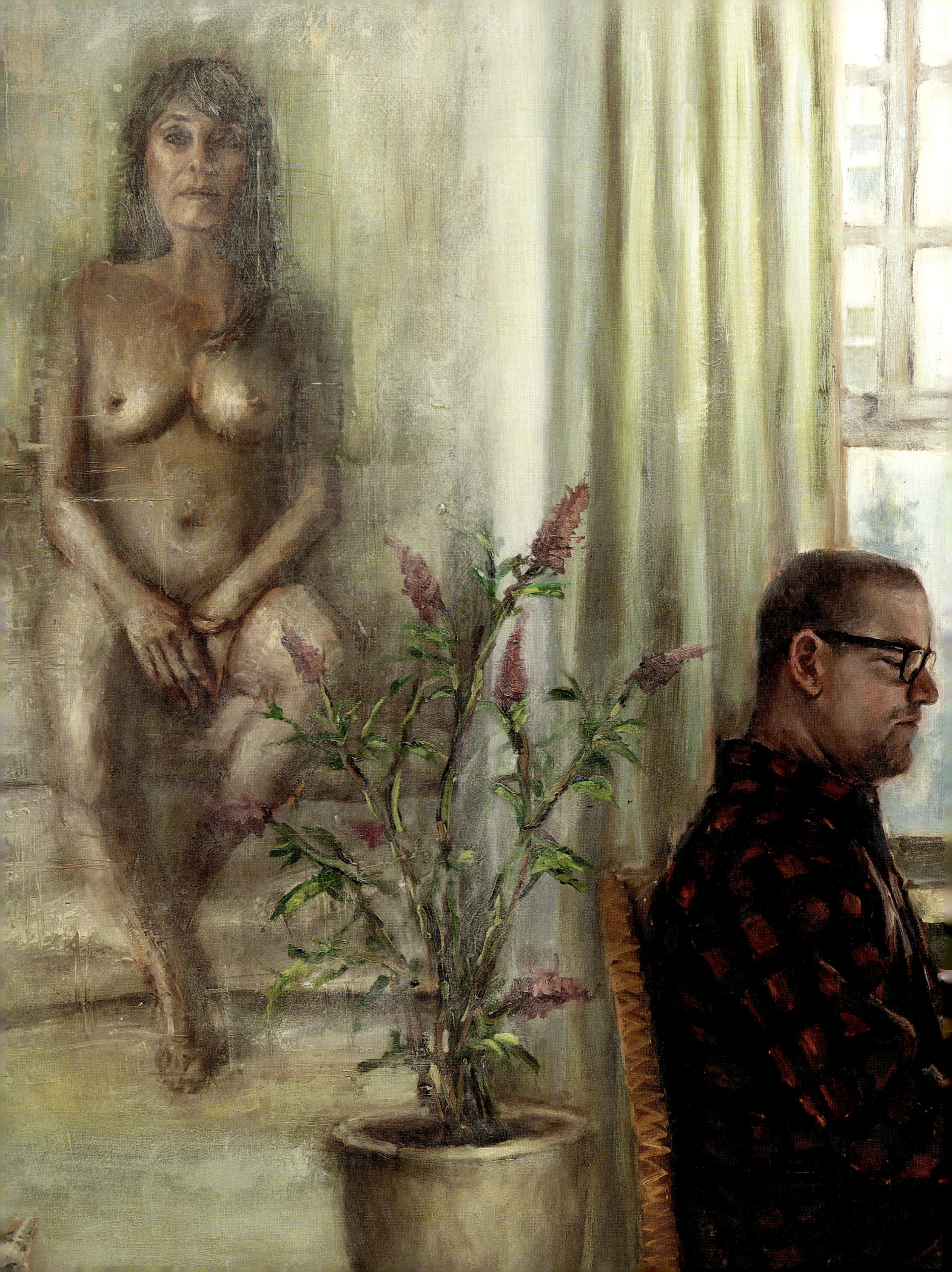

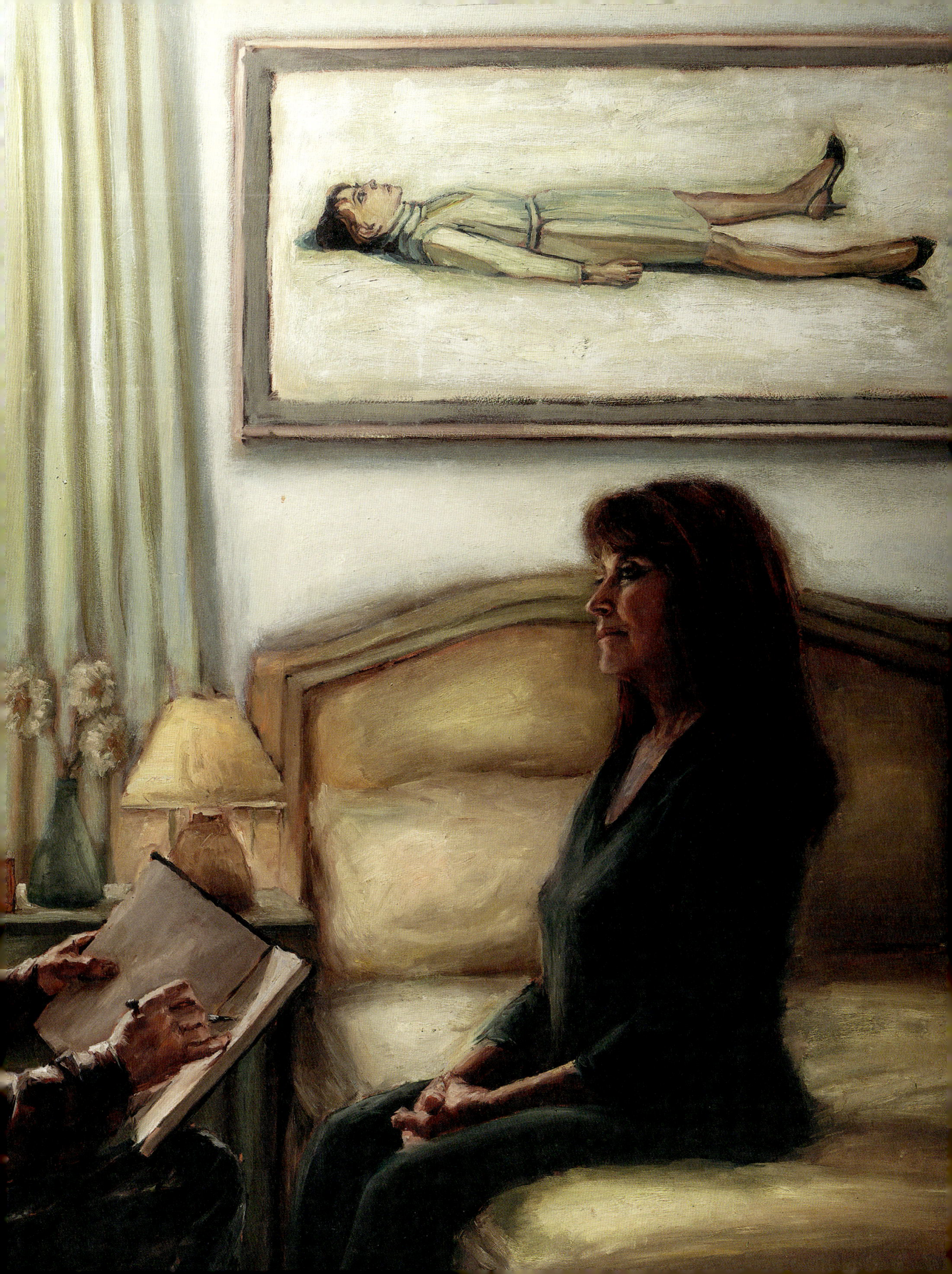

EXHIBITION CHECKLIST

TWINKA THIEBAUD AND THE ART OF THE POSE

Don Bachardy (American, born 1934)

Twinka Thiebaud, 1985. Ink on paper, 30 × 22 ¼ in. Crocker Art Museum, gift of the artist, 2021.37.4.

Tami Bahat (American, born Israel, 1979)

The Elegy, 2022. Archival pigment print, 16 × 20 in. Collection of the artist.

The Encounter, 2022. Archival pigment print, 20 × 16 in. Collection of the artist.

Alexandra Becker-Black (American, born 1985)

Twinka, 2022. Watercolor on cotton rag paper, 22 × 36 in. Private collection.

Kim Campbell (American, born 1970)

Beguiling, from the *Deep in Between* series, 2017. Archival pigment print on fiber paper, 15 × 10 in. Collection of Kim Campbell.

Biding, from the *Deep in Between* series, 2017. Archival pigment print on fiber paper, 15 × 10 in. Collection of Kim Campbell.

Perceiving, from the *Deep in Between* series, 2017. Archival pigment print on fiber paper, 10 × 15 in. Collection of Kim Campbell.

Ellis Christopher (American, born 1970)

Untitled, 2015. Gelatin silver print, 12 × 8 ⅜ in. Collection of Twinka Thiebaud.

Lucien Clergue (French, 1934–2014)

Twinka at Pebble Beach, Monterey, CA (Falling Sand), 1975. Gelatin silver print, 14 ¼ × 9 ⅜ in. Collection of Twinka Thiebaud.

Twinka at Pebble Beach, Monterey, CA (Hand and Breast), 1975. Gelatin silver print, 14 ¼ × 9 ⅜ in. Collection of Twinka Thiebaud.

Twinka at Pebble Beach, Monterey, CA (Looking Ahead), 1975. Gelatin silver print, 14 ¼ × 9 ⅜ in. Collection of Twinka Thiebaud.

Fred Dalkey (American, born 1943)

Untitled (Twinka Portrait), 2014. Pastel on paper, 9 ⅛ × 8 in. Collection of Twinka Thiebaud.

Untitled (Twinka Seated), 2014. Pastel on paper, 10 ⅛ × 7 ½ in. Collection of Twinka Thiebaud.

Lorijo Daniels (American, born 1965)

In the Lace, 2020. Tintype, 7 × 5 ⅛ in. Collection of Twinka Thiebaud.

You Name It, 2020. Tintype, 5 ⅜ × 5 in. Collection of Twinka Thiebaud.

Double Allium, 2021. Tintype, 5 ⅞ × 5 in. Collection of Twinka Thiebaud.

Judy Dater (American, born 1941)

Twinka and Lace Curtain, 1970. Gelatin silver print, 13 ½ × 10 ⅜ in. Collection of Twinka Thiebaud.

Twinka Thiebaud (Twinka and Tree), 1970. Gelatin silver print, 12 ⅞ × 10 in. Crocker Art Museum Purchase, 1978.2.4.

Imogen and Twinka at Yosemite, 1974. Gelatin silver print, 9 ¼ × 7 ¼ in. Crocker Art Museum purchase with funds from the Shirley & Forrest Plant Fund, 2017.81.

Twinka with Lifemask, 1975. Gelatin silver print, 11 ⅞ × 9 in. Collection of Twinka Thiebaud.

Woman in a White Slip, 2014. Archival pigment print, 20 × 15 ⅞ in. Collection of Twinka Thiebaud.

Ralph Gibson (American, born 1939)

Untitled, 1976. Gelatin silver print, 8 × 12 ⅜ in. Collection of Twinka Thiebaud.

Eikoh Hosoe (Japanese, born 1933)

Twinka under the Tree Shadow, Yosemite, 1975. Gelatin silver print, 12 ½ × 10 ¾ in. Collection of Twinka Thiebaud.

Ron Jacomini (American, born 1941)

Twinka, 1974. Gelatin silver print, 9 ⅝ × 9 ½ in. Collection of Twinka Thiebaud.

Chris Johnson (American, born 1948)

Twinka, 1974. Gelatin silver print, 8 ¼ × 7 ⅝ in. Collection of Twinka Thiebaud.

Kevin Kadar (American, born 1955)

Twinka's Dream, 2011. Oil on museum board, 24 × 18 in. Collection of Twinka Thiebaud.

Larry Keenan Jr. (American, 1943–2012)

Untitled, 1975. Gelatin silver print, 9 × 5 ½ in. Collection of Twinka Thiebaud.

Michelle Magdalena (American, born 1985)

For Imogen, 2014. Gelatin silver print, 6 ⅜ × 4 ⅞ in. Collection of Twinka Thiebaud.

Soulshine, 2014. Gelatin silver print, 6 ⅞ × 3 ⅞ in. Collection of Twinka Thiebaud.

Kathleen Malan-Thompson (American, born 1953)

Twinka at 65, 2014. Gelatin silver print, 10 × 8 in. Collection of Twinka Thiebaud.

Mary Ellen Mark (American, 1940–2015)

Henry Miller and Twinka, Pacific Palisades, Los Angeles, 1975. Gelatin silver print, 7 ⅞ × 11 ⅞ in. Collection of Twinka Thiebaud.

Michele Mattei (French)

Duality, from the *Emerging Essence* series, 2014. C-print, 19 ¾ × 15 ⅜ in. Collection of Twinka Thiebaud.

Emerging through Time, from the *Emerging Essence* series, 2014. C-print, 12 ⅜ × 11 ⅞ in. Collection of Twinka Thiebaud.

Einar Moos (German)

Twinka and Sierra, 1980. Gelatin silver print, 6 ¼ × 5 in. Collection of Twinka Thiebaud.

Arnold Newman (American, 1918–2006)

Untitled (Twinka Seated), 1975. Gelatin silver print, 9 ⅝ × 6 ⅜ in. Collection of Twinka Thiebaud.

Untitled (Twinka Standing), 1975. Gelatin silver print, 9 ½ × 6 ½ in. Collection of Twinka Thiebaud.

Elizabeth Opalenik (American, born 1947)

Twinka Floating in Red, 2011. Archival pigment print, 14 ¾ × 22 in. Collection of Elizabeth Opalenik.

Bird in Hand, 2011. Archival pigment print, 9 × 13 ½ in. Collection of Elizabeth Opalenik.

Twinka in Morning Light, 2011. Archival pigment print, 9 × 13 ½ in. Collection of Elizabeth Opalenik.

Twinka, the French Look, 2013. Archival pigment print, 33 × 16 ½ in. Collection of Elizabeth Opalenik.

Untitled 1, 2013. Archival pigment print, 11 ⅝ × 8 ¼ in. Collection of Twinka Thiebaud.

Untitled 2, 2013. Archival pigment print, 11 ⅝ × 8 ¼ in. Collection of Twinka Thiebaud.

Eva Rubinstein (Polish-American, born Argentina, 1933)

Twinka on Rocks, Yosemite, 1974, 1974. Gelatin silver print, 5 ½ × 8 7/16 in. Collection of Twinka Thiebaud.

Twinka, Yosemite, 1974, 1974. Gelatin silver print, 5 ½ × 8 ⅛ in. Collection of Twinka Thiebaud.

Bradford J. Salamon (American, born 1963)

Triple Twinka Study, 2015. Pencil on Bristol vellum paper, 22 × 29 ½ in. Private collection.

Triple Twinka, 2015. Oil on canvas, 72 × 105 in. Private collection.

V-V #15 Twinka Thiebaud, 2021. Charcoal on canvas, 84 × 60 in. Private collection.

Pete Saloutos (American, born 1947)

Twinka Desert, 1974. Infrared black-and-white film, 6 ½ × 9 ½ in. Collection of Twinka Thiebaud.

Twinka on Fallen Tree, 1974. Gelatin silver print, 8 × 10 in. Collection of Twinka Thiebaud.

Twinka and Juniper Tree, 1974. Photo print on metal, 24 × 36 in. Collection of Pete Saloutos.

Twinka at the Beach, 1976. Infrared black-and-white film, 4 ¾ × 7 in. Collection of Twinka Thiebaud.

Susan Seubert (American, born 1970)

Entwined, 2014. Digital pigment print from wet plate collodion negative, 18 × 14 ½ in. Collection of Twinka Thiebaud.

Aline Smithson (American, born 1953)

Twinka Turned, 2017. Archival pigment print, 30 × 30 in. Collection of Aline Smithson, artist.

Twinka with a Cake, 2017. Archival pigment print, 20 × 14 in. Collection of Aline Smithson, artist.

Twinka with a Donut, 2017. Archival pigment print, 29 × 26 in. Collection of Aline Smithson, artist.

Twinka, from *Fugue State*, 2021. Archival pigment print, 24 × 24 in. Collection of Aline Smithson, artist.

Wayne Thiebaud (American, 1920–2021)

Untitled, n.d. Pastel on paper, 6 ¼ × 4 ¾ in. Courtesy of Twinka Thiebaud.

Untitled, 1948. Watercolor on newsprint paper, 17 ½ × 13 ¾ in. Collection of Twinka Thiebaud.

Twinka Thiebaud, Age 4, 1949. Charcoal on paper, 23 ⅛ × 16 ⅜ in. Collection of Twinka Thiebaud.

Untitled, 1949. Charcoal on paper, 11 ⅜ × 12 ⅜ in. Collection of Twinka Thiebaud.

Twinka, 1951. Oil on canvas board, 19 ⅝ × 15 ¾ in. Collection of Twinka Thiebaud.

Mallary Ann and Twinka, 1962. Pencil on paper, 24 × 18 in. Collection of Mallary Thiebaud.

Twinka Posing, 1963. Pencil on paper, 17 ¾ × 11 ½ in. Collection of Twinka Thiebaud.

Supine Woman, 1963. Oil on canvas, 36 × 72 in. Crystal Bridges Museum of American Art, Bentonville, Arkansas, 2009.17.

Twinka Thiebaud, 1964. Ink on paper, 14 × 17 in. Collection of Twinka Thiebaud.

Untitled, 1965. Pencil on paper, 14 ¾ × 16 ¾ in. Collection of Twinka Thiebaud.

Green Dress, 1966/2017. Oil on canvas, 72 × 60 in. Collection of the Wayne Thiebaud Foundation.

Twinka (in Hat), 1968. Pencil on newsprint, 11 ¾ × 17 ½ in. Collection of Twinka Thiebaud.

Untitled, 1968. Pencil on paper, 6 × 12 in. Courtesy of Twinka Thiebaud.

Untitled, circa 1985. Pastel on Schoeller's Parole paper, 27 ¾ × 21 ⅞ in. Collection of Twinka Thiebaud.

T. K. Thompson (American, born 1947)

Twinka, from the *Garden* series, 2014. Platinum/gold print, 10 ¼ × 13 in. Collection of Twinka Thiebaud.

Arthur Tress (American, born 1940)

Twinka, Age 40, Bombed Paper Mill, Arles, France (Missile Columns), 1985. Gelatin silver print, 7 ½ × 7 ½ in. Collection of Twinka Thiebaud.

Twinka, Age 40, Bombed Paper Mill, Arles, France (Outside Tunnel), 1985. Gelatin silver print, 7 ½ × 7 ½ in. Collection of Twinka Thiebaud.

R. Michael Walker (American, born 1950)

Twinka at Wawona/Yosemite National Park, CA, 1974. Archival inkjet print, 13 ⅝ × 17 ⅛ in. Collection of Twinka Thiebaud.

Twinka in Henry's Garden, Pacific Palisades, CA, 1975. Gelatin silver print, 14 ⅝ × 14 ¼ in. Collection of Twinka Thiebaud.

Untitled, 1975. Gelatin silver print, 7 × 7 ⅛ in. Collection of Twinka Thiebaud.

Twinka, Portland, OR, 2011. Archival inkjet print, 14 ⅜ × 14 ½ in. Collection of Twinka Thiebaud.

Jack Welpott (American, 1923–2007)

Twinka (Torso in Light/Dark Contrast), 1970. Gelatin silver print, 9 ¼ × 7 ⅛ in. Collection of Twinka Thiebaud.

Twinka (Tilted Head), 1970. Gelatin silver print, 9 ⅛ × 7 ¼ in. Collection of Twinka Thiebaud.

Twinka, 1970. Gelatin silver print, 12 ½ × 8 ¾ in. Collection of Twinka Thiebaud.

Untitled (Seated with Curving Spine), 1971. Gelatin silver print, 10 × 8 in. Collection of Twinka Thiebaud.

John Reiff Williams (American, born 1954)

Twinka Crying, 1987. Gelatin silver print, 13 ⅝ × 9 ⅝ in. Collection of Twinka Thiebaud.

Twinka Portrait, 1987. Archival pigment print from solarized Polaroid process, 14 ⅝ × 11 in. Collection of John Reiff Williams.

Twinka: Nude in the Chair, 1987. Gelatin silver print, 14 ⅛ × 11 in. Collection of Twinka Thiebaud.

Twinka: Nude in the Chair "C," 1987. Gelatin silver print, 14 ¼ × 11 in. Collection of John Reiff Williams.

Twinka: Nude in the Chair "F," 1987. Gelatin silver print, 14 ⅜ × 11 in. Collection of Twinka Thiebaud.

Untitled, 1987. Gelatin silver print, 6 ½ × 9 in. Collection of Twinka Thiebaud.

Untitled (Twinka: Nude in Chair, Hands on Knees), 1987. Gelatin silver print, 6 ⅜ × 6 ¼ in. Collection of Twinka Thiebaud.

Untitled (Twinka with Eyes Crossed), from the *Funny Faces* series, 1987. Archival pigment print, 16 ½ × 11 in. Collection of John Reiff Williams.

Untitled (Twinka with One Eye Looking Up), from the *Funny Faces* series, 1987. Archival pigment print, 16 ½ × 11 in. Collection of John Reiff Williams.

Untitled (Twinka Straining Neck), from the *Funny Faces* series, 1987. Archival pigment print, 16 ½ × 11 in. Collection of John Reiff Williams.

Untitled (Monster Face 2), 1987. Archival pigment print, 16 ½ × 11 in. Collection of John Reiff Williams.

Untitled (Monster Face 5), 1987. Archival pigment print, 17 × 11 in. Collection of John Reiff Williams.

Untitled (Monster Face 7), 1987. Archival pigment print, 16 ⅝ × 11 in. Collection of John Reiff Williams.

Twinka Thiebaud (with Model 1), 1991. Gelatin silver print, 7 ⅞ × 5 ⅞ in. Collection of Twinka Thiebaud.

Twinka Thiebaud (with Model 2), 1991. Gelatin silver print, 7 ⅞ × 5 ⅞ in. Collection of Twinka Thiebaud.

Untitled (Twinka Reflection), 2011. Archival pigment print, 6 × 4 in. Collection of Twinka Thiebaud.

Untitled, 2011. Archival pigment print, 6 × 4 in. Collection of Twinka Thiebaud.

Untitled (Twinka with Sheet 3), 2011. Archival pigment print, 6 × 4 in. Collection of Twinka Thiebaud.

Untitled (Twinka with Sheet 4), 2011. Archival pigment print, 6 × 4 in. Collection of Twinka Thiebaud.

Untitled (Twinka with Sheet 5), 2011. Archival pigment print, 6 × 4 in. Collection of Twinka Thiebaud.

Untitled (Twinka with Sheet 6), 2011. Archival pigment print, 6 × 4 in. Collection of Twinka Thiebaud.

Untitled (Twinka with Sheet 7), 2011. Archival pigment print, 6 × 4 in. Collection of Twinka Thiebaud.

Untitled (Twinka with Sheet 8), 2011. Archival pigment print, 6 × 4 in. Collection of Twinka Thiebaud.

Untitled (Twinka with Sheet 9), 2011. Archival pigment print, 6 × 4 in. Collection of Twinka Thiebaud.

Untitled (Twinka in Wet Slip), 2013. Archival pigment print, 16 × 10 ⅝ in. Collection of Twinka Thiebaud.

Untitled (Twinka's Eye), 2016. Archival pigment print, 16 ½ × 11 in. Collection of John Reiff Williams.

Ephemera

Wayne and Patricia Thiebaud with baby Twinka. Courtesy of Twinka Thiebaud.

Twinka Thiebaud, 1947. Courtesy of Twinka Thiebaud.

Twinka Thiebaud, age 12, circa 1957, New York. Courtesy of Twinka Thiebaud.

Twinka Thiebaud, high school graduation photo, 1964. Courtesy of Twinka Thiebaud.

Wayne Thiebaud with *Green Dress*, n.d. Courtesy of Twinka Thiebaud.

Twinka Thiebaud and Eva Rubinstein in Yosemite, 1974. Courtesy of Twinka Thiebaud.

Life Special Report: Remarkable American Women, 1776–1976. January 1976. Private collection.

Twinka Thiebaud posing, circa 1985. Photograph by Phillip H. Seymour. Collection of Twinka Thiebaud.

Twinka Thiebaud posing in Arles, France, 1985. Courtesy of Twinka Thiebaud.

California, September 1986. Collection of Twinka Thiebaud.

Twinka Thiebaud with daughter Sierra Le Baron Mellinger, circa 1990. Collection of Twinka Thiebaud.